DATE DUE		

When Tutor Meets Student

When Tutor Meets Student

Second Edition

Edited by Martha Maxwell

Ann Arbor

THE UNIVERSITY OF MICHIGAN PRESS

Copyright © by the University of Michigan 1994
All rights reserved
Published in the United States of America by
The University of Michigan Press
Manufactured in the United States of America

1997 1996 1995 1994   4 3 2 1

*A CIP catalogue record for this book is available
from the British Library.*

Library of Congress Cataloging-in-Publication Data

When tutor meets student / edited by Martha Maxwell. — 2nd ed.
    p.   cm.
    Includes bibliographical references (p.).
    ISBN 0-472-09532-3 (alk. paper). — ISBN 0-472-06532-7 (pbk. :
alk. paper)
    1. Tutors and tutoring—United States—Case studies. 2. Peer-
group tutoring of students—United States—Case studies.
3. Interpersonal relations—Case studies. 4. English language—
Composition and exercises—Study and teaching—United States—Case
studies. I. Maxwell, Martha
LC41.W48 1993
371.3'94—dc20   93-40871
                                                            CIP

Acknowledgments

The following stories appeared in an earlier edition of *When Tutor Meets Student: Experiences in Collaborative Learning,* edited by Martha Maxwell (Kensington, MD: MM Associates, 1990), and are used by permission of Martha Maxwell:

"Tutoring? Why Should I?" by Lynn M. Schuette

"Ours *Is* to Wonder Why" by Matthew J. Livsey

"Patience and Persistence Please" by Tammy Medress

"Achieving Rapport with Quiet Students" by Mark Yardas

"Learning to Write for Readers" by Susan Vincent

"Getting to Know You: Building Relationships as a Tutor" by Karen Castellucci

"Persistence Pays Off" by Barbara McClain

"Tutoring via the Objective Eye of the Video Camera" by Antonina Pascale

"I Have Been Meaning to Write for Some Time" by Judith Wolochow

"On the Level" by George Durgerian

"A Little Enlightenment in the Golden Bear" by Susanna Spiro

"Close Encounters with Feminist Ideology: A Case Study" by Linda Irvine

"A Minority Writing Tutor at the Golden Bear" by Eduardo Muñoz

"Session from Hell: The Dark Side of Collaborative Learning" by Jason Buchalter

"Coping with a Learning Disability" by Robert Derham, Jr.

"Before Ideas: The Preliminaries of the Student-Tutor Relationship" by Jennifer Fondbertasse Royal

"Getting Real" by Holly Holdrege

Grateful acknowledgment is made to Muriel Harris, editor of *The Writing Lab Newsletter* for permission to reprint the following stories:

"Ours *Is* to Wonder Why" by Matthew J. Livsey

"Patience and Persistence Please" by Tammy Medress

"Tutoring as Two-Way Learning" by Susan Enfield

"Getting to Know You" by Karen Castellucci
"The Journey Continues" by Vincent Harris
"Orthodoxy and Effectiveness" by Dina Fayer
"Expectations of a Tutor: Reflections of a Former Tutee" by Helen Woo

Preface

If you want to succeed in college, pay to be a tutor, don't pay a tutor.

—W. J. McKeachie (1990)

Why This Book?

I have long sought better ways to evaluate academic support programs than the traditional descriptions and statistics that seldom reveal much about what we actually do in our work with students. However, many approaches proved unsatisfactory. For example, when I asked tutor supervisors to write case studies, most read like recipes, or lab reports, or sugary testimonials. When Thom Hawkins inquired about ideas on how to get writing tutors' work published, I saw a chance to help tutors while getting the kinds of information I wanted by suggesting a contest, in hopes that writing tutors might welcome the opportunity to win prize money as well as the prospect of being published.

The stories in this book are the result of that contest. They won cash awards for their authors in the M. Maxwell Contest for Writing Tutors between 1987 and 1992. Eighteen of the stories appeared in an earlier edition of *When Tutor Meets Student,* and a number have been published in *The Writing Lab Newsletter.*

Most of the authors were student tutors enrolled in a tutoring-for-credit course at the Student Learning Center, University of California, Berkeley (UC Berkeley), and their students were taking freshman composition. (For details about the UC Berkeley tutor training course, see the Appendix.) These stories reflect the enthusiasm of many UC Berkeley tutors who often report that tutoring was their most important learning experience at the university.

For many years I have observed that tutors gain much from the tutoring experience, perhaps even more than the students they tutor, and I felt that the tutors' stories would confirm this. Tutors were asked to write about how the experience of being a tutor had affected them and to address their stories to an audience of new tutors. So we now have a book by tutors and for tutors. Of course the stories are biased and subjective, for they represent mostly the tutor's view, not the student's nor the supervisor's, although occasionally you'll find some comments from supervisors. Despite this, almost everyone will be interested in the situations they describe.

Some Recurring Themes

As you read the tutors' stories you'll find recurrent themes. Some describe the painful self-consciousness and anxiety beginning tutors feel and how frightened they are that their students might reject them. The authors discuss their feelings openly and honestly. They remark, as novices in any field do, "If I had it to do over, I'd do it this way," or "Do as I say, not as I did," reflecting their discovery that hindsight can be crystal clear.

As the tutors describe their efforts to help students improve their writing and thinking skills, they relate their successes as well as their frustrations and failures, discover new insights and blind spots, and explain their techniques and strategies. Certainly not all their efforts are successful. Some are worst case scenarios, like Jason Buchalter's "Session from Hell," where the tutor harbors murderous thoughts about his student, and Rachel Levin's "Prejudice and Power Plays," where tutoring degenerates into a power struggle. Perhaps we can justify including more stories about successes than failures by citing Bradley T. Hughes' 1990 review, "Too many of the stories may seem to be unqualified successes. . . . But new tutors reading this book need the encouragement it offers." Nevertheless, in this edition, we've tried to include more stories that describe equivocal results.

Another limitation of the stories is that they are snapshots of events, rather than complete documentaries, a reflection of the fact that tutors rarely know the ultimate outcome of their efforts—

even whether their students pass the course, much less whether they live happily ever after, or at least until graduation.

Since tutors tend to be high achieving and high aspiring students themselves, it is not surprising that they view tutoring as another opportunity to succeed, and their fears about failing surface early. "I want to be the best darned tutor the Student Learning Center has ever seen," seems to be an implicit goal of many tutors. Their determination to be the best, coupled with their intense need to be liked by their students, causes some conscientious tutors to assume the role of parent—becoming over-protective and emotionally involved and willing to take full responsibility for the student's success. These tutors shrink from being tough on deceitful students because they fear being disliked and avoid discussing important issues because some topics might make students feel uncomfortable. Even when they recognize that their student needs to become independent, they might find themselves reinforcing the dependency rather than helping the student overcome it, as Karin Cintron describes in her story. But later, they usually realize what they should have done.

Another recurrent theme is how tutors change their initial assumptions as they work with students. A determination to cover everything gives way slowly to the realization that students must work at their own pace and that, in tutoring, sometimes less can be more.

In some stories, women tutors describe how they felt and what they did when male students tried to intimidate them. (See stories by Fayer and Levin.) I personally find it fascinating to read about how different tutors reacted to similar stressful interpersonal situations, such as the male tutor's frustration with the passive female student or the student who hoodwinked his tutor into thinking he was working when he was not.

A number of stories concern the definition of the tutor's role, another almost universal problem for beginning tutors. In a story by an experienced professor who became a tutor, Edwin Chin-Shong describes succinctly the differences between tutoring and college teaching.

Some tales describe how the tutor tries to get an uncommunicative, passive student involved. On the other hand, the opposite situation occurs when a quiet, reserved tutor is working with a very talkative student. Esther Sam describes how the quiet tutor must learn to be more assertive and interrupt if she is to be effective.

Rare and Unusual Situations

There are also stories describing unusual situations such as the student whose instructor feels his writing problems are insoluble due to his disability, the girl who gives up and stops studying rather than risk losing face if she studies hard and fails anyway, and the reluctant writer who only wants to get through the English requirement and never plans to write again. Also there's the over-enthusiastic tutor who tries to build up his student's confidence only to find that the student has grown overconfident and no longer feels he needs to study. There are tales about how tutors handle uncomfortable situations such as Po-Sun Chen's experience with a girl who couldn't keep her hands off him and the woman tutor whose student is a marine who only wants answers, "Ma'am."

The tutors' stories also reflect the institutional context in which they operate and its problems—the struggle of a highly selective university to implement affirmative action and maintain academic standards, the problems of multiculturalism, issues such as political correctness, the difficulties of existing simultaneously in a university and an inner city environment, even the impact of an earthquake on the tutoring relationship.

Although many of the selections describe specific techniques for tutoring writing, such as Robert Derham's story about working with a student with cerebral palsy, this book is not intended to be a how-to-tutor manual. You will find references to tutor manuals in the Works Cited, but this book is designed to supplement other training materials with stories of real-life tutoring situations. In a sense, it presents the social dynamics of tutoring—the interpersonal relations that sometimes overpower both tutoring strategies and learning. Concerns about the relationship between instructors and tutors surface in several stories, and Jackie Goldsby's "Teamwork" suggests ways tutors and teachers can work together effectively. She also addresses ethical questions and gives an example of a confidentiality conflict.

These stories should provide the focus for some excellent discussions at tutor training sessions but can also be used in many other ways. New tutors can be given the stories to read and asked to respond to the questions in their journals. Instructors can read the stories to get a clearer idea of what happens in tutoring writing and to reduce their fears that tutors are doing their students' work for them.

The range of situations depicted by the student-authors offers many other choices. The stories can be used as a basis for discussion with groups of old and new tutors even in the absence of a tutor training course or to inform any faculty member interested in improving composition about some of the problems, issues, and strategies that are used.

They can be a way to inspire tutors to write their own stories and share them with others, and they are a good way to let others (administrators, even your own family) know what it is that you do in a writing center. They might even be used selectively to help students who are being tutored realize what tutoring is and how it can help them.

If you are a beginning tutor, I hope that, in reading this book, you will find stories that speak directly to you and that you will be encouraged to record your own experiences in tutoring and share them with others.

I'm grateful to each tutor who wrote a story and to the excellent work that Thom Hawkins, Rosaisela Rodriguez, Yvette Gullatt, Liz Keithley, and Anya Booker did in supervising and training the tutors, reviewing drafts of their stories, and contributing in many ways to the shape and substance of this book.

Contents

Introduction

What do you need to know to tutor well? In this volume, the peer writing tutors at UC Berkeley's Student Learning Center (SLC) offer their answers to that question as well as to many new questions that grew out of their attempts to find answers to that first one. After reading these essays, you might agree that tutoring is the art of asking questions—of yourself, of your students, of what we think we know about learning to write. I hope that you will join in the discussion and ask your own questions and share those questions with your fellow tutors. Questions trigger reflection, and reflection gives rise to stimulating writing and to tutoring that responds to an author's writing process.

The excitement in these essays comes from the sense of discovery as the tutors uncover each student's personal writing process. The longer I tutor writing, and that's been twenty years now, the more pleasure I derive from the variety of creative solutions students apply to the problems they encounter in drafting, revising, and editing. Tutors who meet regularly with the same students share in a privilege of confidence and insight that is often impossible for the overburdened classroom teacher. We see the writer at work over time, and we can intervene in that process to artfully demonstrate alternative solutions. I believe there is a secret to the phenomenal growth and success of programs that provide individual and small group tutoring to developing writers of all ages (when do we stop developing?): Tutors know from experience that writing improves when students draft, revise, and edit. Drop a link in that chain, and the writing weakens. That's why we never relent in our insistence that students come to their sessions with a draft and that they allow the time to brainstorm and prewrite before and to revise, edit, and proofread after. No one has ever driven them so hard and so compassionately to stop turning in first drafts written the night before and to get real, to write like most writers write. As Steve North (1984, 438) puts it, "Our job is to produce better writers, not better writing."

Few students come to us fully aware of how writing develops over time in recursive steps. They have not discussed among themselves, as tutors do, Flower and Hayes's (1981), Sommers's (1980), or Murray's (1991) models of the writing process. Many will hear about such procedures for the first time as their tutors devote the first few sessions to making clear the purpose of tutoring. At our center, tutors review with clients a two-sided handout (see appendices C and O) that lay out what we expect from students and what they can expect from us. But is that enough? Dan Aronson writes in Chapter 1 about going beyond the obvious nuts and bolts of tutoring and establishing a "contract" with your client—a mutual understanding that establishes clear goals with a rationale and specific methods. Tell students why you will be asking so many questions—that you want them to learn to ask themselves the same questions because you won't always be by their sides when they're writing. Explain to students why drafting, revising, and editing works—that writing is thinking and thinking is messy. And describe to them how you're still struggling with your own writing process and how that process gets reinvented when you change genres and audiences. Let them know that no one ever finishes learning to write, but promise them they'll get better if they work very, very hard at drafting, revising, and editing.

Before you can have a contract with your student, you must have a contract with yourself, to define your role much as the tutors in the first chapter attempt to do. Peer writing tutors are practitioners of collaborative learning—students learning from students. No matter how thorough your training might be, you will find that you learn the most by tutoring because each student is unique. By responding with energy and creativity to your clients' range of problems, you become resourceful and focused on what students are bringing to the tutorials, not on what you've been taught to expect. But while you're tutoring, you need to reflect on what you're doing and use the resources available to you to refine your skills. The resources in your tutoring program might include regular seminars; readings on composition research and teaching or tutoring practices; journal writing; videotape or audiotape analysis of tutorial sessions; exercise and handout files; word-processing and computer assisted instruction; and individual consultations with your students' classroom instructors, your training supervisor, and your fellow tutors, especially the more experienced ones who might act as your mentors. (Seek out resources you don't have.)

Of these, what do you think is the most valuable resource? Yes, the people, because ours is a community of writers, and we learn from each other. But would you be surprised to hear that within this community, new peer tutors find that their most valuable resource is one another? In the seminars, in the tutoring area, and any place they meet and talk about writing and tutoring together, new tutors, most of whom have never tutored before, provide one another with fresh insights and valuable suggestions. By asking how writing is learned and by close examination of students' successes and failures, new tutors produce a text for learning to tutor that is as applicable as anything in publication. And now, collected in one place for the first time, here is a significant part of that text, written by tutors at the end, in most cases, of their first semester of tutoring. I invite you to experience the vigor and utility of this community of peers. Join in our discussion, and you will strengthen all of us as you guide your students to discover themselves as writers.

Thom Hawkins

As in any freewheeling discussion among people who share a common concern, elements of the discussion often overlap because distinctions between categories tend to be blurred. Thus, you can read the chapters or the essays in this book in any order you wish and find yourself bumping into many of the same issues expressed from different perspectives. Some essays seem to fit perfectly in their chapters, while others could just as easily appear in two or three different chapters. In some sense, for instance, every essay, not just those in the first chapter, is about defining your role as a tutor.

Yet, as we five tutor supervisors read through all the essays, they seemed to fall into natural groupings based on certain themes. We tried to listen to the tutors and to let their voices tell us what those themes are. Once we were able to identify the themes, we ordered the resulting chapters in a sequence that closely parallels the syllabus for our tutor training course and the development of tutors' relationships with students. For instance, tutors find it essential to be clear from the start about their role with students, and they must waste no time in examining and refining their own reading and writing skills. To some extent the other chapters are interchangeable, since there is no rigid, correct way to learn how to tutor, and every class of tutors finds its own unique path to the same goals. We end the book with the very special wit of Jennifer Brunson, because imagination, humor, and a light touch will help carry you through your most demanding challenges as a tutor.

Anya Booker
Yvette Gullatt
Thom Hawkins
Elizabeth Keithley
Rosaisela Rodriguez

1 The Tutor's Role

Tutoring? Why should I?
Lynn M. Schuette

Lynn describes some unanticipated benefits of being a tutor.

Unless we begin to hear other's stories, we'll keep walking around
like strangers in an airport.
    —Joseph Featherstone, *Growing Minds: On Becoming a Teacher*
      by Herbert Kohl (New York: Harper and Row Publishers, 1984).

. . . the romance of teaching is related less to individual students
than to the phenomena of growth itself. It is wonderful to witness
young people discovering that they can have power and to be able to
help them acquire the skills and sensitivity they need to achieve the
goals they come to set for themselves.
    —Herbert Kohl, *Growing Minds: On Becoming a Teacher*
      (New York: Harper and Row Publishers, 1984).

It's the first week of your English 117 class, and all of a sudden
this (what you think is a) dweep comes into your class and starts
pushing this tutor stuff onto the class. "What's that? Who, me?
Tutor?" you ask. And rightfully so; after all you've been cramming
already (in the first week), you forget what your better half looks
like, and you're breaking out. You need to take on another responsibility like you need another thirteen units, right? Even if
you did make the time, what can you get out of tutoring anyway—
besides another three units?

I remember sitting in the back of a classroom, just like you,
minding my own business and trying to put out my own fires. I
couldn't begin to think of writing my term papers, let alone someone else's. And my grammar—sheesh! I crossed my fingers and said
a few "Hail Mary's" when I turned in my application to the English

Department to declare my major. To tell you the truth, I ventured into the Student Learning Center because I did need another three units, but I'm coming back for the things that I get out of it . . . and can contribute.

The day that my tutoring application was accepted, I really started to doubt my writing; that's the first benefit of tutoring: humility. It was like Dickens' *Christmas Carol*, Berkeley–English major style; the ghosts of bad-papers-past floated before my eyes. I remembered my science paper from the fifth grade. I got a C– on it. I guess the teacher figured out that I copied most of it from the *Encyclopedia Brittanica* (like everyone else). Then there was one of my first papers at Cal; it was about the "Wife of Bath" from *The Canterbury Tales*. The teacher totally railed on me for my interpretation; "I think that you are too hard on the W.O.B.," he said.

The night before I met my first tutee I went over, for a second time, the papers that my senior tutor and supervisor handed out to me. I paid special attention to the pieces that related to the collaborator role. I felt there was truth to the idea of working with the student instead of teaching or editing papers. I remembered the English teachers who had the biggest impact on my writing and why they did. That was the second benefit I received from tutoring: reflection. I was forced to think about what tools I'd been given in my writing career and how I could share them with my students.

I was extremely relieved to know that I wasn't responsible for writing the students' papers for them. I tried a few leading questions on for size in front of a mirror.

"So . . . what do you . . . like about this paper?"

"So . . . *what* do *you* . . . like about this paper?"

(You can imagine my embarrassment when my grandmother walked past my room and said, "the funnies.")

Walking to my first tutoring session was like going on my first (and last) blind date. What would my students be like? Would they be as bad as the bad student characterized in my training seminar, or would they be good students? I pictured all kinds of awful sessions.

"So what do you like about this paper?"

"The title . . ."

Or, "So what do you like about this paper?"

"The first sentence."

"OK, what do you like about it?"

"It's the only sentence in the paper so far."

Or, "So what do you like about this paper?"

"Isn't that what you're here for?"

"Well, if you want, but I think it would be better if you analyzed your own work."

"You really mean that you don't know what you're doing. Where do I sign up for a new tutor?"

Thankfully, none of my students turned out to be as bad as I first imagined, although I must admit that I've had some challenging moments. I remember one student who was skeptical of my writing abilities. It wouldn't have bothered me so much if he wasn't a Subject A student, but since he was, I felt duty bound to prove myself to him—for his sake. (I didn't want him to leave the Learning Center feeling as if we tutors were nothing more than a group of brown-nosing students.) I believe that nobody had ever collaborated with him on his writing and that he mistrusted any pedagogical type whose questions numbered more than her answers. Somehow I sensed that every time I asked, "What do you think?" he assumed that I did not know the answer. I persisted in playing the collaborator role—in spite of his apparent dissatisfaction; I gave him as few answers as possible. Rob responded to my questions curtly, as if he were frustrated by my apparent inability—or aversion—to instruct him. We had three sessions of near frustration until our fourth, when he first seemed to understand the function of tutoring and his role in the collaborative effort. In this particular session I noticed that Rob wasn't as irritable as usual; he answered my questions in a (comparatively) thoughtful manner. I can still see him sitting forward in his chair at the end of that meeting and saying "Yes, I think that these sessions are beneficial. Can we meet again this week?" Patience was the third bonus I gained at the Learning Center.

When it was time for me to write my first papers at the fifth and sixth weeks of the semester, I realized one of the biggest advantages to being a tutor. As I wrote each paper, I could imagine a tutor sitting next to me asking leading questions such as, "What is your thesis statement?" "How does this quote support your thesis?" "Is this point relevant to the thesis?" and horrors on horrors, "What do you like about this paper?" Instead of writing in my usual haphazard manner, I realized a new efficiency in my writing. I have always been a good writer, but somehow serving as a collaborator to others helped me to do the same for myself. All the tips, pep talks, and thought-provoking questions that I asked my students came back to me as I pecked away at my computer. At this point my humility was counter-balanced with a sense of accomplishment, pride, and self-confidence. I was no longer the writer who knew everything, nor the pre-English major who had reason to believe that she might not be good enough for Cal.

Right around midterms, most of my students started to catch the midsemester slumpies; in fact, I was not immune to this phenomenon either. Not only were my academic pressures building, but I was also in the middle of a major breakup (a five-year commitment gone sour). I was feeling physically and emotionally sick. I didn't want to go to school; I just wanted to curl up in a ball under my covers and hibernate until the end of the semester. I was so bottomed out that, at the very peak of my depression, my sole reason for going to school was for my students. One day I was on the verge of tears as I hurried in for my first appointment of the day; I had cut my morning class because I couldn't get out of bed, traffic had been a nightmare, and I was feeling very alone. Even as I hurried into the SLC I was in the process of beating myself up for being a bad student and a bad human being.

While waiting for my student to come in, I psyched myself out so that I wouldn't transfer any of my bad vibes to her. Rachel arrived five minutes late, full of apologies, and was visibly upset; she was particularly apologetic about the fact that she did not have a paper ready to discuss. Before I could catch up to her swirls of nervous chatter, she asked me if she could talk to me as a friend. Somehow, in the big hole that I had dug myself into, I could see Rachel reaching in to pull me out, even though she felt helpless herself. We spent the hour talking about her frustrations about being a student at Cal and her personal problems. I played the role of collaborator because I sensed that any decisions that she would make should be her own. I asked her questions related to her personal well-being: was she eating properly? taking care of her feelings? reaching out to friends and teachers for help? resting properly? I also directed her to various resources that could help her cope with her problems.

By the end of our session, Rachel seemed calmer and more at ease. Before she left though, I noticed hesitation and the tears welling up in her eyes. I asked her if she needed a hug. She immediately put down her back pack and said, "Yes." As we hugged, it became apparent to me that she helped me as much as I helped her. As we parted, I told her to be easy on herself and said that she was a very special person. Like with my leading questions and helpful writing hints, it became clear to me that I needed, once again, to take my own advice. We both left our session feeling better.

I don't need to wonder anymore about whether tutoring is worthwhile for me; I know it is. By being a collaborative tutor, I let my students discover the tools that are available to them, and I rediscover these tools for myself. Tutoring humanizes the learning process. It has personalized my education in a very profound way, and I can now fully appreciate the role my teachers, past and present, play in my educational career and in my life. I have learned this semester that we are the sum total of all the people with whom we have collaborated.

Supervisor's Comments

Lynn discovered that who you are as a tutor ultimately depends on who you are as a person and what you and your student bring to the sessions; as such, with each student and each session you will constantly re-create your answer to that ubiquitous question, "What is a tutor's role, anyway?" Oddly enough, it seems easier to approach this question backwards first, by listing things a tutor is not: no, you're not an editor or a proofreader; no, you're not a teacher; no, you're not the students' nagging parents, their counselor, their best friend. The list seems endless. But backwards though it may be, this approach is an important part of defining the tutor's role, because you need to look at the academic context you find yourself in and understand how the role you play is different from that of anyone else in your students' world. (To compound the confusion, the role of academic support units themselves often remains only vaguely defined by the academic community.)

Students often come in with expectations that are based on the same models you are trying to differentiate yourself from. So the need to establish a separate space for this role we call tutor is very real indeed.

Once you've been able to push aside all these competing identities, you can explore what it is that you are uniquely positioned to offer your students. Many of the tutors in this book write about exactly this process of discovery, finding unexpected possibilities, as well as some unexpected limitations, to what they can accomplish. Having rejected many familiar roles, you are without their reassuring guidance but also blessedly free of their constraints: you are a teacher who doesn't give lectures, a reader who doesn't give grades, a fellow student who is not a competitor, a role model who is not always perfect. It is up to you how to combine the best of all these possibilities as you work with your students. Your creativity and intuition mingled with humor and compassion will guide you in discovering the best combination for each of your students.

—Elizabeth Keithley

Ours *Is* to Wonder Why
Matthew J. Livsey

> If a tutor can get the student to ask critical questions about her own writing, those questions can work wonders.

One of the duties of writing tutors at the Student Learning Center at UC Berkeley is to keep a journal of their tutoring experiences. The following journal entry was written after a particularly productive session with one of my tutees. I have appended a discussion of what I see as the major implications of this session.

Journal Entry for 30 September 1988

Today Blair decided that the matter most requiring our attention was the upcoming in-class midterm exam. She said that the topic involved selections from the class reader and that her instructor had suggested that the students concentrate on one of three essays. Blair had made her choice and had begun to outline her thoughts about the essay. From this basis, we embarked on a forty-five minute question-and-answer session, sharpening Blair's focus on the major points of the article. Every time she brought up a new aspect of it, I asked questions and challenged her statements, narrowing the terms of her description, until she suddenly lit up and quickly scrawled some new insight. A particularly difficult moment came in differentiating between the first and second points of the essay. Through this constant clarification and distillation of ideas, I think Blair made an important step toward questioning her own writing; this questioning, I believe, is something that she will be able to take away from our tutoring experience and use throughout her academic writing career.

The essay was a discussion of the language of advertising, and the author first stated that ad language needs to be "edited and purposeful"; next he claimed that ad language has to be "rich and arresting." We covered the reasons behind the first statement: "Ads have limited time and space, have a definite purpose (to glowingly describe a product in that short time and space), and are therefore constrained to short, punchy messages." On to the second point.

Myself: "So, what's the second point?"

Blair: "That ads need to be 'rich and arresting' to be effective."

"OK, what does that mean?"

"Well, they only have a limited time to sell something, so they have to grab your attention and make an impact."

"All right. How is that different from what you said about 'edited and purposeful'?"

"Ummmm . . . uhhhh . . . well . . . they sort of mean the same thing, I guess . . . I don't know."

"So O'Neill says the same thing twice."

"Sort of."

"Paid by the word, was he?"

"No . . . there must be something different."

"What makes something 'rich and arresting'? What does 'rich and arresting' mean that 'edited and purposeful' doesn't?"

"Well, it's not about time."

"No, I guess not." It was time for a new approach. "Let's assume that the advertiser has me right where he wants me. I'm going to sit here and read this entire ad. Time and space are no longer problems. What will 'rich and arresting' language do for the advertiser in this case?"

"It will make you buy," Blair ventured, apparently wondering whether I was really so dense as to not realize this point on my own.

"Aha!"

"What?!!? You scared me!"

"There! You just said it!"

"What!? All I said was that 'rich and arresting' would make you buy the product!"

"So isn't that the point of this section?"

"Uh, of *course*. I just said it was. 'Rich and arresting language persuades people to buy the product.' Let me write it down before we go on to the third point."

Ruthless clarification led to Blair seeing the difference between the two points, and to her better understanding of an essay that I have never read.

Later in the session, during the discussion of one of the other points in the essay, Blair informed me that the "simple" language of ads was a bad thing. Although I could certainly understand why she would take exception to the mindless language of ads, that sort of intuitive argument will not suffice for academic writing. She needed to be better able to defend her assertion. Before I could say a word, nay, before my lips could form a sound, she blurted out "Why!" I leapt nearly out of my chair. "Why did you do that?" I asked meekly. "I wanted to say it before you did," she smugly answered, "and I did."

Part of tutoring is to make yourself obsolete; I think today I saw an important step toward my own antiquation.

In the weeks since that session, Blair has continued to progress. I met with Sheila, Blair's instructor, after that midterm was graded; she indicated that Blair's major writing problem seemed to be incoherence. Her papers lacked an underlying order; there seemed to be no cogent, logical argument. Blair and I attacked that problem and continued questioning her ideas. Now when Blair brings in a rough draft of a paper, she anticipates the questions that I will ask and the challenges that I will make. Most importantly, she clears up her basic logical errors before she ever gets to me. An exercise that really seemed to bring home the importance of self-questioning was when she was preparing a persuasive speech a couple of weeks ago. By imagining a hostile audience, Blair was able to challenge her own work. Her speech was convincing because, as she later explained to me, she kept in mind what a hostile audience would be thinking after she made each point. And aren't all academic audiences hostile?

Tutoring involves asking many, many questions. Some of them are aimed at grammatical difficulties or sentence construction problems, some at more global organizational troubles. The most important questions we can ask, however, are those questions that the students can learn to ask of themselves. We can give advice, we can challenge statements, we can cheer success; but if we don't give our students the tools to survive the years of writing that face them (without someone beside them to advise, challenge, and cheer), can we say that we've really done anything at all?

Asking the questions that inspire self-questioning might seem like the perfect solution to every tutoring problem; how, then, does one do it? Here's the really challenging part of the whole idea: I don't think that there exists a single plan of action that will inevitably succeed. It seems mostly to evolve as a natural result of the interaction between tutor and tutee. When Blair belted out, "Why!" I was really unaware that the monosyllabic query was such a large part of my tutoring vocabulary; apparently I had asked it enough that Blair realized the question's importance to academic writing. If she could rob her audience of the opportunity to ask "why?", her logic would be a great deal more sound. That is precisely what she has done. Having finished a rough draft of another assignment, she prepared to read it to me. She prefaced her speech with "I think it's pretty good. After everything I wrote I asked 'why?' I don't think there are any questions now."

I could go for the storybook ending here, but tutoring isn't like that. Of course there were questions left to be asked. But they were new, more complex questions. We left behind the simple "why?" in favor of questions about transitions, and rhetorical values, and even style. One question will never solve all writing difficulties. But if the student asks the question of herself, she is well on the way to developing writing strategies on which she can rely after the tutorials have ended.

1. Do you think that the student might have felt that the tutor was being obnoxious by asking so many questions? Explain.
2. How was the tutor able to get Blair to question her own writing?
3. Can you think of other ways a tutor can help students ask appropriate questions about their writing?
4. Do you agree with the tutor's statement, "Part of tutoring is to make yourself obsolete"? How well do you think Matthew succeeded in doing this?

More Than Worth the Effort: The Importance of the Tutoring Contract to Productive Tutoring
Daniel Aronson

> Daniel finds that each of his students has a different expectation of what a tutor does, and none of them coincides with his perception of effective tutoring.

The initial tutoring contract, where you and the student each communicate your needs, is one of the most important ingredients in a successful tutoring relationship. Although you might be wary of focusing on your job in the first meeting with your student, it is more than worth the effort; a proper understanding of your role as a tutor—as well as the student's role in being tutored—will help you avoid unpleasant misunderstanding in the future.

Although it might be difficult to tell your students that you are not there to correct papers or to serve as a teacher, they will appreciate your directness later, when they know how to respond to your suggestions and how to give you the kind of response that you need.

The first meeting is always somewhat difficult because for many students it is their first experience in tutoring, and my students were uneasy about needing help from a tutor.

Although I did my best to put them at ease, they continued to hear their own little voices telling them that they were failures for not being able to write as well as they wanted to without tutoring. One of my students, Mark, responded by considering me his proofreader; another, Cecilia, passively waited for me to be her teacher;

and Tracy abdicated all responsibility for what we would be doing by hiding behind "I don't know." Each of these responses might have been prevented, at least to some extent, if I had effectively communicated what our relationship was going to entail at the start, in other words, by giving them a tutoring contract.

This isn't to say that I didn't establish an agreement with my students about our common goals and purposes at the beginning of the semester—we spent most of our first session talking about our goals for the semester. The importance of students communicating their goals to me at the beginning of our relationship should not be underestimated. Without the communication that did occur in our first session, our relationships would have remained without direction and of minimal value to the students. We might have fluctuated from sentence to sentence, paragraph to paragraph, paper to paper, without any idea of where our journey was taking us. Like the proverbial blind man and the elephant, we would have been so lost in the details that we would have missed the nature of the beast altogether.

Still, the agreement we had about our goals and objectives was insufficient. Certainly it was a start, but a clumsy one. Although we had talked about goals, we didn't spend sufficient time defining how we planned to arrive at these goals. Like the papers of so many inexperienced writers, my students and I tried to build our relationship on a vague and insufficiently developed foundation, and like those inexperienced writers' papers, we could not escape the fundamental limitations on our effectiveness imposed by our inadequate beginning.

The result of our inadequate communication was not the complete failure of our relationship—that could only happen if both my students and I were not willing to work through the difficulties. In all three cases, both the student and I adapted to the realities of our situations. However, the students were not able to adapt to my expectations, simply because they did not know what my expectations were. So I ended up trying to adapt to their actions. In each of the cases, this solution was not the ideal. While tutors must have a flexible approach, I felt that in adapting to their needs, I had to use techniques that were not comfortable for me and were not beneficial for my students. I ended up doing more proofreading than I wanted with Mark, asking more leading questions than I wanted to with Cecilia, and providing more answers than I was comfortable with for Tracy. I felt forced to make these changes that left me feeling uncomfortable and ineffective, and I felt I was cheating my students of the best I as a tutor had to offer.

Although I knew something was wrong and did my best to remedy it, I finally realized that my students were not relating to me as I had expected. In fact, they had fundamentally different ideas about our relationship and my role. This led to their defining their own roles in ways I was not comfortable with. So I made it a point to begin my next session with a description of what I expected my role to be in our sessions, with my part explicitly and completely defined. This did not force them to act out an inflexible script, but within the framework of their own personalities, they were able to modify their responses so I got what I needed—a chance to help them discover what the answers were for themselves instead of having me lead them or outright tell them the answer. Because I got more chances to tutor in ways I was more comfortable—and did well—with, they got the maximum benefit from our time together.

My detailed explanation of what my job was did not go over well with all my students, however. Mark had continually frustrated me throughout our association. He came only rarely, usually canceling or wanting to postpone our sessions, and when he did come, he only wanted me to correct his papers for him, not to help him develop as a writer. We had indeed discussed the fact that I would not correct his papers, but I had been too worried about appearing unsympathetic to his needs to be absolutely clear about mine. As a result, he ignored what little statement of them I had managed to muster. This meant that throughout the semester I had refused to correct his papers and he always seemed uninterested in listening to me try to explain how to be a better writer since he did not see why he should. I ended up pointing out a few errors each time, explaining how he could correct them in the future. The day I made it perfectly clear that I would help him write better, but not correct his papers, was the most productive session we had together. He did not ask me to correct his paper, and I felt comfortable for the first time. He called me the next week and told me he didn't want to meet that week—in fact, that he didn't want to meet again.

I look back on my experience with Mark with regret. I regret that I became so frustrated with his expectations that I be an editor, not a tutor. I regret that he did not get what he wanted, but most of all I regret that I spent so much time and energy trying to tutor him and that I was not clear with him about my role sooner—for both our sakes.

My experience with Mark, as well as with Cecilia and Tracy— with whom I now have far more productive sessions—demonstrated to me the value of having an explicit, detailed tutoring contract. As uncomfortable as it might be for you to try to spell out exactly what you need and expect from your students in tutoring to be an effective tutor, both you and your students will benefit from the effort.

DISCUSSION QUESTIONS

1. Striking a balance between what a student expects and wants from tutoring and what the tutor sees as the best way to help the student is often a problem for beginning tutors. Do you think that Daniel protests too much about how uncomfortable he was in trying to adapt to his students' varied expectations of tutoring, or do you think he was frustrated in trying to make them conform to his way of doing things? Explain.
2. Why do you think Daniel didn't get around to clarifying his role with each student sooner?
3. Do you think Mark would have dropped tutoring at the beginning of the semester if Daniel had clearly explained that tutors are not editors and refused to correct any of the errors in his papers? Why or why not?

The Dynamics of Passivity in Tutoring
Erin K. Getty

> Erin thought that her student's silence signaled passivity and coldness until she found that silence can indicate high mental productivity.

The day started out like any other. Reyna came to the table smiling meekly, sat down, and began to tell me what she wanted to work on for the hour. She said she was still having trouble understanding the assignment she had been given a week earlier, particularly the question, "What is imagination and what does it accomplish?" We had struggled with this question for over an hour in our previous session and had made little progress. She was getting restless to start writing, and I was hoping she would soon be able to do more prewriting, such as brainstorming and outlining. After I asked several probing questions and she gave her answers, silence pervaded the table and silence continued. I wondered, "Should I end an unproductive pause or silently encourage a fruitful incubation period?" I waited. She stared vacantly across the room. I shuffled in my chair. "Is she thinking?" I asked myself, "or is she someplace else today? Or is she on the verge of a revelation and just trying to find words to express it?" I waited one more precious minute and then it happened. She burst forth with the *idea*, one that might have been lost in an ill-timed torrent of questioning. I was right in sweating out the silence that seemed to last a hundred years.

The above vignette suggests a situation in which a tutor might be tempted to consult an implied thermometer of interpersonal discourse. This is how it works. Imagine a thermometer in the mind of the writer, one that can be influenced by the heating or cooling influence of the tutor, a catalyst. A freely flowing discussion might be considered productive and the thermometer would be warm, or when questioning is unproductive or silence dominates the thermometer would be cool. At the extreme, when the tutee has a swarm of ideas, swarming in chaos, the thermometer would be hot, but the tutor might consider asserting a cooling, organizing influence. However, if the indicators show absolute zero, the tutor might spark more mental heat by asking questions. Whatever the condition, the tutor's goal should be to avoid extremities, maintaining an overall body temperature of 98.6 degrees. This temperature would suggest good working conditions where ideas are born and develop but are not suffocated by superfluous competitors.

However, gauging the tutee's idea making in this fashion is too facile and problematic to be useful in peer tutoring. For instance, in those moments when conversation drags, is it true that the tutee's mind is frozen? Or should the tutor really attempt to cool those moments when the tutor is inspired? Wouldn't that thwart the tutee in her most brilliant moment? Silence might not be counterproductive; some of the best ideas are born out of what seems to be a barren silence. I know this from my personal experience in tutoring, for I was once tutored by a well-meaning person who took my silence to be confusion and in trying to question me out of my stupor totally disrupted my chain of thought. I had needed the silence, the mental time, to sort out my ideas and rearrange them so I could express them well.

Expression—this is what the tutor should elicit with questions. But expression can be thwarted by overzealous tutoring. What is needed are a few coaxing, prodding words rather than the insertion of new ideas by the tutor. New ideas cloud whatever conceptions the tutee is trying to establish on her own. If the tutor could ask the student to scribble on paper or try to verbalize what she is thinking, no matter how incoherent, the tutor could then determine how to proceed.

Because Reyna's Subject A teacher focuses on abstract ideas (i.e., the nature of imagination) rather than the basics such as plot, character, symbol, etc., Reyna has to concentrate more deeply. Sometimes she is silent for over five minutes before she or I begin to ask questions. As a first-time tutor, I would have thought such a long pause a waste of time because I was so eager to dig in and start her thinking. Now as a one-semester veteran, I don't dare interrupt her silent conversation with her mind. Sometimes as she crouches over her paper and pen, jotting down a word or phrase occasionally, I lean back and think. I have had to think harder for her Subject A class than in a couple of my upper-division courses. As ideas are formed and questions raised inside my head, I begin to see the big picture. Across the table, Reyna carries out the same mental discussion to form her own big picture.

I must be careful not to superimpose my big picture on hers and must suppress my urge to ask her whether imagination might be an escape. Instead I concentrate on her conception and ask her what she means by, "Imagination is hope."

Tutors must draw the line carefully between when to talk and when to wait. The thermometer that indicates that silence means stupor and verbalization means productivity is not a reliable indicator.

DISCUSSION QUESTIONS

1. Despite its unreliability, do you think the analogy of tutor-tutee interactions resembling a thermometer is a useful idea?

2. What mental activities might be going on in the tutee's mind during periods of silence?
3. Have you waited as long as five minutes for a tutee to talk? Is this something that a new tutor would be comfortable doing? Or would it take an example like Reyna's brilliant insight to convince a tutor that silence is productive?

Tutoring as Two-Way Learning
Susan Enfield

> Students often have trouble deciding on a topic when the professor gives them the chance to choose their own. Susan describes how she helped Marion decide and also clarified her own writing dilemma.

Giving students the confidence to have faith in their own ideas is not an easy task. Their lecture classes don't encourage them to think for themselves, often requiring that they only regurgitate information processed by their professor. And even when it comes time to write a paper in which they can express their own ideas on the subject, many students find that instructors have already formed their own opinion on the topic and will downgrade a student for not conforming to their ideas. So what results? Students who do not believe that they have anything worthwhile to say—after all, they aren't the experts; the instructors are, right? Maybe, but not always. Working with my tutees this semester, I have faced the challenge of trying to convince them that they do indeed have good ideas and should rely on their own thoughts more than they do. Marion is one tutee who was more than ready to have someone encourage her to follow her own ideas.

It's 10:00 a.m. Monday morning and Marion, a tall and extremely bright freshman English student, has just joined me at my table for one of our weekly tutoring sessions. We chat for a few minutes, indulging ourselves in a lighthearted discussion about our classes and our weekends before plunging into work for the rest of the hour. About ten minutes pass, and we both decide that it's time to get down to business, and our business is writing. So Marion begins by pulling out some scribbled sheets of notebook paper and says, "My assignment is, well really I don't have a specific assignment. My teacher just wants us to write a paper on Spike Lee's movie, 'Do the Right Thing,' that we all saw together as a class."

"That sounds great. You have a lot of freedom with this assignment, since it seems that your teacher wants you to come up with your own topics, basically. So what have you come up with so far?"

"Well, I went through some of my old English questions and read about some critical approaches [This did not sound good to me!], but I had a hard time understanding some of them, and others didn't seem to be very interesting. The one I'm considering working with is a question about how the story's actions determine its having a specific ending, but I don't know."

Instantly the words *students as slaves* rang through my mind. Here was an exceptionally bright student with a rare opportunity to write about anything she could think of, yet she had been cautioned by other teachers to consult the critical approaches of some literary expert rather than formulate her own ideas. She had to be stopped. She couldn't go on not allowing her own wonderful thoughts to surface and show themselves to the world in a paper. I had to take action. So I said, "Well, tell me what *you* thought about the movie. Did you like it? All or only some parts? What was it that interested you most? Remember, in this paper, you just have to talk about some aspect of the movie that you consider important, so try to find something that genuinely affected you—made you angry, sad, or even left you feeling apathetic?"

"We did read a description of the movie that Spike Lee, himself had written, which I did not totally agree with."

"Aha," I thought, "now we're making progress."

"He said that one of his characters really was a racist in the movie, but I don't think he was. I don't know if I could get a whole paper out of this idea, though."

"OK. Why didn't you think he was a racist, and why do you think Spike Lee intended him to be one? Also, what implications do you think it has on you as a viewer if you don't share Lee's views? Does it mean that you harbor some racist sentiments? Do you think Lee . . . "

"OK, OK, I get your point. Obviously if I think about this enough I can write a paper about it. And you're right, it is far more interesting than writing about what some critic might have said. I mean, if I disagree with Lee on certain points of the movie, that definitely affects how I view it. But my teacher wants us to follow a question-thesis format . . . "

"Ugh—Formats!" I thought, "Now this poor girl, after deciding to think for herself and give validity to her own ideas, was having to alter them so they would fit into this question-thesis formula— whatever that is!" I realized that we now had another problem to tackle as Marion continued, "I mean how can I word these ideas so that my teacher will accept them as part of a thesis?"

"Well, first of all, [here was my minilesson for the day] a thesis is merely a formal term for what you want to say in your paper. So write down exactly what you have told me, and worry about formatting it later. I know that you have to do the assignment so that it is acceptable to the teacher, so I would ask her if your approach is OK. But your ideas are so good, Marion, that I would hate to see you give up on them just because you can't fit them into a structure. You can't be [was I really going to say it?] a student as slave forever. Have faith in your ideas, and you'll do fine."

Marion nodded, laughing a little, indicating that she obviously knew what I meant. She was experiencing what I have only recently realized was a problem for me too. She was so programmed by all her years in formal education to think in a certain way—which means not thinking that her own ideas were good enough—that she was at a loss when confronted with an assignment that gave her free reign. At the same time, however, she had to corral her ideas into the teacher's desired format. However, she was realizing how to change this, long before I did. She had the guts to go with her own thoughts, which can be risky with some professors. I was impressed and I told her so.

"You know Marion, I think it really takes guts to follow your own instincts rather than rely on someone else's opinion, and I know it isn't easy. If you can do it though, you'll find that you have a sincere interest in what you are writing and that your papers will be much better because of it. I know because I'm trying to do the same thing right now in one of my classes."

"I know you're right, but I'll check with my teacher before I go ahead with it just to make sure. But I really think I can do it. I'll bring you what I have done next week. Thanks. . . . "

And so ended another tutoring session. But this one was some-how unique. We had both learned something. Marion's predicament reminded me of the one that I have so often found myself in— performing rather than writing. Hopefully, I had given her enough encouragement to have some faith in her own thinking, but I knew that she had to decide whether it was the right thing for her to do. Only she can improve herself, but I think she knows that. I see far more dedication and daring in her than I did in myself as a freshman. She has the intelligence to ask for help and open herself up to new possibilities rather than pretend that she has all the answers—an example that I should probably follow more often than I do.

DISCUSSION QUESTIONS

1. In your opinion, is Susan's analogy of the student as slave a good one? If so, why? When might it be inappropriate?
2. Do you think that students who are less verbal than Marion might feel intimidated by Susan's "rat-a-tat-tat" barrage of questions like the ones before Marion says, "OK, OK"?
3. Can you think of other ways tutors might help students discover topics for their essays?

Supervisor's Comments

Susan realizes that by tutoring she can learn as much about writing as, if not more than, her students. But some tutors feel guilty about this realization; after all, it's the tutor's job to help the student master writing skills. Isn't it assumed that a tutor comes to tutoring with all of his or her skills intact? A tutor who chastises a student for procrastinating on a major paper will be painfully aware of her own writing avoidance. Such inconsistencies can encourage someone like Susan to try even harder to apply to her own writing the techniques she is helping a student to master. I've often spoken with tutors who rigorously defend the "writing process" (a term that has been elevated to near-canonical status among tutors) with strong conviction: "My student won't prewrite," "My student won't write a rough draft," "My student won't revise." When I gently question them about their own writing processes, many tutors begin to understand the ways in which they have modified their processes as they have become more experienced writers. Susan and her fellow tutors are writers who are still struggling with expression, still juggling the importance of audience with the authenticity of voice. An increased awareness of their own connection to writing helps tutors remain focused on the needs of less experienced writers.

—Yvette Gullatt

Patience and Persistence Please
Tammy Medress

> Tammy finds that her student needs a very, very long time to get started—more than she had ever imagined. Here's how she did it.

"Well, do you want to go over this paper you just got back or talk about your next one?" I asked Jesse as our meeting began. "That old one is the same old stuff. You know, tenses and stuff. I don't think we need to go over it."

"Well, do you know anything about *Puddinhead Wilson*?" Jesse asked, his words tinged with doubt. "I have to write an essay on it, and I have no idea what to write about."

I had just started meeting with Jesse last week, so this was only our second session. He had come to the Student Learning Center looking for a miracle in the ninth week of class. He expected someone to give him the answers to all his writing problems, preferably in ten words or less, and make his papers perfect. Instead, he got me.

"Actually, I've never read *Puddinhead Wilson*," I answered. "Oh." The disappointment in his voice made me cringe. He had little confidence in me or my ability to help him, and I began to doubt myself.

"Tell me a little about the book," I said—always a good place to start. As he grudgingly reported the few skimpy facts he remembered from the plot, I began to wonder whether this tutoring session could succeed. What was I supposed to do with a student who couldn't even tell me the basic plot of the book?

"So what really stood out in your mind about the book? What did you like best about it?" I asked the always successful, last resort questions. I got a blank stare in return.

Thoughts began racing through my mind: There must be something wrong with me. Why couldn't I ask the right questions? Why was I pretending to be an authority on writing? What was I even doing here? In desperation, I tried again.

"Tell me about the main character. How do things get resolved in the end?"

"I think he might have committed a murder or something. I can't remember. Yah . . . I think . . . "

"Does he get punished, sent to prison?"

"I don't remember . . . I think it just sort of ends."

Trying to remain calm, I began explaining to Jesse in an un-threatening way, that knowing the basic elements of the plot is essential when trying to understand and analyze a book. Minute details like the main character committing murder shouldn't be forgotten, and books don't usually "just end," I urged. He assured me that he had, indeed, read the book, but it was so long ago (last week) and you know . . .

As I continued to ask what felt like an eternity of basic ques-tions, all of which seemed to lead nowhere, the temptation to give up was overwhelming. Jesse kept fumbling around with the same basic nothingness, and I wasn't helping him one bit. In searching for the right questions to ask, ones I couldn't ask Jesse kept popping into my mind. What was I supposed to do? Who did Jesse think he was, coming in here without any solid basis for us to work with? Who did I think I was? I had walked into the Student Learning Center and volunteered my time to help other students write. What made me think I was qualified to do this?

"Did you like the book?" I asked Jesse, trying not to let him hear the desperation in my voice, and knowing that this would at least elicit a yes or no response.

And at some point within the next five minutes, I'm not exactly sure when or why, Jesse began to talk, and intelligent, coherent facts and ideas came out of his mouth.

"Oh yah . . . *now* I remember. He *does* commit murder, with a knife he stole from the twins, and he tries to blame it on them!" Aha! A minuscule detail that might be important, I think to myself, wondering how this could possibly have slipped Jesse's mind.

But soon Jesse has constructed a complete plot summary, and we begin to discuss some of the connections between characters, important symbols, and suggestive meaning. As each new idea was discussed, Jesse's eyes lit up, and I could practically see the cogs of his brain churning away. I finally began to hear some gasps of insight and see smiles of recognition. Statements of intuitive understanding began to spew from Jesse's mouth without any probes from me. Our bleak situation was beginning to look more promising.

And what if I had given up when I was so tempted to do so? What if I hadn't continued to ask questions, even though I felt like a complete moron when I couldn't get any answers? At some point I had found the right approach to get Jesse thinking, analyzing, and discussing. Since every person comprehends in a different manner, it is impossible to predict when this will happen. A tutor's job is to continue trying, probing, asking, and challenging, even when it seems futile. Patience and perseverance are essential, because the very last approach might start the avalanche rolling.

I think Jesse and I both left that session having learned valuable lessons. Jesse had filled two pages with notes of *his* ideas about *Puddinhead Wilson*. He had a good, solid basis for an essay and, most of all, a strong feeling of confidence in himself.

I realized how important it is for a tutor to have patience to help any student grasp new ideas. Sometimes all a student needs is someone who will listen while he gropes around with ideas and who will respond with encouragement. A tutor's job is to be that person. I also really felt satisfied when I heard Jesse say, "God, I never thought of any of this before." Jesse stared down at his notes and proclaimed, "I'm going to write a really great paper!"

Would I ever have thought this session would turn out this way? Would I ever have thought the blank stares I got from Jesse would turn into these sweet sounds of victory?

Whenever I feel frustrated, stuck in a rut with a student, I must remember this session with Jesse and trust that success lies somewhere around the corner. It might be a long block's walk to reach that corner, but it is my job as a tutor to have the patience and persistence to help the student make it there . . . eventually.

DISCUSSION QUESTIONS

1. Jesse seemed to expect a miracle from tutoring and was distressed when his tutor said she hadn't read the book he had to write about. How well do you think Tammy handled this situation? Would you have done things differently?

2. What steps did Tammy take to get Jesse involved so he could begin to discuss ideas for his paper?
3. What was the lesson that Tammy learned from this experience?

How Self-Definition Affects Tutoring:
A Teacher Becomes a Tutor
Edwin Chin-Shong

> After teaching college courses for many years, Edwin tries his hand at tutoring writing and finds his teaching skills a hindrance as he learns that tutoring requires quite different strategies.

As someone nearing twenty years of teaching, my experience as a volunteer tutor might be expected to differ from someone still an undergraduate. At least one might predict that I would find it easier. But personally, I found the first two weeks of tutoring stressful. It was much more difficult than teaching. In teaching, I would be prepared. I'd know what points I intended to cover, and the trick was to find a current event or personal experience to use as a takeoff. The point was to set the stage for talking, so that my intended points would seem the most natural outcome.

After four weeks in the Student Learning Center, during which I had read *The Practical Tutor* twice, I no longer found tutoring so difficult. It was even beginning to be fun with some students. This essay aims to clarify how and why this change came about. I write it with the hope that it will help other new tutors to understand how their definition of their role affects the interaction that follows and how that can make tutoring less difficult, more fun, and, perhaps, more beneficial to the student as well.

I began with the implicit self-definition of being a teacher and hence responsible for teaching my students how to write. I felt that I needed to stage the tutoring as I had my teaching so that good writing would result. This was already a difficult task, as I was not trained as a writing teacher. To make the job even more difficult, I would have to teach material I did not know. The material would be whatever essay the student had brought, and the chance that I knew the content was very small. I tried racing through the material hoping to get an overall picture, but that did not work either. I was too conscious of my student sitting there and my looking at too many errors to note, too many instructor comments, and too many ideas to try to remember. The quick read left me in a blur, and now I had to speak with confidence while walking on quicksand.

I also had to be careful not to lead the student too much. Since I was the "expert," the student assumed that I already knew what was correct. My expertise in tutoring would manifest itself in a string of questions worthy of Socrates himself. My questions would allow the student to personally discover this one true expression that I had in mind, or so I thought. But I found this difficult to do. The injunction from *The Practical Tutor* not to lead the student set up cross-purposes. My questions came out in a cautious, tortured manner, freighted with untold implications. As a result, my students froze.

The solution to this problem, when I found it, was very easy. It was like a Zen illumination, wherein everything is changed but no different than before. There were two key points to the change.

First was the realization that I have no responsibility to teach my student how to write. Instead, I reflect back to the students what they write. I simply say, "This is unclear to me," and "I'm not sure what you are saying," and "Is there another way you can say this?"

The more important revelation was that I did not have to know a single thing about the content to tutor properly. In fact, the less I knew, the better I was able to tutor! How does this work? It is simply this: the less I know, the clearer the writing must be for me to understand. And my job as tutor was now only to say, "I don't understand who this person is," or "What is this new idea doing here?" or "What is the connection?" I repeat that it is the writer's job to take the reader by the hand, down the garden path. If I don't get it or the language sets up distractions, it is my job to let the student know that he or she hasn't delivered the message.

The result is that I feel no pressure to perform or to teach writing because I have nothing to teach. I focus on the student's text to see whether it communicates. If it doesn't, the student is left to think of another way of saying it. The question of leading the student never arises because I no longer use my ideas as a criterion but focus on what the student is thinking. And there often are surprises. The student might have buried in the language a very good idea that I could never have thought up. This way, we both discover something interesting.

Another thing I learned is that Rome was not built in a day. I don't have the responsibility to fix all the problems, particularly if the student's skills are weak. We do what we can for that day and hope for a better day tomorrow.

DISCUSSION QUESTIONS

1. What reasons does Edwin give for finding tutoring so stressful at first? Do you think that undergraduate tutors might consider tutoring stressful too?
2. Can you relate to Edwin's comments about how difficult it is to try to help someone when you do not know the material? Do you think his ways of overcoming his concern about not knowing the material would work for other tutors? Explain.
3. Why do you think his students froze when he first tried to ask them questions?
4. Edwin compares his insights into how to be a successful tutor to Zen illumination. Explain what his insights were and how they relate to Zen. Does his Zen analogy make sense to you?

A Slight Case of Plagiarism
Pam Moody

> It's hard for a tutor who loves literature to accept the fact that her student detests the subject and will do anything, including plagiarize, to get through the English requirement.

Looking back over my journal entries about tutoring Eric, I realized that from the beginning of the semester I had known something about him that I was unwilling to face consciously. Eric hates English, not only because he feels that he is no good at it but also because he sees no use in it. His first statement about why he came for tutoring, "My English sucks," could just as well have been "English sucks." Although I really should have been prepared for this, it came as a shock to me when he finally said it. Most of the people I knew had at least pretended to see the value of studying literature out of respect for my obvious passion for it. And my other two students didn't share Eric's attitude at all. My basic writing student was highly motivated from the beginning of the term and tried to make the best of her not always stimulating class— in fact, she even expressed an interest in becoming an English major. My other student intended to major in political science and study in France, but she too was excited about her comparative literature course. These two students corroborated my enthusiastic assumptions about the glories and benefits of studying the written word but also blinded me to Eric's most critical problem with English: he really just didn't care enough to apply himself and saw his other courses as far more important.

I suppose the problem began immediately, as Eric's only question to me during our brief "getting to know you" talk in our first meeting was one regarding my qualifications. The memory of the worst case scenario in our tutoring training class the week before danced before my anxious eyes. I resisted the temptation to give the answer one tutor did, "No, actually I'm a molecular biology major," mostly because I knew I wouldn't be able to keep a straight face. More than that, I realized that this guy was stressed out; he knew he needed help and was desperately looking to me to provide it. Pleased at feeling needed, I assumed that his motivation for seeking tutoring lay in a real desire to improve his writing rather than, as I later learned, his wish to get a decent grade and finally be done with the evil Reading and Composition requirement.

As time and tutoring went on, sessions with Eric became more and more frustrating. As much as I tried to dispel the notion by being personable, casual, and collaborative, Eric obviously expected me to be the authority, and I often felt that he treated me more like hired help than a partner and peer. As we reviewed his papers, Eric wanted only answers while I provided only questions, much to his irritation. I desperately wanted to believe that he was really interested in the reading assignments but was just having trouble analyzing and writing about them. Certainly there were reasons for my assumptions; Eric intended to double major in math and computer science and was continually under pressure from the demands of these time-consuming and difficult courses. More important, however, is the fact that Eric is Chinese and has only been in this country about five years. He still has significant problems with the English language, not to mention the cultural difficulties involved in reading works of English literature.

His paper on the paramount figure in English literary history, William Shakespeare, proved to be the turning point in our relationship. We worked on his *Othello* paper together for two or three arduous sessions. He brought it to me in two sections, the first half one week and the completed draft, minus the conclusion, the next week, and it was surprisingly good. His language problems had virtually disappeared, and his argument was fairly well thought out and developed. When I commented that he must have spent a lot of time working on it, he just grimaced and didn't say anything. He asked me whether the paper had "unity" and "flow," two things his instructor had emphasized, but in going over the paper, he became really agitated when I pointed out parts that were confusing or incompletely developed. He wanted me to tell him what to write, and when I refused, he would either simply cross things out or say, "Well, I'm not about to change it now." His parting comment on the first day we worked on this paper, after I had refused to "give him a sentence" to end his conclusion with was, "If I can't sleep tonight it's because of you." I was left exhausted and frustrated that our sessions had become more like battles than collaborations and looked forward to giving him a midterm questionnaire the next week so we could finally talk about what was going on in tutoring and, hopefully, reestablish our roles, which I obviously had not made clear in the first place.

When Eric returned the next week, he didn't have a new paper to work on yet and had barely started reading the new novel assigned for class. He asked a few gratuitous questions about *Frankenstein* and then wanted to leave—ten minutes into the session. I gave him a questionnaire to fill out and went up to see his instructor who had office hours at that time. I intended to schedule a time to see her later, but she wanted to talk right away because of a serious problem with Eric, which he, of course, had neglected to tell me about. She gave me the shocking news that Eric had plagiarized his *Othello* paper. Her teaching assistant, who had been reading Eric's papers regularly, had discovered that he had copied the introduction of a different edition of the play almost word for word. When she confronted Eric with this, he at first denied it and then admitted that he had copied it from one of his sister's papers, not knowing that she had taken it from the introduction. I was aghast, furious, and at a complete loss about what to do about it. His instructor suggested that I simply tell Eric that I knew there was a problem with the paper and that he was required to rewrite it.

Back in the Student Learning Center, Eric had long since finished writing his one-line answers to my questions. I set the questionnaire aside without reading it and tried to talk to Eric. I asked him how he felt about our tutoring sessions and said I knew he was having a difficult semester. He said that tutoring was fine, except he felt I was asking him questions that he didn't know the answers to, and he was placed in the position of having to guess what I meant. I tried to explain my position, that I never had specific answers in mind and so on. When I told him I had spoken with his instructor, he looked utterly stricken. I asked if he wanted to work on the rewrite together—I was much nicer about this than I had intended to be—he mumbled, "Later," and virtually ran out of the room.

I was surprised at how strongly I reacted to this situation. I hadn't realized until then just how much I had invested in working with Eric and was terribly hurt and angry that he had blatantly deceived me. I felt like an idiot as well that I hadn't noticed anything particularly strange about his paper, except that it was markedly better than his previous work. His instructor had found the situation almost laughable because it was so blatant, but I took it as a personal affront and a reflection of my failings as a tutor. If I had really been there for Eric, I felt, he would not have been reduced to seeing plagiarism as his only option.

My efforts to talk to Eric failed miserably; he absolutely refused to talk to me about his feelings toward school, and I didn't even raise the plagiarism issue. As much as I wanted honesty between us, I felt the abyss between us would become even greater if I pushed it, and there was never a time that I felt comfortable bringing it up. Eric was obviously abashed about what happened, and I believe he understood the seriousness of his actions without my reiteration. Although neither of us ever mentioned that *Othello* paper again (I found out from his instructor that he eventually rewrote it), after a time and to my amazement, Eric actually began to come around. He unexpectedly opened up to me one day about his strong hatred for English and, to my relief, expressed a real interest in—indeed a love for—his major subjects. I hadn't thought it possible that someone could get as emotionally involved in a math problem as I could in a book, but this is what Eric told me he does. So I had to reevaluate my pretentious assumptions.

After this session, Eric and I seemed more comfortable with each other. I wasn't afraid to be tough with him any more, and he no longer expected me to do his work, although it still drove him crazy that the reason I never gave him any answers was that, in fact, there are no answers.

I couldn't call our parting a heartfelt moment, although I felt a little sentimental because Eric had been my first student and was the first one to whom I said goodbye. I felt as well that although his writing has improved slightly, his attitude toward English had not changed at all. Hopefully, his seeing me as an ally rather than an adversary has helped make English less alienating to him. Eric, however, happy to have only one English paper to write in his college career, took his leave by running by me down the hall yelling, "Have a nice summer."

DISCUSSION QUESTIONS

1. This is another story where the tutor's love for literature blinded her to the negative feelings that her tutee had about it. Can you think of anything that Pam might have done to learn Eric's true feelings earlier? Do you think that people like Pam can be trained to be more aware that students have different attitudes before they begin tutoring?
2. Do you think you would have recognized that Eric's *Othello* paper had been plagiarized had you been in Pam's position? Why or why not?
3. What steps did Eric take to hide the fact that his paper had been copied?
4. What might have happened if Pam had been able to confront Eric about his plagiarized paper? Would it have made any difference? Explain.
5. How do you feel about the way Eric's instructor handled the situation with Eric? In your opinion, was she fair to Eric? to the other students in her class?

Orthodoxy and Effectiveness
Dina Fayer

> Dina faces the problem of what to do when she thinks her student, a
> marine corporal, wants a pro, not a peer, to help him with his writing.
> Her approach might be controversial, but she feels it worked well.

When I hear the word *tutor,* I think of an authority who teaches
other individuals better proficiency in an area of expertise. When
I hear the word *peer,* I think of my own friends and our relationships, which are based on humor, parties, gossip, and fellow feeling.
Now think of the expression *peer tutor.* I can't think of two concepts
more irreconcilable. Who *is* this walking oxymoron called a peer
tutor? How is the new peer tutor supposed to define his or her
role in helping students?

I was introduced to the idea of peer tutoring in a special seminar
that outlined the shoulds and shouldn'ts. I learned that I was expected to follow a format that seemed pretty standardized. As
novices, we were warned against giving students our own ideas,
showing obvious biases for or against their opinions, and editing
their papers. We were also shown videotaped examples of the So-
cratic method of questioning that we were supposed to use. In
other words, we couldn't really give our students straight answers,
couldn't suggest, couldn't criticize, or couldn't expect anything
from the student that he or she wasn't readily willing to give. What
the heck was I supposed to do? I was terrified about my first day
of tutoring. What would happen if I didn't do all of this right?

My first student was Corporal Lou Fiore of the U.S. Marines,
who immediately came across as noncommunicative, professional,
and cold. Now here was a man who was used to dealing with drill
sergeants. I felt ridiculous trying to be a peer when he clearly
expected a semiprofessional tutor who knew what she was talking
about and showed it. But I disregarded my instinct and followed
the method I had been taught. And got nowhere. Lou became
frustrated with what he considered evasiveness and, what is worse,
did not listen to any advice I gave because he did not consider me
a qualified authority. He discarded my own experiences when I
used them as examples and ignored me if I hinted at a writing
approach that was different from his. He made me nervous because
I felt as though he considered me an inferior rather than an equal.

Somewhere toward our third week of hell together, I gave up. I started giving him straight answers, and I began to require more from him. I sat on him until he agreed to free-write and started arguing him into listening to my suggestions. In other words, I assumed the authoritative role of his sergeant. At the same time, I experimented with offbeat techniques and humor to try to make our sessions less grindingly slow and frustrating. And I got results. Lou worked diligently, and our relationship developed into a kind of wary equality. He began to respect my opinion, because by answering his questions directly when it seemed appropriate, I showed Lou that I respected him and his writing. Apparently, he had thought that I didn't think his work was worthy of criticism and that I was questioning him dialectically as a condescension.

Meanwhile, I was feeling guilty. Was I giving away too much? Was I making him work hard enough for answers? Every tactic I used with him was somehow unorthodox. Was my approach permissible? I worried about these questions until he brought his graded third paper to me—a C in a course in which he'd previously been failing. At this point, I figured that this grade and his improvement was the proof of the pudding; I continued using my methods, and Lou is now getting A's. We have a solid friendship based on mutual respect, and our sessions have become productive consultations rather than agonizing power battles. I'm proud of both of us.

So I solved the "peer tutor" dilemma with Lou to our mutual satisfaction, but I'm not saying that we should treat all of our students like I treated Lou. What I do feel strongly about is that it is necessary to let the situation dictate the approach. The peer tutor formula contains good ideas that can be productive, but it does not provide for individual quirks and contingencies. And it seems to me that every situation is a contingency. Whether a student is abnormally shy, abnormally obstinate, or normal, he or she needs to be treated as an individual respectable person and writer.

DISCUSSION QUESTIONS

1. Do you agree with Dina's definition of peer tutor and her statement that the term is an oxymoron? Explain.

2. What evidence does Dina present to support the accuracy of her observations about Lou's perceptions of her?
3. Dina does not mention any conferences with her tutor supervisor. Do you think she avoided consulting her supervisor? If so, why do you think she did?
4. Dina talks about a power struggle with her tutee. What are other ways of working through a dilemma such as Dina's?
5. Assume that you were Dina's supervisor and she came to you after her first session with Lou. What might you have suggested she do?
6. Do you think that Dina might have stereotyped Lou as a typical U.S. marine and might have been responding to that perception? Why or why not?

A Tangible Audience
Jennifer Dike

> Jennifer describes the impact that a teacher's critical comments written in red ink on a student's paper have on the student's writing and how the tutor can help turn these into a positive learning experience for the student.

Sara came to tutoring straight from class. She slumped in the chair, remarking that she had just gotten a B− on her first paper. She read the paper out loud to me and, as she reached the comments written in red at the end, her disappointment turned to anger. "What does she mean by transitional phrases?" she snarled as she flipped through the pages jumping from comment to comment. "And here she says I need to develop my thesis—the whole paper is about how we should legalize abortion. How could she miss that?" All of a sudden I felt like I was supposed to be the referee between Sara and the teacher, judging who was right or wrong.

Sara had spent a lot of time on this paper, and now she felt like she had entirely missed the point. She seemed to forget that the teacher had given her a B−, which suggested that the teacher thought that generally it was a good paper. Hurt, Sara wanted to make changes only in the places where the teacher had marked the paper. She wanted to throw out whatever the teacher had questioned—when the teacher was really looking for a clarification or elaboration of an idea. Her reaction to the teacher's comments made me aware of just how alienating these comments written in red ink can be. More often than not, the teachers use academic terms like *clarity, thesis development,* or *organization* to describe what a paper lacks—terms that are often alien to the student. These comments can reduce a student's work into one or two points that are usually viewed negatively. This robs the student of his or her identity, especially because the experience of writing is so personal. In contrast to other academic disciplines where memorization is the rule, writing is one of the few occasions when a student creates something of her own. Yet so often, teachers use vague umbrella terms to describe a complex and subtle piece of communication.

These terms take the individuality out of a paper. They take the focus off effective communication of ideas and put it on trying to make ideas fit a predetermined mold. Sara felt that her paper did not fit into some a priori pattern that the teacher had in mind, and thus her paper was a failure.

The terms that teachers use need to be positive so they can be used as tools to help construct a paper. The teacher's comments must be interpreted to the student so that she sees them as a way of strengthening her argument. The different applications that a student learns throughout her writing experience become a toolbox that she can draw on to improve her communication with the reader.

It is when I am able to help a student achieve this that I feel that I am really fulfilling my role as a tutor. I feel best when I can play the role of interpreter, explaining what the teacher means by "weak transitions" or other comments, not when I find myself a referee between student and teacher. Sometimes students get so wrapped up in their own mental processes that they cannot see things from another point of view—specifically the reader's. I am best able to convey how to use the teacher's comments when I am reacting at a very personal level to the student's paper by asking questions about the points I don't understand. In a way, I am responding as the teacher might if he or she were to correct papers on an interactive basis instead of through the impersonal jottings of red ink.

The tutor works by translating the teacher's comments—not just by giving a technical explanation of terms. For the tutor robs the student of the writing experience when the tutor merely describes how to fix the mistakes. Doing that does not solve the problem of how terminology alienates the student, because the tutor must show the student how the comment is relevant so that the student will see the comment in a positive light. To gain a better sense of control over writing, the student must use these comments constructively in future writing.

Tutoring has the advantage of helping students realize that writing is communication. That is why the most productive tutoring sessions are a dialogue. Through the give and take of conversations related to the paper, the tutor makes clear what is difficult to understand about an argument and why. Thus the student realizes that a paper is not a one-person endeavor but involves at least two people. That is how the tutor makes the audience tangible to the student, an audience that is not just red ink comments but a person who interacts with the student.

The ability to have a dialogue—a give and take—is crucial to the student's ability to identify the areas to work on in future papers. For the goal of tutoring is not just doing well on the immediate paper but ultimately enabling the student to develop skills to write quality papers independent of the tutor's assistance. Students must learn to adopt the tutor's role and internalize it within their own writing. This way they will recognize the difficulties a reader might have with their paper and anticipate them.

DISCUSSION QUESTIONS

1. Can you summarize Jennifer's description of the role of a tutor in working with a student's paper?
2. Do you think Jennifer is being too harsh on English teachers when she criticizes their written comments on students' papers?
3. Do you agree that the ultimate goal of tutoring is for the student to internalize the tutor's comments and use them to anticipate and avoid the difficulties a reader might have with future papers? Explain. What other tutoring goals might be equally important?
4. Compare Jennifer's approach to helping students understand teacher's terms with Po-Sun Chen's in the "Bungee-Cord Thesis" on pg. 77.

Teamwork

Jackie Goldsby

> Jackie explains the differences between tutoring and teaching
> composition and describes how the tutor and the instructor can best
> cooperate for the benefit of the student.

Whenever I work with a new student, I begin by constructing a profile of his or her writing. Does he know what a thesis statement is? Does he structure his paragraphs well? Does he have grammar under control? In talking with the student and in reading his first few drafts, I look for what he already knows about writing and what he needs to learn. Meanwhile his instructor is doing much the same thing as she assesses his response to the first few assignments. Because the teacher and I look at the same person's work in more or less the same ways, our insights will often overlap. And yet the role each of us plays and the perspectives we gain from tutoring in the Student Learning Center or teaching in the classroom provide us with somewhat different views of both the student and his writing.

From her position as a peer collaborator who does not grade the student papers she reads, the tutor is able to determine how a student goes about his work. Close to the student in age and herself a student, the tutor can encourage the student to talk openly about his school work. He will most likely feel comfortable discussing with her why he has problems turning his work in on time, or if he reads haltingly, he might more readily reveal this deficiency in a one-to-one peer session than in a classroom. The tutor has the opportunity to sit beside him as he writes. What process does the student follow when working on a paper? Does he free-write? Does he develop a thesis? Does he use an outline? Does he get stuck at sentence-level problems, or does he fix his attention on the overall organization of his drafts? What particular problems crop up in those drafts, and how does the student solve them? What happens when he develops a writing block? What is the source of the obstacle, and how does he steer himself around it?

While the tutor comes to know the student's study habits and writing processes at close range, the teacher, through her training and her experience with a wide range of student writers, usually

has more refined diagnostic skills. Thus she can name and cate-
gorize structural and grammatical errors, point out logical inconsistencies, and set stylistic norms. Her responses to the student's
papers tell him—and the tutor—what he needs to work on as well
as what he does well. Just as important is the instructor's ability
to help set priorities. She might direct the student to work on
paragraph structure before he worries about paragraph transitions,
or she might first ask for solid thesis statements rather than eloquent introductions or conclusions. She might suggest that problems
with parallel structure or modification are less pressing than those
of subject-verb agreement or run-on sentences. In drawing on her
experience to suggest an order to the student's efforts, the instructor can help to frame, though she does not rigidly determine, the
tutorial sessions.

Since the context for her tutoring is the writing class, the tutor
functions best when she understands the demands the instructor
places on the student. Therefore, the instructor should make time
early in the term to lay out course essentials. What texts will be
used? When will papers be due? When will exams be given and
how important are they? What topics will be covered? What is the
class format? What will the student need to learn to pass the class?
In addition, since each teacher approaches the teaching of writing
differently, the instructor should briefly explain her philosophy and
idiosyncrasies. The better the tutor understands the expectations
of a particular instructor, the less likely it is that she and the teacher
will work at cross-purposes. Certainly the tutor won't want to
belabor thesis statements if they are to be covered in class two
weeks hence or dwell on passive constructions if style is discussed
at length the following term. Because tutoring time is so limited,
the tutor must clearly understand the instructor's objectives, and
she should feel comfortable about approaching the instructor with
her questions throughout the term, whether they be about the
demands of a particular assignment or about the instructor's attitudes toward experimentation with the thesaurus. And the more
aware the instructor is of what goes on in the tutorial sessions, the
better able she will be to affirm, in a finely tuned manner, what
the student attempts in his papers. Her responses to his efforts and
praise for his successes rewards him for spending extra time on his
writing.

A working relationship between teacher and tutor, then, presents to both the opportunity to share their observations and to combine their resources as they define the tasks and direct the efforts that each member of the learning triangle—teacher, student, and tutor—will undertake. Ideally, the tutor and teacher will meet early in the term to discuss the course, the student's writing, and any learning problems the student might have. Together they can devise a checklist that divides up the work that needs to be done. Their goals will be continuously revised as they come to know the student better, as he expresses his own desires about what he feels ready to tackle, and as he makes progress. It is crucial that communication be open and frequent to accommodate this growth and change. Quick phone calls, comments at the ends of papers, or notes can provide the means for keeping in touch.

Of course the student should be the first to know about this collaboration, for he will be the subject of the discussions. The tutor must remember that some students might not want an instructor to know that they are seeking help in a course, and the instructor should be sensitive about the boundaries of the peer sanctuary. Both tutor and instructor are obligated to honor the confidentiality of their relationship with the student. This is not to say that they must restrict their conversations solely to academic matters, but they should be sure that they do not betray the student's trust. If, for instance, an unmotivated student has difficulty producing good work, the best solution might be a three-way conversation between teacher, student, and tutor. However, in some cases, a student might reveal very personal information to only one of them, information that he might not want shared. A student of mine in a basic writing course at UC Berkeley was having unusual difficulty handling an assignment. While he had plenty to say about the topic, the way alcoholics are portrayed in films, for some reason he couldn't put pen to paper. After some discussion, I discovered that the student's writing block was rooted in the emotions he had about being an alcoholic during high school. We faced a dilemma: the paper was due the following day and he didn't want to share his personal history with the teacher. While I sensed that the instructor would be sympathetic, I didn't want to pressure him to take a step he was not ready for. Moreover, I felt that he would benefit from learning to negotiate with the instructor on his own.

I therefore encouraged him to explain to the teacher that he found the topic personally difficult and to request an extension and a new topic. The instructor spoke with me to confirm that the student had indeed been struggling all week with the topic, but I kept the source of the problem confidential.

Once trust is established and all three members of the team are working smoothly together, the student will steadily learn because the extra effort he expends is consistently directed. The mere ten to fifteen weeks that he has to learn in are not fragmented by misunderstanding or conflicting emphases. Of course, students with numerous composing problems especially benefit from such coordinated efforts. For example, another student of mine found it difficult to harness his ideas into paragraphs, wrote prose riddled with grammatical errors, and had trouble reading college-level textbooks. The list of things-to-do was lengthy, but first the instructor and I decided to confirm that the student's writing problems didn't stem from a deficiency beyond our scope. We agreed that the student's first task should be to take the reading comprehension test administered by specialists in the Student Learning Center. As it turned out, the reading problem grew out of the student's unfamiliarity with academic prose. He took charge of that area by working with the reading specialist on vocabulary building. Next, we decided that the student should bring several of his more serious sentence-level problems under control. So the teacher zeroed in on this area in her comments, and the student and I allotted twenty minutes per session to reviewing predication and agreement. Once his prose was free of those errors, he and I shifted our attention to paragraph structure, and the teacher's critical responses showed him that she was aware of his concern with unity and development.

This plan worked out rather nicely. The instructor, who was teaching two classes and had some fifty students, could spend the brief conference time she had with this student discussing the conceptual and developmental problems of specific papers. I could systematically structure the two hours per week I had reserved for the student so that we covered particular topics in great detail. And while the teacher and I went about our tasks separately, we did maintain contact through the messages she relayed to me on the student's papers. Sensing the harmony of our joint efforts, he felt confident about discussing with me what he hadn't understood in class and saw the teacher's comments on his papers as useful and challenging. He worked harder because he felt that we were both working together for him.

One of the most important things that tutors as well as instructors do for the student is to involve him and get him to write and think for himself. When instructor and tutor maintain contact with each other and involve the student in setting goals, the student assumes an active role in the project and, rather than being uncomfortably caught between two reader's responses, draws on the strengths of the two readers and two learning contexts. Thus any checklist of tasks devised by the tutor and the teacher should serve only as a recommendation that the student evaluates for himself before deciding what goals he wants to achieve. After all, he will be the one to do much of the work, and he must be able to generate such lists for himself in the future. A student might suddenly develop a keen interest in his own introductions, or he might decide that his pride is hurt by spelling errors, even though the teacher finds spelling errors innocuous. The student learns fastest when he discovers his own interest in mastering a skill and draws on his teacher and his tutor as guides to and reinforcers of his learning.

I remember being impressed when, during a rough draft session, a student began by telling me what areas she needed to smooth out in her paper, juggling three critiques that she had solicited on her work: one offered by her instructor, one by me, and one by her roommate. As she debated how each did or did not fit with what *she* wanted to do, and as she explained how she would incorporate several of the suggestions into a revision of the draft, I realized that over the past month she had become more adept, more confident about judging her own work. She was now evaluating her writing and her readers' responses in a critical, probing, questioning manner. The student had begun to understand and to practice writing as a social act. Her prose sharpened in clarity and focus as she discussed her ideas with others; she had turned a potentially isolating activity into one of active engagement with an audience.

Few students, including myself, learn best at the back of a lecture hall or in the dim corner of a library. They must learn how to get the most from the varied and rich educational resources available to them in conversations with tutors, teachers, teaching assistants, study skills counselors, reading specialists, and classmates. Each has her own special insights and can help the student in different ways. The productive collaboration of tutor and instructor, then, does more than assist the student in a given course during a given term; it invites the student to actively participate in the give and take of academic discourse.

The Student-Tutor-Teacher Triangle
Rebecca Weller

> What's a tutor to do when the instructor refuses to acknowledge that her student's writing is improving? Rebecca found an answer.

By the eleventh week of classes, it seemed quite likely that one of my basic composition students wouldn't pass the course. Indeed, to my mind and under the circumstances, it almost seemed preferable, for I feared that a heavy academic schedule would place a disheartening burden on the shoulders of a student who was not truly adept at writing. Over spring break, I'd spent several hours reviewing the videotape I had made with my two basic composition students, and it seemed hard to believe that the two students were enrolled in the same class. Even in the first few seconds of the tape, Phil exuded pleasure in his newly discovered self-confidence as a writer. While he still had many stylistic issues to be addressed, they were just that—stylistic. Now that it seemed certain that he would pass the course, my goals for him were to help him maintain his high degree of motivation and to further his interest in the complexities of strong, insightful academic writing. We both felt that the rest of the semester would be an exercise in accomplishment, and I was delighted to hear him express pride in his writing.

But Maria was another story. As a new tutor at the beginning of the semester, I had been greatly relieved to realize that both my tutees seemed intelligent, disciplined, and dedicated to doing well with the tasks the course presented. My opinion of Maria had not changed during the intervening weeks; indeed, as the semester progressed and we began to unearth more problems than either of us had anticipated, I was impressed by her continued perseverance. Unfortunately, only some of the problems lay in Maria's writing. Difficulties with her instructor, Beth, presented other obstacles to her improvement.

After about the sixth week, I had gone to see Beth for a short meeting because I was interested in getting her perspective on Maria's progress. With her, I reviewed the midterm that she had graded a D+ but had not yet returned to Maria. Beth's grade as well as her comments on the paper distressed me for several reasons. First, Maria had been getting D and D+ grades all term, and I had hoped to see some improvement in her grade or at least in the instructor's comments by then. More worrisome I felt was the fact that, despite its grade, this essay seemed to be a vast improvement over Maria's previous work, yet these changes went unnoticed.

Because her writing was plagued with all sorts of problems, from immature thought to logical discontinuities, from lack of structure to several significant sentence-level problems, Maria and I had worked on idea generation and overall essay structure, for it seemed that my first task was to help Maria begin to explore how to discover and arrange her thoughts. While her previous week's practice midterm had been, to my mind, a near-total disaster, I was astonished to find that this in-class theme had incorporated all of the major considerations we'd been stressing in the previous week. To be sure, the sentences remained somewhat garbled, and those that were clear revealed some immaturity, but the essay's framework was sound and well-considered. While it is often terribly difficult for a student to "waste" the first few minutes of an in-class exam just thinking and organizing, Maria had clearly taken the time to read the essay questions carefully, consider the relevant issues, and compose an outline based on those aspects she wanted to address. To my eyes, the exam demonstrated a clearer recognition of the fundamental tasks of an academic essay.

But Beth had made no comment whatsoever about structure, nor had she said anything about the essay's content. Instead, she picked apart sentence construction, rewriting whole sentences, reminding Maria to control her "wordiness" and to "watch those commas" with no further explanation. Essentially, she gave Maria the task of incorporating notions that the student did not understand, a task that would mystify, mislead, and ultimately dishearten her. To me, the teacher seemed to be abdicating her teaching responsibility while inadvertently punishing Maria in the process. In response to my enthusiastic comments about the paper's improvements, Beth seemed to recognize some of the things she had over-looked, but the fact remained—the paper was graded and the judgment had been made.

Reviewing the tape of our tutoring session over spring break confirmed my fears. In the face of persistent criticism and failing grades, Maria had begun to retreat from the real purpose of the class—to develop an understanding of the process and basic skills of academic self-expression. To be sure, Maria had never shirked the work, and until the midterm she had maintained faith that her efforts would pay off in better skills and higher grades. But it was clear to me that since the midterm fear had replaced her faith. She no longer saw writing techniques as tools that could, with dedication, be developed. Instead, polished academic prose suddenly became something out there beyond her grasp, something that you either had or didn't have. She became more passive in our sessions together and tended to retreat into the rules of grammar. When asked to rewrite an earlier paper, she clung stubbornly to the task of trying to "put in what Beth wants," rather than daring to try to write something new.

Her instructor's rigid teaching methods seemed to have rein-forced Maria's sense that writing is about rules, rather than about self-expression. In watching our videotaped sessions, I realized that I had reinforced this academic oppression by allowing Maria's fears to drag us into an examination of grammatical details. Despite my distress over my complicity, I didn't feel that I could in good faith simply encourage her to forget the rules and just write what she thought. I knew that any such attempt would be undermined by her instructor's relentless emphasis on using correct grammar. But for me to continue to try, as I had in our taped session, to explain the rules of grammar was to alienate her further, making writing seem tortuously contrived. I knew that writing needn't be so per-plexing for her as she was more than articulate in ordinary con-versation, and the grammatical errors displayed in her writing simply weren't evident in her speech. Further, I had read a paper she had written for a sociology course in which many of the gram-matical errors disappeared when she didn't feel she was embarking on a mystifying minefield called "sentence-level problems."

Despite my fears that I might be overstepping my bounds, when she and I met after spring break I expressed some of my concerns about her change in attitude and confidence and said I thought we should talk about that. She talked at length about her frustration over putting in so many hours of effort and receiving so little in return. Somewhat defensively, she confessed her surprise that she might fail the course and revealed a lot of resentment toward her instructor. I was pleased that she had attributed her problems to insecurity and frustration rather than saying she felt she just wasn't smart enough to understand what the teacher wanted. I asked her if she would talk with my supervisor and me as I wasn't sure of how to proceed, and she readily agreed, seemingly glad to have all of this out in the open.

After listening to Maria and discussing what had transpired, Liz, my supervisor, suggested that maybe Maria would like to have me accompany her to a conference with Beth. Liz and I emphasized that some of what Maria was experiencing was beyond her direct control and that her instructor should be informed of how alienating her constant barrage of small criticisms had become. Maria set up the appointment, and she and I met with Beth in her office later that week.

It was clear from her opening remark, "So I guess you two must have an agenda," that Beth was uncomfortable by the apparent necessity of having a tutor mediate between her and a student. However, after listening to Maria's account of frustration and to my observation that many of the grammatical errors seemed to be a result of anxiety and poor structural process, Beth seemed more responsive and sympathetic. The three of us agreed to try an experiment for a few weeks: Maria would hand in a rough draft of each assignment a day before the official due date, and Beth would respond simply to the content and structure of the papers. Only after that initial review would Maria go back to address whatever sentence-level problems she might perceive, and only that second draft would be graded.

Maria's improvement was astonishing. Her next paper was coherently structured, reasonably well-considered (if not sophisticated), and virtually devoid of sentence-level problems. It earned her a respectable B. While she still has to write one more paper and to take the final exam, it is now apparent to all of us that Maria has the ability to pass the course with ease.

I can't pretend that it was simply a change in an instructor's grading policy that allowed Maria to find her own voice in academic writing; in the final analysis, that might be a minor element. The reading, writing, and analysis she had done in all of the semester's assignments were essential training. Surely, the nature of one-to-one tutoring intensified her examination of the process of analytic composition. But her improvement stems much more directly, I believe, from redefining the terms of the teacher-student relationship. She didn't simply take her mistakes to a teacher for further instruction or swallow them and try to work around them. Rather, she discovered that it might be valuable to ask the teacher to consider her differently, to try something else.

After the meeting, I taped another of our sessions together. Because she was again given an assignment to rewrite an earlier paper of her choice, we used the first twenty minutes to make a nostalgic survey of the semester's work. It would be hard for a disinterested observer to tell which of us was the tutor and which the student. Maria did almost all of the talking, analyzing with great ease and confidence the flaws she now saw in her early work. When she decided which paper to rewrite, the most obvious change was her markedly increased sense of confidence. Maria had known all along that she is smart; what she discovered, I think, is that personal and social issues lurk behind so much of the university experience.

DISCUSSION QUESTIONS

1. If the tutor had spent less time on grammar early in the term, do you think that Maria might have improved faster? Why or why not? Explain.
2. What do you think was the most important factor in Maria's metamorphosis from D student to B student? Why?
3. Do you think the other students in the writing class might have resented the experiment that Beth, the instructor, arranged with Maria? Why or why not?
4. Recent research suggests that poor college writers often don't understand the comments and suggestions instructors write on their papers and generally ignore written feedback. Does Maria's experience support this conclusion? Explain.
5. Do you think this same approach would work with other stu-

dents? If you do, describe the conditions under which you feel it might work.

Twelve Steps to Great Tutoring
Candida Ellis

> Candida explores the notion that there's no easy trick to tutoring well. It's all in the wrist—or is it?

When I studied for the GRE exams, I resisted the notion that the complex analytical problems had to be solved by a series of painstaking steps. "There's a trick to it," I assured my husband. "Once you learn the trick, it's easy." What occurred to me even as I spoke was that underlying my attitude lurked a conviction that there was an easy way to do everything. All that was needed was to master "the trick."

Uncovering the trick is a national hobby. *The New York Times* best-seller lists swarm with "How To" titles because Americans can't resist the notion that book covers can hide a magic trick capable of altering the course of life: how to lose weight while eating and drinking everything that isn't nailed to the refrigerator, how to exercise while napping, or how to make a zillion dollars by spending an hour a month on the telephone talking to a good friend. Or how to toilet train a kid or housebreak a dog while never once having to deal with the waste products of consumption. Or how to bring peace and tranquility to the battle for excellence. It's all in the wrist!

As tutors, most of us show up for duty with a bundle of similarly banal assumptions about the art of tutoring shoved under one arm. Face it, the reason you're reading this story is you're hoping against hope that I can tell you that little secret something that will sweep you into a tutoring relationship filled with satisfaction and success, devoid of the unpleasant suspicion that anything you're doing could possibly be a waste of time.

When we arrive at the Student Learning Center with our bundles, we might be surprised to meet our tutees carrying rather large packages of their own tucked up high in their armpits. The contents of their packages in many respects seem to correspond with the contents of our own: tutoring should be fun; writing should be easy; the paper in question needs to be an A paper; there's a way to do this stuff. But the burden thrust on us by most of these mutually held assumptions, that of having to know everything, usually makes us urge our tutees to unload. Sometimes tutees do change their expectations, and sometimes they don't. Yet whatever the tutee does, neither he nor the tutor is likely to take any notice of that rather awkward package the tutor is still lugging. With a little bad luck, most of us are certain to make it all the way to the end of the semester with that unwieldy parcel intact.

Proof of this emerges whenever our tutees face a due date. We feel pressured to find extra time, either in face-to-face meetings or over the telephone. Our response to this pressure (whether internal or external or both) can signal a need to remove from our armpit that rather large ungainly item labelled *ego*. That particular package contains a number of unwrapped assumptions about how this poor tutee cannot possibly get along without us and about how only with our help may he or she squeak by this perilous due date with a C, or (if *we've* really done a good job) the well-assisted student might have a shot at a B or even at an A.

What we've done in this case is to extend the fairly logical premise that our job is to help the student stay in school and improve scholastically into the idea that grades are all important, an idea that makes all goals immediate. Suddenly we're either amplifying our students' thesis statements or going over their papers like an automated grammar checker or revising their interpretation of the book they are discussing or pointing out overlooked arguments for or against in a way that is more directive than helpful. *Help* becomes a word bloated well beyond respectability. Suddenly *help* is drunk with purpose.

Ironically, in our swelling confusion about the meaning of the word *help*, we hold back the very information we probably ought to offer routinely, such as, "You need a comma there," or "You misspelled *anitdisestablishmentarianism.*" Instead we cryptically interrogate our befuddled tutees. "What's *wrong* with this sentence?" A change in tense probably doesn't need to be discussed unless a student truly does not know the difference between present tense and any other. But in our zeal to redefine *help*, we soberly ask the tutee to ponder a pronoun with the wrong referent instead of casually reminding him or her that pronouns refer to the immediately preceding noun and quickly moving on to something more challenging such as, "Tell me exactly what your thesis is in one short simple sentence."

Yet we feel, nursing our cultural assumptions, that we have been asked to do something that ought to be a great deal easier than it has turned out to be, and probably more fun than we seem to be making it. Clearly the fault is our own. Hair prickles at the back of our necks when the tutee plops down with a grimy sheet of mangled paper and announces, "This is due tomorrow."

Let's dump our sacks and start from the beginning. Let's refuse to accept the Christian premise that the grade we save might be our own. Let's look at tutoring as a process instead of rapid movement to an end. If we see ourselves as engaged in collaboration and see our role as reflective and inquisitive, even occasionally resourceful because we happen to know that a comma is misplaced or how to fix a dangling referent, we might start having fun, and we might even be more helpful. And if you send me $29.95, I'll send you my pamphlet, "Twelve Steps to Great Tutoring."

DISCUSSION QUESTIONS

1. Examine the assumptions in Candida's recommendations for great tutoring. What assumptions is she questioning?
2. Do you agree with her statement that in our zeal to redefine *help,* we sometimes stress the insignificant aspects of writing?

Achieving Rapport with Quiet Students
Mark Yardas

It's hard for a talkative person to learn to tutor a very quiet student.

I guess I should have felt suspicious. I had been hanging around the Golden Bear tutoring the tutees and enjoying a strange sense of harmony considering it was my first week on the new job. Strange indeed, since I have not seen harmony's smug mug in my vicinity since back in Ohio, right before the Great Flood of '68; rarely do we part company in the gentlest of circumstances. Perhaps my guard was down the first week. Except for the never ending pile of Xerox copies of reading materials, everything seemed cool and easy. My first three tutees all brought drafts to work on, and they even smiled occasionally. In each session, we quickly established a friendly rapport before starting to work on writing, and they all had clear ideas of what they needed to work on. Most importantly, they all *communicated* these ideas to me, so I felt involved with their struggles to write more clearly. Each evening, I left the Golden Bear with another pound of tutoring handouts under my arm, feeling a sense of oneness with humanity, as I strolled home in the warm September air. "I am needed. I belong," my spirit sang.

But I should have been suspicious. I should have known that everything could change, as it did the following week when I met my fourth tutee: the young woman I will refer to as The Quiet One.

It must have rained that morning. I can still see her peering at me through a pair of fogged lenses as thick as hamhocks. I held out my hand. "I'm Mark," I said.

"I'm The Quiet One," she returned with an icy handshake. As she sat down and began staring off at a land she alone inhabited, my skin began to crawl like a gila monster infested with army ants. I hoped that the goal-setting worksheet might loosen up our conversation. As instructed, I started out by trying to focus on her strengths as a writer. "Are there any aspects of your writing that you feel particularly good about?"

Silence.

"Any times when you feel yourself enjoying writing?"

More Silence.

"Maybe something about writing that you don't completely hate?"

After awhile she looked up at me as though she had just realized that she was not sitting at the table alone. "No," she answered. "I hate writing."

I appreciate directness. "Okay," I said. "What do you hate about it?"

"You never get a clear answer. In math you know if something is right or wrong. In writing everything seems wrong."

"Sure," I said, relieved that we were talking. "Even the greatest writers feel constantly dissatisfied with what they've written. They're always trying to express their ideas perfectly, but there can always be a better way to say something. But that's also what makes writing interesting. It forces you to confront some of your deeper thoughts and communicate them to others." She looked unmoved, and I felt like I was talking too much. I like to talk. "Are there any aspects of your writing that you feel you need to work on? The goal-setting worksheet here is divided between grammar and sentence structure, essay structure, and writing process. What type of writing problems are you having that we should work on?"

"Everything, I guess," she mumbled. She is an expert mumbler. If I wanted to make progress with The Quiet One, I would have to slow down and get my ears cleaned.

I am an extrovert from a family of introverts. At some point, I learned that it was easier for me to talk out the problems I was having rather than keeping them stored up inside. Once I started expressing myself, I never stopped. I often wonder if I go too far. Sometimes I feel that a real strength resides in silence, that one who is quiet is perhaps more in touch with himself. But there is also another form of silence, one that relates to various fears: the fear that one's ideas are not intelligent or interesting enough to be communicated, the fear of becoming vulnerable by expressing feelings that are deeply personal, or even the fear of delving into such feelings in the first place. As The Quiet One's tutor, I needed to determine the nature of her silence, so that I could help her overcome it if it were caused by fear, or so I could learn to be comfortable with it if it were not.

As weeks passed, though, she engaged more openly in light conversation before and after the sessions, so I concluded that one source of her silence was shyness. I instinctively felt it was important to tone down my own expressiveness so that she would feel more comfortable expressing herself and so that the rapport between us would feel more balanced. This sense of balance is essential in a tutorial relationship. To achieve it, a tutor must learn to listen — not only to the tutee but also to himself. I slowly learned that listening is indeed a skill and that its usefulness definitely extends beyond tutoring.

At first, the long stretches of silence unnerved me, and I would attempt to break them by asking different questions or filling them with my own comments. Not only did these methods fail to draw

The Quiet One out, they seemed to cause her to withdraw even more. Clearly, I had to change my tactics, or our peer tutoring sessions would turn into lectures.

One afternoon, she brought a watch advertisement picturing an Olympic runner next to a giant watch. When I asked her why she thought the advertisers juxtaposed the two images, she grew tense and quiet. I felt that it was important that she answer this question herself, though, so I settled back in my seat, and I waited. (I noticed in my videotaped session with The Quiet One that she seemed more at ease when I sat back from her, thereby conveying patience by giving her more physical space.) She began fidgeting, looking at me as though she expected an answer.

"Take your time," I reassured her. She continued to fidget, and I continued to listen for an answer. Finally she said, "They're taking something really small and trying to make it seem really big." We both burst out laughing, probably due to a sense of comic relief.

"Sure," I said. "Any other reasons you can think of?" From there, the session took off. Once The Quiet One felt her ideas were valid, she expressed them much more freely. I learned that it was important to pace our sessions according to her speed and to center our discussions around her ideas.

I noticed that her periods of silence usually began when I asked questions that led her into areas of abstraction. If I asked her a question regarding the text she had read, she would start slowly thumbing through it, looking for an answer. If I asked her to come up with something off the top of her head, she only stared at me blankly. I found that asking open-ended questions proved helpful in this regard. How did she feel about the author's opinions? Did she like the essay? What stood out in her mind most from the reading? Initially, such questions clearly intimidated her, but as the semester progressed she began answering them with greater ease and depth. Also, examining her feelings on what she read enabled her to get more involved and interested in the author's ideas. Needless to say, learning is much easier when one is interested in the subject.

The success of peer tutoring depends on the tutor's sensitivity to the student's needs. I doubt if I would have learned this lesson so concretely if I had only tutored the other, more expressive students. The Quiet One's silence forced me to listen more patiently and ask the kinds of questions that could draw her out. As a result, my ears are a little keener, and The Quiet One is not such a quiet one.

DISCUSSION QUESTIONS

1. Mark describes himself as an extrovert. What made him realize that he'd better "slow down and clean out [his] ears" if he wanted to work successfully with this student?
2. What kinds of questions seemed to intimidate his student the most, and what did Mark do that helped her answer these?
3. Do you think that Mark might be insensitive in referring to his tutee as The Quiet One? Why?

2   The Tutor as Writer and Reader

When the Tutor Suffers Writer's Amnesia
Alicia Rojas Wainer

> Alicia found that by concentrating so hard on her students' writing as a tutor, she had been ignoring her own writing problems.

I placed my paper, titled *Mind over Matter*, a comparison of Shakespeare's Sonnets 97 and 98, on the table in front of the professor and breathed a sigh of relief. The agony was over, or so I thought. As I walked away from the class, had anyone asked what my paper was about, I wouldn't have been able to tell them. My writing had disintegrated since I had been tutoring. I hadn't paid much attention to my own writing while I had consistently examined and reevaluated my students' writing. My first reaction to this disintegration was that it was the result of being excessively critical or of overanalyzing. The vast amount of information about writing that a first-semester tutor reads gives any student the tools to critically assess and revamp their own writing. A person competent enough to become a writing tutor in the first place already has strong writing skills, but under close scrutiny and criticism, a writer's whole approach could be decimated, appearing riddled with faults.

Overanalysis was not my problem though. In the long run, my writing would probably have been better if I had deliberately taken a good, hard, objective look at it, the same way I had with my tutees' papers. My problem was that I didn't have a definite writing process to examine. Writing had always come naturally to me, and I'd never really needed to assess it. Nor was I aware of any major problems in my writing. When I began to tutor writing, I was exposed to massive amounts of information about building and improving writing. If I had inspected my own writing closely using this information, I might have realized how amorphous my writing process was. Instead, because I had not consciously analyzed my writing, I was wide open to any potshots my subconscious chose to take.

My intuitive relationship to writing presented problems to me in tutoring as well. I'd never had trouble activating the passive voice, but I did not know how to explain passive verb form transformation to developing writers. Moments like this made me aware that one of my major weaknesses as a tutor was my lack of command of the technical and grammatical vocabulary related to language. So although tutoring initially weakened parts of my writing, it made me confront the soft spots as well.

To be totally honest, the problem paper I wrote wasn't prepared in an ideal time frame; rather, it was produced under the time constraints demanded by my many academic responsibilities. This particular incident was different from other times when I've procrastinated, because in the past, after the postpaper nausea had passed, I would think back on the piece and know what the strengths and weaknesses of my paper were. This time, I couldn't recall anything. Even after I'd gotten the paper back and was reading the professor's comment, what he wrote made absolutely no sense to me. It was a case of ex post facto writer's block!

I'd failed to go through the revision stages as described in *The Practical Tutor* when it presents the idea of an "other self," a part of the writing mind that detaches itself from the writing person. This other self assesses the strengths and weaknesses of a paper, discriminates between what's necessary and what's superfluous, and helps pull the writing person out of the mire of his or her ideas. The breakdown of this process left me stuck in the mud. This was my first paper after a long summer break, and I found writing awkward. Not only had it seemed hard to write, but I was unable to analyze literature gracefully, and I found myself digressing at every possible juncture. Under most circumstances I would consider this normal; either a result of not developing my ideas sufficiently or not focusing them. One can usually clear these problems up in the revision process, but this time I couldn't. I wasn't able to look at the text I'd written and discriminate between meat and fluff either analytically or linguistically.

The first line of the professor's comment says it all. "Cia, this is not very successful." So much for the rule that positive reinforcement should come first. My professor was right though, and as I reread the paper I had to laugh, because I was guilty of awkward prose, talking around ideas and text, digression, and contradiction. As a result, I'm very tempted to consider myself a victim of circumstance, because when I mentioned to a friend and fellow tutor what had happened to my paper and wondered whether it had anything to do with tutoring, she said, "Your writing is the first thing to go."

In the long run, however, I see the experience as positive. I got one bad grade on one paper out of the thousand I'll probably write in college.

Since then, it's been back to the writing board for me. I have had to grasp the essentials of essay writing—thesis, development, focus, logic—and tackle my amorphous process. Strangely, this process inspires me and heartens me, and I feel I am beginning to build a solid foundation for strong and reliable writing. I am cultivating good writing habits rather than relying on inspiration and the ability to improvise.

Best of all, I'm learning not to be intimidated by writing. In the past when I turned in a paper, I felt like I'd just climbed the highest peak of Mount Everest. The feeling of satisfaction was tremendous, but the process was often traumatic. Tutoring has taught me to move beyond these anxieties. Not only has my writing begun to improve tremendously, but I think I am doing a better job of helping my students because I am helping myself.

DISCUSSION QUESTIONS

1. Do you think that Alicia's losing the ability to critique her own papers happens to other tutors who rely on improvisation and inspiration? If so, can you think of ways this problem can be avoided?
2. Is this amnesia of one's own papers something that new tutors should be alerted to? If so, how best might this be done?
3. In what way will the experience Alicia describes make her a better tutor? Explain.

Tutor Writing Blocks
Kyle Ikeda

> Thinking that he, as an English major, should have all the answers
> set the stage for Kyle's fall when he found himself experiencing
> writer's block. After suffering bitterly for a while, he realized the
> answer could be found in talking to other tutors.

"What's up?" the girl asked. She had just taken off her back pack
and put it on the table while easing into her chair.

"Well, I'm having a tough time starting my essay," the guy said.
"I've got a bunch of ideas, but don't know how to organize them."

"How do you usually go about organizing your ideas?"

"I kind of just see what goes well together. Usually I've got a
better idea of how to connect my ideas. Right now I don't know
what's wrong. By now I usually know what point I'm trying to
make."

"Well it sounds like you know what's missing. Have you tried
figuring out what point you're making or what your thesis is?"

"Yeah, but I guess I haven't tried hard enough. I still don't know
how my main point is connected to half of my ideas. Sheesh, I'm
so stressed I feel like I'm going to die right now. I feel like I don't
know how to write. I suck."

"Oh, be quiet. You're a good writer, otherwise you wouldn't be
a writing tutor. You're stressing right now. All we have to do is
get you past this writing block, and everything will be just fine."

The dialogue above depicts one of the most rewarding and
beneficial parts of being a writing tutor: having the opportunity
to get the support of and counseling from other tutors. Of course
much of the sharing between tutors takes place in seminar. Often
prompted by our supervisor, we are able to offer suggestions on
various tutoring difficulties while receiving many insights into our
own problems. By merely sharing a story about an encounter with
a student whose writing appears racist or sexist, the entire seminar
group can benefit from the forewarning. Yes, most of the problems
discussed in seminar concern our student's writing. What my little
story depicts is a conference that concerns my own writing obstacles. Of course this support and counseling usually takes place

outside of seminar. Every tutor should be aware of the opportunity to get help on his or her own writing from peers.

My writing blocks resulted from my tutoring experiences. I'm sure of that. In my tutoring sessions, I'd been in the habit of always trying to know the answer to a particular writing problem. I saw myself as a guide presenting wonderful strategies and tactics that led to good prose. After all, I am an English major, a writing tutor, and a senior with three years of experience at this silly campus. Heck, I should know how to write by now.

This attitude led to problems when I ran into trouble working out difficult ideas for my own papers. Suddenly, I no longer had all the answers. I'd begin to panic and torture myself over my incompetence. Yet, I was supposed to be extremely competent. I'm supposed to know what to do. "If I can't write this paper, then it's impossible!" I'd think to myself. So I'd just sit at my desk, staring at blank paper for a couple of hours worrying.

See, I couldn't scream or ask for help. My roommate wouldn't understand because he's a music major. Running to my professor would be too impersonal because he doesn't know who I am. Talking to a reader or a teaching assistant would be even worse because I don't even know who they are. Furthermore, I felt too embarrassed to ask for help. After all, I'm supposed to have all the answers. I finally built up enough courage to share my problems with my roommate. As I expected, the poor guy just didn't understand my predicament. Instead of getting sympathy, he replied, "You're supposed to be the English stud, I can't help you." That really made matters worse.

I then began to doubt not only my ability to finish the paper but my ability to finish my English major. Mentally, I made a mountain out of a mole hill from the situation. I'd think to myself, "If I fail this paper, then I'll fail the class. If I fail the class, then my GPA will be shot. If my GPA sucks, then I won't get into grad school and I'll never get a job!" The one skill that I thought was keeping me at this university was blanking out on me. I felt I was the only English major who had problems writing papers.

Well, of course that isn't true. Unfortunately, when you are in the middle of your own problem, it's hard to find a solution. Furthermore, I had fooled myself into believing that I had all the answers and that those around me couldn't help. Luckily I decided to call someone from my tutoring seminar. After all, a fellow tutor isn't as intimidating as a professor or a teaching assistant; a tutor should know who you are after sharing weekly seminar meetings.

Talking to a fellow tutor made me realize that I'm not the only English major who has problems writing papers. In fact, it is a relief to know that writing discomfort is normal—or at least that I'm not alone in suffering it. Furthermore, getting help from a peer was more comfortable than seeing a professor, because a fellow student has a better understanding of what you're going through. This observation has helped me change my attitude toward tutoring as well. Surely if I get intimidated by my professors, then my tutees might be scared of me. Instead of trying to have all the answers, I now try to act more tentative when working with my students. By not having the answer, I force them to find solutions for themselves. Hopefully my sessions haven't been that intimidating and have allowed my students to develop confidence in their writing.

In any case, I found there are great benefits in having close contacts with other English majors. I've been able to give and receive great advice on which professors to avoid and which to take. I've received advice as well as sympathy concerning problem students. I've been there to listen to fellow tutors complain and indulged in the pleasure of complaining myself. In any case, the spirit of the Student Learning Center is to help students, so we might as well help ourselves and each other.

"Oh be quiet. You're a good writer. You're a writing tutor. You're just stressing right now. All we have to do is get you past this writing block and everything will be just fine."

"Yeah, you're probably right. Sometimes you just need someone to reassure you that everything will be all right. Just knowing you're here to help makes all the difference in the world."

DISCUSSION QUESTIONS

1. What were some of the factors that helped Kyle break through his writing block? Explain.
2. Do you think that it is appropriate for tutors to help each other with their writing problems? How about the ethics of sharing the experiences they've had with different professors? Should

tutors give advice to each other about which professors to take courses from? To their students?

3. How do you feel about Kyle's statement that he learned that it's OK to be more tentative with his students?

Supervisor's Comments

In Jackie Goldsby's essay, "Teamwork" (chap. 1), she talks about extending collaboration to include the instructor and describes the benefits for students when the instructor-student-tutor triangle works in harmony. Some tutors, like Kyle, find instructors intimidating and avoid contact with their own teachers as well as their students'. Even though they've read Jackie's essay in their first week as tutors and even after hearing other tutors talk in seminar about how important their meetings with instructors were to their students' success, they still won't contact instructors. Then something happens that spurs them to action. Maybe it was the interesting discussion the day a composition instructor came to seminar, maybe it was the concern expressed by the supervisor in the midterm conference, maybe the teacher called the tutor.

Once tutor and teacher start talking, the tutor inevitably wonders what there was to be afraid of. Sure, some instructors are more helpful than others, but any kind of information, including bad vibes, helps you serve your student better. Bad vibes happen, but not as often as you might think. Most of the time you find that you share a common bond with the instructors in your students' composition classes, and your students look to your behavior as a model for academic achievement. If you break the ice with the teacher, there's a good chance that the student will follow and take advantage of the individual instruction most composition teachers are willing to give. And who knows, you might even be inspired to go talk with one of your own instructors about your writing.

Nevertheless, every writer, even those like yourself who are expected to be more advanced, needs readers, plural, more than just the one instructor. The habit of talking through ideas for a paper or showing a draft to people who can be representative of your audience can be cultivated either informally or formally in your tutor training program. At UC Berkeley in the first week or two of their training, each new writing tutor is asked to write a rough draft of a 500-word essay describing his or her writing process, and the tutor is then tutored on that draft by his or her senior tutor. Despite this exercise, despite the feedback supervisors give tutors about their writing, and despite the seminar discussions about their own writing processes, tutors like Alicia and Kyle experience writer's block. More is needed. We encourage tutors to tutor each other, to respond to each other's papers, and to form small reader response workshops that meet regularly. At times in the past we have even made these workshops a formal part of the training. Any tutor training program that builds in reader response workshops for tutors is admirable, but if your program doesn't, you can form your own groups or at least seek each other out for individual feedback on papers in progress. You and your fellow tutors are a community of writers, and tutors as well as teachers need to continue to develop as writers so they can better understand their students' development.

—Thom Hawkins

Expectations of a Tutor: Reflections of One Who Has Been Tutored
Helen Woo

> Helen became a tutor because she wanted to help others avoid the nightmarish experiences she had in her basic writing course. However, she learned that trying to play hero can lead to disappointment when she found that other students did not share her fears about writing and had different expectations.

I remember how I first learned about the need for tutors at the Student Learning Center. It was at the end of my junior year when I was walking by Sproul and somebody handed me a pink flyer. I was about to toss it, but when I saw "Tutor for Credit," I thought it might be interesting. However, when I thought about it, I realized I couldn't get committed to something this big just for the credits. I needed a more meaningful reason to be a writing tutor. As I reflected, I recalled my own nightmarish experience in my freshman composition class. I remembered how painful it was to write an essay; each word was a struggle. Only after I took my next composition class was I really able to begin to write. That was due largely to the dynamics between me and my own writing tutor.

Thus I arrived at two very personal reasons for becoming a writing tutor. First, I knew first hand how downright painful the basic composition course can be, and second, because of my own struggles, I would be able to relate with some degree of compassion to my tutees. I also saw myself playing a sort of "Florence Nightingale" role to those wounded English composition students, healing their paper cuts, not with another stinging solution of grammar but with a soothing ointment of understanding writing, not just fixing it.

Before going into that pivotal period of my own writing when I was at the receiving end of tutoring, I would like to address my first reason for becoming a tutor—understanding the frustration of the developing writer—by giving you a little background into my own experience as a first semester freshman in English composition. I usually call this experience The Nightmare for reasons soon to be apparent. I suppose it started after I handed in what I thought was the most brilliant piece of writing I had ever done. That brilliant piece of work got a failing grade. I remember getting the paper back in a required personal conference with the instructor. When she told me that she didn't understand a word I wrote, I literally thought she was talking to someone else. (I turned around to see if there was someone behind me.) Her comments that day and throughout the semester were mostly mechanical, and she made corrections sentence to sentence and did not address the essay as a whole.

"OK," I thought, "this is my first failure, but it is also my first essay." But things did not change much after that. In fact, they got worse. As I continued to receive failing grades, I progressively lost self-esteem, because I thought writing reflected on me as a person, not just as a writer. I got more and more discouraged as I tried harder and harder to make everything come out mechanically correct. I tried never to use the passive verb *to be* and tried to use *one in which* as often as possible. The next paper made me literally delirious. I had a fever, and after a night of trying to define *family* as it is perceived in modern society, I was more confused than when I began. That night I had a nightmare about my English class and the paper topic. I was on a game show in which the bonus question was, "What is the definition of *the family*?" For the life of me, I just couldn't get the right answer. The game show host was my English teacher, and she just wouldn't stop laughing. Experiences like this continued through the whole semester. By the end, I was in a pit of literary despair.

Because of my own nightmarish experiences as a novice writer, I hoped I would be able to give a bit of understanding to the frustrated student writer. I realize that many students perceive writing as putting not only their reputation as writers at stake but also their reputations as thinking, intelligent individuals. I realize that failing grades on papers often become blows to self-esteem, and enough of these blows can floor a student and make it very difficult to get up. Therefore, I think that just becoming aware of the seriousness and intensity that writing can play in a student's life can help a tutor become less of an evaluator and more of an understanding, sometimes even sympathetic, writing companion.

Two semesters after The Nightmare, I found myself sitting in another English composition class. But I was determined that things would be different this semester; I would get myself a tutor. My tutor did not merely change things in my writing; rather, we worked together to set my writing straight. We threw out all the mechanics of writing and looked at writing as a process. (I did not even know that writing was a process.) I did not need another grammar lesson to evaluate syntax or diction; what I needed was a serious attitude change. I began to see that my writing was a selfish and rude affair because I was entirely unaware of the reader's presence. I was writing for myself; any other reader just happened to be there. I finally realized that writing is not a private conversation with oneself or simply a list of ideas but an earnest attempt to communicate with another human being. Only after I understood the issues I was discussing, how each idea fit with other ideas, what the flow of my argument was, only then could I begin to communicate with the reader. Perhaps the most significant thing that happened to me was that writing began to be fun. The point is that the role my tutor played was actually pivotal to, if not the genesis of, my becoming a writer. So my second reason for becoming a tutor was that maybe I, too, could facilitate a revolution in a student's understanding of writing. I would offer not only sympathy but real advice about the proper attitude of a writer, explain how writing well is thinking well, present writing as a process, not just as a way of putting words on paper. In other words, when I got through with my students, they would never look at writing the same way again.

After a semester at the Student Learning Center, I am better able to examine my own expectations. I have come to realize many things—mainly that my own experiences with writing and tutoring are not universal. Not every student has harrowing experiences with writing; not every tutoring session is earth shattering, and so on. After realizing that my own writing experiences are unique, you might wonder if I am disillusioned or bitter. I am neither. Although tutoring has been different from my original expectations, it has been a rewarding and satisfying experience. I realize now that each student progresses at a different rate but nonetheless progresses. I have learned to celebrate not only revolutionary changes in writing but also the smaller ones like being able to formulate a thesis or to use transitional words, or even to use commas correctly. These are the things that keep me going. Moreover, I have realized that putting any self-glorifying expectation on the tutoring experience, let alone the students, is in itself bad. Wanting to play Florence Nightingale is sure to lead to disappointment. Instead we should always keep in mind that we might not necessarily reap a harvest of all A writers, but we might be planting the seeds for future ones.

DISCUSSION QUESTIONS

1. Do you have a "Florence Nightingale" reason for wanting to be a tutor? If so, where do you think it comes from? Explain.
2. In your opinion, what was the major reason for Helen's difficulties in her first composition course?
3. Do you think that it was unsettling for Helen to realize that most students did not share her fears about writing?
4. How did she resolve the differences between her expectations and reality?

[Editor's note: For more information on one of the issues raised in this story, you'll want to read Karin E. Winnard, "Codependency: Teaching Tutors Not to Rescue," *Journal of College Reading and Learning* 24, no. 1 (Fall 1991): 32–39.]

Learning to Write for Readers
Susan Vincent

> After years of writing for herself, Rosa learns from her tutor and her instructor that readers have certain expectations.

The topic for the first paper that Rosa showed me was "Why is it hard to write?" Her answer, painfully elaborated, was that she was inhibited when she knew she was going to be evaluated. In the course of the semester of tutoring, we came to realize that her fear stemmed from unconscious confusion about whom she was writing for.

Rosa had been writing prolifically in her journal for several years. No one else read her entries, so she had developed a style that was loose and obscure, and since the purpose of her journal was to explore her feelings, her perspective was entirely subjective. She had obviously received little, if any, constructive criticism of her writing in high school.

The instructor's response to Rosa's first English 1A paper shocked her. There was barely anything left of it. Whole paragraphs had been crossed out, and the rest had been marked with notations of errors. Of course, Rosa thought that reaction only proved what she had been trying to say in her paper.

In the first few sessions I concentrated on going over the writing process with Rosa to make sure she understood the steps. She had told me that she spent hours and hours in futile attempts to perfect her sentences, and I wanted to show her ways to use her time more economically and productively. She was discouraged and defensive, not wanting to believe that her writing was as deficient as the instructor's comments indicated it was.

For our third meeting I decided to go over the terminology of the paper corrections as explained in the handout on Subject A grammatical and structural errors. I wanted to be sure she understood what the instructor was trying to tell her about her writing. This session turned out to be a breakthrough for Rosa. By first discussing the meaning of the various errors to which she was prone, and their relevance to her paper, Rosa was able to see that she actually did make those mistakes. She was surprised because before, not understanding the jargon, she had felt she was being unfairly attacked. Since she had been writing in a confessional style, she felt particularly vulnerable. Now she was able to see that she herself wasn't being criticized but that only her writing errors were and that once she understood them, she didn't have to make them any more.

This realization was unpleasant for Rosa at first, as it meant accepting the fact that she still had a lot to learn about writing. However it marked the beginning of a crucial change of attitude. She knew from then on that she had control of her writing and that she didn't have to feel threatened by the instructor's remarks. Having started to drop her defensive attitude, Rosa was then open to finding out why her journal writing style was not appropriate in the context of a college English class.

The clouds parted then, and Rosa started applying her strong analytical ability, which had been developing through the introspective activity of her journal writing. Our next project was synthesizing information from paragraphs. Rosa was good at it. This was an opportunity to focus on sentence-level problems without the distraction of having to relate them to an entire essay. Now we were addressing her habits, such as her roundabout way of saying things, another legacy from her journal writing.

Rosa once spent an entire session telling me about her personal problems. It happened when we were brainstorming for a definition paper. She wanted to write about guilt, and I, knowing the trap she could fall into writing a whole paper about her emotions, was trying, unsuccessfully, to steer her away from it. In any case, she poured out her feelings to me, and as it turned out, she didn't want to write about guilt after all. She chose instead to describe a social group at her high school. I think that, having had the opportunity to express her feelings orally, she wasn't compelled to put them into her paper.

Putting Rosa's problem into perspective and relating it to my own experience with writing papers at UC Berkeley, I realize that readership is all important. That is, to know who your reader is helps you to formulate your argument and to use appropriate language. In Rosa's case, she needed to find out that she was writing for someone else. The tutorial—where she actually saw someone reading her papers and had the opportunity to discuss them in an atmosphere in which she didn't have to impress somebody for fear of her grade—gave her a tangible and healthy sense of a sympathetic audience. She now knew she had to make her papers understandable to someone other than herself.

DISCUSSION QUESTIONS

1. What did Rosa seem most afraid would happen with her writing?
2. How did the tutor help Rosa become aware of and less defensive about her writing errors?
3. Do you think you might have encouraged Rosa to write a theme about guilt when she seemed to want to do it? Why did Susam steer her away from this topic?

Supervisor's Comments

Your ability to read critically has contributed to your development as a writer, and in turn, your experience as a writer has made you a more sensitive reader. As you have assessed the strengths and weaknesses of published writing, you have developed an internal critic who applies similar criteria to your own writing. Yet sometimes that critic, that "other" you, can be too harsh. Too harsh for you, and too harsh for your students. How can you keep your harsh interior critic from overwhelming a student?

Sue Vincent concludes that you can suspend judgment and describe to the student your experience of reading his or her paper. One effective way to do this is by making "I" observations:

I'm not sure what this word refers to.
When I read this paragraph I get distracted from what I thought the paper is supposed to be about.
I would like to know more about this example.
I don't understand the significance of this illustration.
I've never heard this argument before, and I'm really intrigued by it.

You can also ask the kinds of open-ended questions a critical reader would ask:

Are there other events or scenes in the novel that either support or refute your point?

What are the important themes in each scene?
How does each theme relate to similar themes in other scenes?
Why are those themes important to your thesis?

These and many similar practical techniques are fully explained in books like *The Practical Tutor* (Meyer and Smith 1987) and *Talking About Writing* (Clark 1988). When you regularly give a student this unique reader's view, uncluttered by judgmental language, the student will begin to hear in his or her own head the tutor-reader's side of the conversation when the tutor-reader isn't there. Such a conversation in the mind of the writer forges arguments and prose that are sensitive to a reader's needs, what Linda Flower (1979) calls "reader-based prose." While refining your role as a nonjudgmental reader for your students, you will develop an "other self" who will be less harsh and will allow your own writing to open up in ways that will probably surprise you.

—Thom Hawkins

Collaboration with Students Who Write Well
Theresa Rigney

> When she began tutoring, Theresa, influenced by the stories about basic writers she'd read about, expected the worst from her students. But this soon changed when she realized they were all good writers. Then the problem she faced was how to help them become even better, more confident writers.

I remember how scared I was sitting across the table from my new students that very first week at the Student Learning Center. I wanted to be the best darn tutor the Center had ever had, and I was going to do everything by the book so my students would show rapid improvement in their writing. I'd read all the reading assignments, brushed up on my grammar, and reviewed the requirements for the basic composition course. However, I soon realized I wasn't prepared at all. Sure, I was ready for the faltering student that Jackie Goldsby (1981) scared me into thinking I was going to work with—the student whose essays lacked structure, focus, and good grammar. But I was definitely not prepared for the students who actually came and sat across the table from me. Those students wrote well!

My student's writing had very few structural problems and only minor stylistic flaws, yet they sat there waiting for me to turn B+ papers into A papers. Because I was utterly unprepared for this type of writer, I thrashed about during the first two weeks trying to give my students the help they needed. As much as I thought these students were good writers, I also knew that they had committed themselves to me for the rest of the semester. Obviously they wanted and needed help. This was a difficult problem for a new tutor to face. Instead of simply working on their easily detectable grammar and structural mistakes, I had to find a way to tutor students who face the same writing difficulties that I face every time I write a paper for an English course. They struggled as I struggled.

How can a peer tutor help lower classmen who write well? My answer was collaboration. Not exactly the collaborator model given in Adele Karliner's essay (1979), although that served as a base; but rather, the collaboration between two equal students, each helping the other to interpret, analyze, and argue on paper. My students came to realize that I did not have all the answers and that I was not going through their papers as a professor might, but as a peer. In essence, my students became my fellow writers.

Of course, my students were not prepared to accept this idea any more than I was. They wanted a pseudo–teaching assistant. The wanted me to go through their papers with a red felt-tip pen and write "good" or "bad" in the margins. They wanted a yes or no answer. Imagine how disappointed they must have been when they received an "I don't know, what do you think?" answer to most of their questions.

Nonetheless, our sessions developed into what I like to think of as mutual collaboration meetings. That is, we developed the understanding that I would not be an editor or an evaluator, to use Karliner's terms. I was not going to tell my students if and when their papers were good enough to turn in. After all, I did not know myself. I didn't know what the professor was looking for. All I could do was to talk to my students, tell them what I got from their papers, and ask them how they felt about their work. I explained what I thought about their writing, and they explained what they thought about their papers to me. Together we tried to come to an understanding about the point of the essay. This is what I mean by mutual collaboration.

By the end of the fourth week of tutoring, I began to see results from these mutual collaboration sessions. And boy did I ask them a lot of questions! But I did not ask the "Why did you start a new paragraph here?" structural questions but rather the "I don't understand what you mean" or "Why do you really think Sethe killed her child?" content-based questions. And for a full hour, my students were able to verbalize what they thought about the paper and what its strengths and weaknesses were in their own eyes. All I did, all I was qualified to do, was to talk about the issues or emotions they brought out in the essay and the things that I did not understand. My fellow writers began to realize that writing means not just writing down words in so-called academic paragraphs (topic sentence, example, quote) but verbalizing ideas, thoughts, opinions, and objections in a meaningful yet coherent and understandable way. They saw that writing is not really about the order of the words or the placement of commas, as they were taught in grammar school. It is about the personal expression of thoughts and feelings.

Collaboration, then, came to be redefined as the exchange of ideas and opinions between fellow writers. I would have my students read their papers aloud, and we would spend the rest of the hour discussing the issues brought out in the paper. In most cases, I had not read the literature discussed in the paper, so I asked a lot of questions about the book itself. Although they were disappointed that I was not able to come up with a thesis statement for them despite my vast understanding of literature, I felt it was more beneficial for them to articulate the questions and opinions they had to address in their papers. "So Kafka had this guy turn into a bug? That's kind of weird, isn't it? I mean, why not turn him into a puppy or something?" is an example of one of my more intellectual questions. I think these questions excited my students and were much more interesting to them than comments like, "I think you need a semicolon here."

I like to think my silly, naive questions helped them realize that the red felt-tip pen is not the main consideration in the writing process after all. In fact, they became less and less interested in an evaluator. They didn't need one! They didn't need to worry about some grammatical specter. What they needed was a chance to discuss the issues, to verbalize their own thoughts, and to formulate an argument in the process of explaining their thoughts and emotions about a piece of literature. And the great thing was, we all won—they were able to verbalize and strengthen their papers, and I learned all about Kafka's *Metamorphosis*.

Of course, the collaboration session was not all metaphysical expression. I did use a few "tutoring techniques." In talking with other tutors, I found out that whether one is working with struggling basic composition students or A-average comparative literature students, it is useful for them to leave the tutoring session with a piece of paper with their own writing on it. My students agreed that they wanted to walk away each week with concrete evidence of progress, no matter what we worked on. As one student commented, "I like to go home with the idea that I worked on my paper, not just *thought* my paper." So even if we spent most of the time brainstorming, my fellow writers left the session with a few notes of what we discussed, including thoughts, emotions, epithets, or simply a comment like, "MacBeth is a wimp." (That particular student expanded his sentence into a great essay on the issue of manliness in Shakespeare's play.)

Mapping was another technique I found useful when discussing the early stages of paper writing. I asked my students to make a diagram or draw a picture of the points they were including in their paper. Each did this in his or her own way—one student used different sized bubbles strung on a line, another visualized her paper as a kite, a third simply used arrows—but all said they preferred mapping to the standard outline.

However, no tutoring technique will solve the problem facing most writers, especially less experienced writers—lack of self-confidence. They wanted someone with a red felt pen to tell them their papers were good. My job, as I saw it, was to help them see that they can write good papers if they ask themselves the same questions I asked. And they needed to realize what I observed when I met them—they write well.

DISCUSSION QUESTIONS

1. Do you think that Theresa's techniques would have worked as well if her group had consisted of very poor writers? Or of students for whom English was a second language? Explain.
2. Some have described the tutor's main role as that of cheerleader.

Do you see any evidence that Theresa was serving that role? If so, what were some examples that demonstrate her cheerleading?
3. Have you tried any of the techniques Theresa mentions such as mapping and making sure tutees carry some written work away from the session? How successful have these been for you?
4. Do you think there's a danger that Theresa's experience tutoring good writing students will lead her to expect that all her tutees will be like these students? Why?

Writing through Thoughts
Marcia Teusink

Marcia always felt that her thoughts were not complete until she wrote them down. Now she has to convince her student, Anne, that the same technique will work for her.

I have always felt that my thoughts are never truly complete until I write them down on paper. My head gets clogged with ideas and writing them opens a trap door that allows my thoughts to run out, leaving room for new, clearer ones to develop. But, my thoughts are not complete when they leave my brain. I need to force the amorphous ideas into concrete visible words, arrange them in a logical manner, and then possibly build these ideas into an essay. Tutoring and witnessing the writing of my peers this semester has helped me see more clearly how writing influences thought development. Especially on the level of sentence construction, I came to see how the physical act of writing is vital to the completion of thought.

As I watched my students develop their thesis statements, I witnessed how grammar, word choice, and syntax force writers to think precisely. I found that my students and I could spend an entire period revising a thesis, yet I knew that they would do well when they went home and revised the rest of the paper. This was especially true of one student, Anne. She must have spent ten minutes on one sentence, getting the syntax and word choice exactly right. Her paper was on a character named Cesar, in *The Mambo King Plays Songs of Love* by Oscar Hijuelos. She wanted to discuss how Cesar had suffered a terrible childhood, devoid of love from his father; how he repressed his pain for years by living in the fast lane; and how he fell into unending despair when his brother was killed in a car accident. Anne was trying to assert a casual statement between the events in Cesar's life, but we were both unclear about what was cause and what was effect. By writing and rewriting, Anne progressed from the statement that,

> Cesar had a rough childhood that he tried to forget, so his brother's death sent him into a depression,

to,

> Because Cesar had repressed all of his childhood pain, his brother's accident not only shocked him but aroused years of pain he could never forget.

The difference is a very subtle one, but it is crucial. For one thing, the first thesis is not really a thesis. It lacks the crucial *because* to set up an argument, something she could then explain and back up with examples from the text. It is these seemingly minute word choices that not only make a better thesis but ultimately clear up one's thoughts.

The difference between thinking words and writing words, at least for me, is that on paper the writer must work with groups of words on a line; she must organize them in some kind of order to create the meaning she intends. Perhaps some people can form clear sentences in their heads, but many of us need to see them on a page first. I do not always think in sentences; I seem to think of a whole concept without thinking of it in the form of words. But the idea remains vague until I actualize it in sentence form; I need the restriction of writing sentences to really clarify my ideas. Words like *because*, like in Anne's case, set up a relationship between ideas. Then the order of the sentence shows what caused what. The relationships between the words creates meaning. For me, and in this case for Anne, the relationships only become vivid when they are written and worked through.

Since I made this revolutionary discovery, I have been more persistent in asking my students about their theses.

DISCUSSION QUESTIONS

1. Did you find the description of how thoughts become clearer when they are written down helpful? Is this an idea you can use in working with your students?
2. Do you think that reading the example of Anne's attempt to write a thesis statement might be helpful to your students? Do you think they could understand the difference between the first and final thesis?
3. Can you think of other ways Anne might have been helped to clarify her thesis statement?

Bungee Cord Thesis: Helping Students Find Theses through an Unusual Method
Po-Sun Chen

> It takes a lot of ingenuity to think of ways to help students understand some of the terms their writing teachers use. Po-Sun thought of a clever analogy for *thesis statement* that delighted his student and helped her grasp the concept.

What is the one thing that a paper absolutely cannot function without? Is it good spelling? Well, *Tale of Two Cities* would probably still be a classic even if Charles Dickens had managed to misspell *their* as *thier* throughout the entire novel, so that's not it. Could it be transitions? Probably not, since, if your paper were functioning in every other sense, you'd at least have a jumble of working paragraphs—as fragmented and unrelated as they might seem—so that's not it either. What would be problematic is if you managed to write a paper from introduction to conclusion without a thesis of any sort. If you did this, you would have managed to throw together sentences with no central concept. That's why I want to spend some time discussing how I managed to combine the deadly art of establishing a thesis with thoughts on an unusual and nearly as deadly sport and to show how drawing these parallels between a thesis and bungee jumping helped more than one unhappy student conceptualize the function of a thesis and make it work for her.

But before I begin, let me explain exactly what bungee jumping is. In short, it is the act of attaching (very securely) one end of an elastic cord to a very high bridge or crane, attaching the other end (even more securely) around either one's waist or ankles, then jumping (very tentatively, I'm sure) off. Proper laws of gravity and elasticity permitting, the cord is supposed to stretch only so far and rebound you up to near your original jump point. The process repeats itself several times, keeping you bouncing up and down until it decides to stop or you decide to lose your lunch. That's bungee jumping. How it applies to tutoring the function of a thesis is a little more complicated but much less stomach churning.

During this, my first semester of tutoring, I had a student (whom we will call Amy) who had repeated difficulty in conceptualizing and forming theses. To solve the first problem, I referred to the fifth chapter of *The Practical Tutor*, which discusses "The Nature of Concepts." I had her read two sentences, one that stated something that would require demonstration and another that did not. The one that did not require demonstration read,

This paper will discuss Henry Kissinger. (Meyer and Smith 1987, 91)

The sentence that did require demonstration read,

This paper will show that Kissinger influenced Reagan to distinguish his administration's handling of the hostage crisis in 1985 from that of the Carter Administration during the Iranian hostage crisis in 1979. (Meyer and Smith 1987, 92)

Both sentences express ideas. However, assuming that readers all have personal opinions, only the second sentence says some things that the writer can prove to his audience. To prove the pseudothesis, "This paper will discuss Henry Kissinger," simply requires that I write several loosely strung sentences about the man. This little tidbit from the *Practical Tutor* showed Amy the difference between something that was a thesis and something that was not. But she still had to learn how a thesis functions within the context of a paper before she could effectively write her own. That's where bungee jumping came in.

I sat there thinking for a few awkward moments, struggling to draw some sort of nifty illustration that could help explain this point that I thought so important for her to know. I couldn't. Eventually my mind began to wander, and I started thinking about skiing, skydiving, parachuting, and that's when it hit me: bungee jumping. Somehow it all came together, and I explained it like this:

"Oh! so you *do* know what bungee jumping is! Good. Well, think of it this way. Your thesis is like that bungee cord, which is the only thing attaching you to the insanely high bridge that represents the point you are trying to make. If your writing has produced a good thesis, then no matter how far down you jump, and no matter how far along in your essay you go, you'll always come back to your main point, the bridge. If your bungee cord is not securely fastened, and you have no thesis, then not only would you be a bloody mess at the bottom of the ravine, but you would have no main point from which subsequent points and paragraphs could be related back to."

Granted it was a pretty verbose explanation, but Amy got the point. She even laughed. Actually, she laughed for quite a while. In any case, I'd drawn my illustration—now I would have to put it to good use. Using a sample topic, I told Amy that I wanted to use this thesis: "This paper will show that dogs were created by some higher being for the distinct purpose of eating cats." In theory then, this sentence would be my thesis and bungee cord. If so, no matter how far along I go in this paper, that sentence should serve as a stable point to which all subsequent points could relate. So the first point would be, "The average dog's stomach is just the right size to fit an average whole cat, because it was naturally designed for the specific task of digesting cats." Now, if my first point really was a thesis–bungee cord, then it should naturally rebound me from my first subpoint back to the main point of my introductory paragraph. It should facilitate the purpose of giving overall significance to each and every point made. Thus, the thesis gives my first subpoint—"the average dog's stomach is just the right size to fit an average whole cat"—a greater significance. The qualifying statement "because it was naturally designed for the specific purpose of digesting cats," not only serves as a reminder of the thesis but also gives the subpoint significance. Without the thesis, it would be very easy for a reader to get lost in the confusion of a series of subpoints. A well-written essay will make the main point as clear as possible to the reader throughout the entire work. For all these reasons, I used the bungee cord analogy.

Needless to say, Amy got a lot out of the session, and we both got a good laugh as she helped me piece together the eccentric analogy. Again, a well-set up bungee cord thesis will constantly rebound the reader back to the main point of the paper. A bogus, pseudothesis will only break under pressure like an untied bungee cord, which will inevitably leave the reader only a little better off (in terms of understanding) than if he had fallen off the edge of a bridge.

DISCUSSION QUESTIONS

1. Does the bungee-cord thesis analogy seem reasonable to you? Do you think this is an analogy that your students might relate to?
2. Can you think of another analogy for thesis statement that might help students understand?

My Attempt to Teach Intuitive Writing
Nicole Reader

> Nicole found that she intuitively wrote well despite her lack of knowledge of grammatical rules and stylistic concepts. However, as a tutor, she faced the problem of helping students improve their grammar and develop their own intuitive skills.

Perhaps I was badly suited to be a writing tutor since I do not know some of the official rules of writing and I lack knowledge of technicalities—the names for grammatical errors and concepts such as the difference between passive and active voices. In some ways this hampered me, for when my students presented me with grammatical questions, I was as mystified as they. I could recognize their errors without fail, but I could not explain why they were errors nor what they were named. All I could say to the students was, "Well, can't you see it *sounds* wrong that way?" I could not teach the rules; I could only demonstrate an intuitive feeling for good writing.

I am as unfortunate as many of my students—high school failed all of us when it came to teaching us to write, and in my case, junior college was of no additional help. Together, my students and I examined grammar worksheets for clues that would teach us things like the difference between passive and active voices, something no one had ever attempted to explain to us. Several of my students knew more about the parts of speech and the proper names for grammatical errors and had a better command of semicolons than I. I don't think my lack of understanding of grammar lowered me in their esteem. I feel they realized that although I knew as few rules as they did, I was still a good writer and that I had an intuitive sense of what was good and poor writing. I hope my competence as a writer showed them that it takes more than technical know-how to make a good writer.

I feel that developing this intuition—what I consider to be an instinctive feel for good writing—was the most important thing I taught my students. I did try to teach spelling, rules of grammar, and the proper form of an essay, but I explained that knowing these would not help unless they also developed an intuitive sense of good writing. I relied heavily on my intuition when I helped students with their papers, and I made a point of sharing this fact with them, hoping that this would inspire them with the desire to develop their own intuitive ways of judging their own writing.

Two of my students responded well to this and began to use their own intuition toward the end of the semester. Instead of my having to point out an awkward sentence, they would catch it while reading the paper aloud and rephrase the sentence. Of course, they did not notice every section that was poorly written, nor did their rewriting always improve the section, but they had discovered how to write intuitively. This freed them from having to depend so heavily on me, for they were able to recognize their own grammatical or stylistic errors on the basis of how good writing sounds, instead of using memorized rules.

My attempts to teach intuitive writing did not always go smoothly. One student became irritated with me when I suggested that one of her sentences was awkward. "So what's wrong with it now?" she asked. I assured her that there was nothing technically wrong with it, but her choice of words, phrasing, and organization greatly detracted from the point she was trying to make. Eventually she realized what I was trying to show her and reworded the sentence, greatly improving it.

Some of my students, of course, were not ready to use intuition. They needed me to let them know when something was wrong, not when it might be phrased better. Sadly, some never learned to recognize their own errors because they had not developed an intuitive sense of their own. This was especially true of a woman who had been speaking English for only a few years. She needed special attention since her knowledge of correct English was undeveloped. I tried to give her a sense of the sound of good writing, but since she was still struggling with the peculiarities of idiomatic English, I usually had to point out her errors, as she could not identify them herself.

Perhaps I was poorly suited to be a writing tutor, but I don't think so. Despite my limited knowledge of grammar, I saw most of my students progress in writing over the semester. They improved their ability to judge the quality of their writing. What I feel helped these students the most was their exposure to intuitive writing, the instinctive feel for the sound of good writing.

DISCUSSION QUESTIONS

1. Do you feel that Nicole was justified in deemphasizing the rules of good writing in her efforts to help students develop their intuitive abilities? Explain.
2. Did you get some ideas about how to deal with students who have a better knowledge of grammar than the tutor does from reading this article?
3. Can you think of some other ways students can be taught to recognize good writing?

Supervisor's Comments

Nicole talks about being mystified by grammar and feeling that her students can learn grammar anywhere. It is not unusual for qualified, effective tutors to be grammarphobic, confused, or merely indifferent to the subject. They write just fine without a formal command of the rules of Standard English, and if they learned without the rules, so can their students. I have to admit to being in that camp once myself, that is, until I faced student after student who couldn't learn intuitively, who had to have the guidelines of formal grammar. The longer you tutor the more you realize that even though your feel for the language is one of your greatest strengths, relying exclusively on intuition can rob you of some useful grammatical instructions for assembling sentences.

Our training seminars, texts, and handouts offer tutors many opportunities to learn grammar. We ask that they learn grammar along with their students, freely acknowledging their limitations but demonstrating their willingness to improve so that they can be of the greatest possible help to their students. Grammar can be fun if you play with it in regular, short periods with friends and colleagues who can help make it seem more like a game, somewhat like learning a foreign language but not quite as intense. Sometimes we end up spending a good deal of time on grammar in seminars, and I caution tutors not to overwhelm their students with all the fancy terminology they're learning. (Chapter 8 of *The Practical Tutor* (Meyers and Smith 1987) explains how to tutor the grammar of a sentence without using traditional grammatical terms.) It's important to see understanding grammar as only one of many skills that contribute to improving writing, and I encourage tutors to debate among themselves the best way to achieve a balance between intuitive writing and a more conscious application of the rules of Standard English. The worst thing you can do is ignore grammar, because it won't go away and makes a better friend than an enemy.

—Thom Hawkins

3 Increasing Confidence

Try a Little Tenderness
Jennifer Leonard

From the beginning, Sara seemed reluctant about tutoring and resentful of her instructor. Jennifer describes how she helped Sara overcome her negativism and develop more confidence in her writing ability.

Somehow Sara found me among the bustle of the Student Learning Center that first session. I had arrived ten minutes early for no apparent reason—anxiety perhaps. As I sat impatiently reading my *Daily Cal* newspaper, I glanced up periodically searching for my unknown tutee. I tried to remember all the things we should cover in our first meeting—discussing the role of a tutor, setting long-term goals, getting vital information. After straining my feeble vision for another five minutes, I returned to the article on the latest budget cuts.

"Are you Jenny?" The moment of truth!

"Yeah, you must be Sara," I answered, removing the clutter from the table. "Oh God!" I thought, "She doesn't look exactly thrilled to be here," and immediately forgot all my presession goals. She plopped down on the chair with an audible sigh.

"So you're taking Subject A? Do you like it?"

"Not really," she looked disgusted with the topic.

"Who do you have?"

She told me her professor's name, making a face as though she didn't like her professor.

"Sounds like you're not too psyched about her," I smiled at her sympathetically. "What's she like?"

"She's a bitch!" I laughed, appreciating her frankness. She told me she was having a lot of problems in general and that her Subject

A professor wasn't making things any easier. As we talked, I gathered that Sara was basically experiencing the trials and tribulations of the freshman year. She felt extremely homesick for the east coast and Manhattan ("A real city"), she had been sick on and off all year, her roommate drove her crazy, and her boyfriend was in San Diego. It all sounded familiar to me! I told her about my miserable first year at Wellesley, how I had longed for the west coast, my friends, my boyfriend, home-cooked meals, my doggie. She finally smiled, and I felt my self-confidence returning.

At last we returned to the topic of writing. From what she had told me, I concluded her professor expected a great deal from her students, especially from Sara. I could understand why. Skimming one of the papers she handed me, I couldn't believe that the writer was the same bright, articulate girl sitting next to me. Her title was, "Religion as Harmful to the Individual," and she began the paper with the phrase, "Since the beginning of man . . ." The writing tutor within me tried valiantly not to cringe. Her paper was full of generalizations and undocumented information and lacked any real structure or continuity. Her professor had given her an F on the essay.

I kept the essay to look over and told her that I was going to meet with her professor the next day. Although I had predictably forgotten to ask her all my rehearsed questions, I knew that the information I had gathered about Sara would prove invaluable to future sessions. It was clear that Sara resented all the negative feedback she'd been getting from her instructor. I also sensed that she really lacked confidence in her ability to write, and I could tell that she hadn't put much effort into her papers—thus the amazing amount of generalizations, the unsupported arguments, and the weak structure of the paper she had shown me.

The Ogre

I dutifully made my way to Dwinelle annex the next day to meet with Sara's professor. Although Sara had provided me with a vivid portrait of this woman, I reminded myself that I should form my own opinion of "the ogre." She wasn't exactly Ms. Warmth when I spoke to her, but she did have a very good idea of Sara's potential and told me that she expected Sara to work harder on her writing.

We agreed that Sara needed to focus on prewriting, on developing her argument, and on finding evidence to support her ideas. But although I respected the professor for challenging her students, I found her extremely negative. She told me, "The way it stands now, Sara won't be passing the course." The message I received was that the professor knew Sara could do better but didn't really believe that she would.

Donning the Cape

Considering her personal problems and the negativity of her professor, I was not surprised that Sara was discouraged with her writing. I knew that tutoring could help Sara gain confidence in her writing and improve her interest in her own ideas, arguments, and opinions. She obviously did not respond to her professor's scare tactics nor to her criticisms, but perhaps she simply needed the encouragement and personal attention a tutor can offer.

Super tutor to the rescue! When we first began to meet, I had made a concerted effort to make her feel comfortable and to gain her trust. I tried to balance my critical comments with positive and complimentary ones. I played devil's advocate to force her to develop and argue her points, and most importantly, I let her know I cared about all aspects of her life, not just her writing. During the first month, Sara and I met up to three hours a week. Tutoring seemed to give her encouragement and guidance that she was not getting from her professor; she had the opportunity to discuss and develop her ideas collaboratively, without the pressure of grades. She began to enjoy the sessions, smiling more frequently and often staying to talk with me after the session.

The Light at the End of the Tunnel

At last Sara was beginning to understand the writing process. She learned to avoid generalizations, to develop more sophisticated arguments, and to use quotes to support her points. It seemed almost too easy for me to tutor her. In those three or four weeks her grades improved dramatically. She had been receiving C− 's, which were failing grades in her course, but the first paper we worked on got a B+ . I was really excited for her when she told me, but she didn't seem to share my enthusiasm. When I asked her why she wasn't more excited, she replied, "I just don't think I can do it again." I started teasing her, asking if she thought she'd been visited by her fairy godmother while she was writing the paper. But her next two papers were A's and I could see her confidence grow with every "Bravo!" her professor wrote.

Collaborator or Crutch?

Sara was a tutoring success story, but after taping a session with her, I began to wonder if I had been too involved in her writing. I admit that I talk a lot, and when my enthusiasm overflows, I can't keep my mouth shut. But had I created a monster? An SLC dependent? Was Sara relying too much on my input, my involvement? In our next few sessions, I made a conscious effort to let her do the talking. Then I realized that I had not done any irreparable damage, just the opposite.

At first my new silence seemed to bother her, and she kept looking at me expectantly for answers. But she soon understood that I wasn't going to give her all the answers, and she began to race ahead of me with her ideas and to develop her arguments before getting my approval.

It reminds me of when I was learning to ride a bike. My shiny new Schwinn was evil incarnate—I hated it with all the passion a five-year-old can muster. Somehow my father convinced me to take it out to the concrete playground near our house and learn how to ride it. He gripped the back of the vinyl seat and ran with me as I peddled for my life. I felt secure knowing that he wouldn't let go and that he was in control, not me. One time I started riding with dad huffing and puffing beside me. When all of a sudden I didn't hear his feet on the pavement next to me, I panicked and crashed into the metal fence. So it wasn't a graceful maneuver, but the point is that I had been riding all by myself without even knowing it. That is how I see my tutoring relationship with Sara. In the beginning, I was like the guiding hand of my father, reassuring her and helping her. But soon, without her realizing it, she was paddling through the writing process on her own. It doesn't matter that she still *thought* she needed me to help her produce a well-written essay, the truth is that she didn't.

Hearing Voices

But what happens when she realizes that I'm not there guiding her? Would she panic and crash as I had done? I am confident that I have given her the ability to criticize and analyze her own writing. Sara and I talked a great deal about the process of writing, what kinds of things to avoid, what to look for when revising an essay. She often got frustrated with me when I answered her questions with a question, when I forced her to clarify her ideas, to revise whole paragraphs, to find evidence to support her argument. Yet all that annoyance and exasperation has been worth it.

I have been able to get inside her head and firmly establish my nagging voice. Every time she reads her essay, she hears that voice asking her to clarify, to explain, to support, to develop, to stick to the thesis. The critical, negative voice of Sara's professor had only undermined her confidence and left her confused and discouraged. My tutor's voice, however, provides her with both the tools to criticize and analyze her own writing and the encouragement and reassurance she needs to remain confident.

DISCUSSION QUESTIONS

1. What were some of the specific tactics that Jennifer used to help Sara?
2. Can you think of other ways Sara might have been helped more quickly?
3. How do you feel about implanting a tutor's nagging voice in Sara's mind as a way of helping her edit her own papers?
4. Can you explain why Sara's instructor was so responsive to the improvement in her papers?
5. Do you think that Sara really needed tutoring? Explain why or why not.

Supervisor's Comments

Writing is so personal, such an expression of the individual psyche, that it is almost impossible to write an effective paper without a strong sense of self-confidence. (To expect otherwise is to see writing as purely artifice: an act, a performance, detached from the real thoughts and perspectives of the writer.) Without confidence, the writer vacillates, hides in ambiguities, twists her sentences so that no one can see what she is really thinking. Or she bluffs, holding out to the reader an easy fake, hoping that the superficial or over-simplified will not be challenged. In either case neither the writer nor the reader is satisfied. There has been no true communication from one mind to another, no honest development or exchange of thought, which are the greatest pleasures of reading and writing.

For the writing tutor, the issue of the student's confidence is both urgent and extremely delicate. Many of the writers we see feel somewhat lost in their new academic environment, unsure of their footing and the changed expectations in their writing courses. This sense of unfamiliarity shakes any writer's confidence, but for many the issue is complicated by both real and imagined gaps in their writing preparation and skills. The tutor who blithely reassures her student "Oh, I'm sure you'll do okay" does no more to help her student's confidence than the tutor who greets his student with a stack of grammar handouts. Jennifer went much farther than applying such Band-Aids; she met with the instructor and put considerable time and effort into the tutoring—she invested herself in her student. Jennifer was convinced Sara could succeed, and Sara gradually began to believe in herself as much as her tutor did.

—Elizabeth Keithley

Persistence Pays Off
Barbara McClain

> It took more than patience and persistence to turn this student around—it took active pursuit plus a wake-up call.

She came to the first workshop session looking as if she were burdened by more than freshman stress at Cal. In a barely audible voice, Lupe acknowledged her presence and then returned her gaze to the tabletop. As I surveyed the group, I noted gladly that among the five students, only Lupe appeared troubled and uninterested in the particulars of the meeting. She avoided eye contact with me and everyone else when she related personal information for our interest. She didn't smile or joke around like the others; in fact, she was downright miserable. While I went over procedures, Lupe just put her papers together and kept her stare fixed on the tabletop.

Just getting into the right English 1A section was an exercise in perseverance for Lupe. She followed instructions on her computer form rather than those from the Student Learning Center that coordinated class and workshop times. Consequently, she didn't show up for the first session, and the professor dropped her from his roll. After several phone calls to him, he agreed to reinstate Lupe. It wasn't that easy, though. He had second thoughts, and bureaucracy intervened. He said he couldn't exceed the assigned enrollment, eighteen. As week two progressed, Lupe wondered if she would ever get into a 1A section. As I encouraged her to do, she attended class, stayed in touch with the professor, and, clearly agitated, called me each class night to report her status. Thankfully, someone dropped the class on the last day of week two; Lupe reclaimed her place in the assigned section.

I knew another of Lupe's problems. In the initial writing assignment, she spelled it out: One of her roommates bugged her. She didn't think the girl liked her, and she couldn't understand why. They didn't talk to each other, and when they did, it was with sarcastic exchanges. Tears sat on the rims of her eyes as she spoke about her unhappiness. Now I was the one who stared at the tabletop.

From the second week of school, Lupe started missing workshops, and I thought the stress from the roommate situation contributed to this. I called to remind her of the attendance policy, and she swore she would honor it. I also began to wonder if she, like the other students, was uncomfortable about the planned computer use in the workshop. None of them was prepared for that. Besides, Lupe whispered, she didn't want to learn to use Microsoft Word; she had her own IBM system at home and was perfectly happy with it. I had hoped the computer would be a catalyst around which to draw the students and focus their attention on the writing process. After week four, however, the students agreed unanimously that they didn't want to use the computers. In fact, they didn't even want to meet in the room with the machines.

After Leonard and Bruce found too many gorgeous females to

survey at the Terrace restaurant, Liz came to the rescue with good old Room C as our new meeting place. Lupe attended sessions in smoldering silence. When she missed a couple of sessions without advising me, I knew that the computer, the location, and her roommate were no longer problems. Lupe and I had to talk. At the end of one workshop session, I took her aside and suggested that she seek counseling if her problems were more than she could cope with. She said she had already seen someone and that she would follow up the visit. She never did.

In spite of the fact that I was spending so much time checking up on Lupe, I felt it was time well spent because I wanted to see her resolve her problems and get on with her schooling. I didn't want her to become another minority dropout statistic, and she seemed to be going down that road. Her attendance didn't improve and, regardless of the time of day or night I called to talk with her, she was never there. Instead, I got a variety of excuses from her roommates: She was in the shower; she couldn't talk on the phone just then; she has already left for school. The professor also noted that she had missed several class meetings; he wanted to know from me what was up. I decided to drop her from the workshop because I thought she just wasn't interested, and I didn't have the time to keep checking on her whereabouts. I had given my supervisor a note about dropping Lupe from workshop, but I changed my mind after I received a neatly written, two-page letter that explained her just-resolved problems. It was like a confessional; her crises were over, and she wanted to clear her roommates' names with me. They had covered up her unscheduled, out-of-town visit to straighten out problems with her boyfriend.

With her personal problems now under control, Lupe's attitude toward workshop attendance and class changed. She said she didn't want me to drop her from workshop. She hadn't intended to behave the way she did; it was just that her personal problems were so overwhelming. I advised her about talking amicably with her roommate. She took my suggestions, and the two of them reached a tolerable truce. She asked that I call and wake her up, so she couldn't say she slept through the snooze cycle on her alarm clock anymore. I obliged, once, and she was grateful. My persistence in urging her attendance had paid off.

One of the things the professor asked that I do in workshop was review comments on student papers. He wanted them to know how to improve their work by understanding and utilizing suggestions from comments in paper revisions. In this area, Lupe demonstrated her changed attitude about class and workshop. The professor noticed a change in her attitude, as well as the quality of her work, and he let her know through comments on a particular paper she wrote about western destruction of Aboriginal culture as told in Bruce Chatwin's *Songlines.*

An example of Lupe's new-found interest in her work was the way she used the professor's reader response sheet. She reproduced it on her computer in a different letter size and type style, made it quite decorative, and attached it to her paper. The professor noted that he liked the style of the sheet, and Lupe was impressed that he actually completed the form rather than writing comments at the end of her paper. He showed by example how he expected his students to respond as critical readers to the group's writing. The other students in the group were particularly impressed with Lupe's originality. In one act, she got specific comments from the professor, learned from them how she could respond to papers from her writing group, and showed her classmates how they could also benefit from specific responses to their writing.

Lupe's story doesn't end there. Her determination to manage her time better and give enough of it to school work paid off in personal benefits. She smiles naturally now; it isn't at my prompting. She is on time, and we can hear her comments clearly—no more whispering while she looks at the tabletop. Above all, she changed from a reluctant participant to an active contributor to the workshop. I don't have to cajole her into giving ideas or opinions on her classmates' papers, and they don't have to feel as if they are imposing on her for comments on them. Lupe told me that this new-found confidence extends to her other classes. Because she sought help, followed advice, and didn't give up on the possibility of overcoming her problems, Lupe also learned that persistence pays off.

DISCUSSION QUESTIONS

1. What would you have done if you were tutoring Lupe and recognized the many problems she had?

2. Do you think that it was appropriate for the tutor to call Lupe in her dorm? to talk to her roommates? to agree to give her a wake-up call? If not, what other strategies might have worked?
3. What seemed to mark the turning point in overcoming Lupe's problems?
4. What do you think was the most important way that Lupe changed?

Tutoring via the Objective Eye
of the Video Camera
Antonina Pascale

> The tutor videotapes a session to try to find out why there seemed to be so much tension during her tutoring sessions. When she viewed the tape, the reasons became obvious.

I shared my most rewarding learning experience as a writing tutor with my Subject A student, Allison, a shy, pretty, black freshman. At our first meeting, she told me bits and pieces about herself: she did not like to speak in class, but she enjoyed the readings and was determined to pass Subject A. During our first few sessions, I felt a tension growing—a tension that came from Allison's frustration with her writing and my eagerness to eliminate her frustration quickly. I wanted to help her develop self-confidence and motivation, but my encouragement often led to sessions in which I found myself answering questions for her instead of allowing her to generate the analysis. The turning point in our relationship came only after I had watched a tutoring session of ours on videotape and received additional feedback from my fellow tutors in our tutoring seminar.

I never realized how much a video could help me improve my tutoring until I thought back on the sessions with Allison before I made the video. In the beginning, Allison's frustration with her writing stemmed from problems with writing style. She wrote her material in a free-writing form, filled three pages with terrific examples but lacked a clearly stated thesis, organized paragraphs, and a conclusion. She did not have a clear idea of what she was writing about—she was simply writing. I explained that free-writing is excellent for brainstorming, but it was important to go on to the next step. She must generate a thesis from this free-writing and decide which examples she wished to use. She became even more frustrated because I told her she needed further work on her paper. However, I wanted her to understand at the start that all writing calls for constant editing and revising.

During our next session, she was even more frustrated because she'd received her first grade in the Subject A class—a C+. I wrote in my journal, "I tried to tell her that this is a good grade. I tried to concentrate on the positive aspects of her paper." I also discovered more of her problems since in one part of the paper she had used incorrect pronoun references, which made her ideas unclear. I asked her about a particular sentence, "If you take this sentence out of the context of the paper, would anyone be able to read and understand it?" She thought for a long while before replying, "No." Then I asked her what she could do to make the sentence clearer. She replied by specifying the subject, and completing an unfinished idea. The sentence sounded a thousand times better! She smiled as she reread the sentence and told me she saw a noticeable difference between the two sentences. I happily agreed, but unfortunately she still seemed unhappy and depressed about her grade. I again sensed the contrast between her frustration and my eagerness and decided to make a videotape of our next session in hopes of finding something that worked.

The following week I nervously asked her if she minded if we videotaped one of our sessions. My approach was to say something like, "Well, as a tutor, I am required to videotape one of my students, and I would really like to make the video with you. I want you to understand that this is for my benefit. I want to be the best tutor I can be, and videotaping will help me a great deal. But I will understand if it makes you feel uncomfortable. What do you think?" She acted very nonchalant about the idea of videotaping but said it would be "all right."

She was depressed again because she had received a C– on her in-class midterm theme, and we spent the rest of the session editing the introduction of the essay her instructor had graded. I wanted her to look carefully at it, and I asked her specific questions about her intentions. She had a very difficult time answering. I felt she could not understand that she could change her writing even after it was graded. It was as though she wrote with permanent ink and each word sat heavy on the page, unchangeable. Yet, once she reread the edited paragraph aloud, she told me she could see the difference. What I wanted her to do next was to be able to revise a piece of her own work.

When we videotaped the next session, my expectations were high. I knew that Allison was feeling better about presenting her writing in a clearer form, but I still felt a tension between us during the session.

At the beginning of the video, we discussed a punctuation exercise that I had asked her to finish at home because she had been having problems with the use of commas. Then, we discussed her paper topic, for which she was supposed to bring a thesis and outline. Instead, she presented some free-writing material and told me she was having a difficult time with the topic. I decided that talking about the topic might help. She seemed to know what she wanted to say but couldn't put her thoughts down on paper. As we discussed the topic, I felt as though I were pulling teeth. "What did you just tell me?" I'd ask. "How can you put that into a thesis?" Silence. Finally she mumbled, "Well . . ." But then she stopped. I asked again, "What did you just tell me?" She sighed deeply and blurted out, "I don't know. It's just hard for me to put it down." I asked other questions but found myself constantly rephrasing each question because she gave no answers. The tension mounted as the session continued, and I couldn't help but wonder, Why?

When I viewed the video with my senior tutor, I realized the cause of the tension. As soon as I saw myself objectively—that is, on the screen—I noticed how I hovered over Allison like a little helicopter. As my senior tutor observed, "It seemed to me, and to you too, I think, that you were so overcome by a desire to help her that you sometimes lost control and crowded her a little and even gave her a little too much information." I was disappointed in the way the video had turned out. In all my efforts to help Allison, I felt that I was overdoing it and not allowing her to express her own thoughts. I felt frustrated with myself and even more frustrated for Allison. When I watched myself on camera, leaning toward her as she leaned away from me, I knew I needed to give her more space.

Looking back at the two sessions that followed the video, I now think that I reacted too drastically. I wanted to give Allison space, but I went to the extreme. I gave her too much space, too much room to swim around aimlessly in her own ideas. My questions to her were too general, and often she didn't understand what I was asking. Many silent moments passed while I wondered, "Does she understand my question? Should I say something else?" While she stared at the page with her brows knit and then finally mumbled, "I don't know." My frustration mounted as nothing seemed to work.

The next week I showed the videotape to my seminar. As they watched the first ten minutes, I sat looking at my hands and not the screen. Afterwards, I explained I was becoming increasingly frustrated and asked the group what I should do. Everyone had terrific suggestions! One person suggested that I count to twenty-five after I ask a question to let the student think. Another suggested that I give the student some time alone to formulate a thesis statement; I could leave her for ten to fifteen minutes, then return and discuss what she had written. This way I would not feel that I was "hanging" over her.

We watched another tutor's video in which she and a student looked at an A paper and discussed why the paper worked. Watching the tutor use more specific questions, I realized that many of my questions had been too general for Allison to answer. It was as though I expected her to know what I was thinking! I needed to be more gentle and specific, but I needed to know where she was coming from too. How could I approach her with such a request?

Fate answered my question the next week when out of the blue, Allison asked me "Whatever happened with the video?" Here was my chance! I told her I learned a great deal from the video about myself as a tutor, how I felt I crowded her too much and asked her very demanding questions. I also explained that I felt I helped too much and that I wanted her to generate ideas and examples on her own. She told me that although I did ask many difficult questions, she felt they helped her get on the right track. She added, "Sometimes I needed help with the questions." I agreed and explained to her that there were times when she did not need help and simply volunteered answers.

After a long discussion, we agreed on a compromise. I told her that I would try and ask more specific questions, giving her ample silence to think. She responded by telling me that she would come to our sessions prepared and attentive and that if she did not understand a question, she would tell me immediately. Although such courtesies might seem natural, in our case they were not. We needed to state them out loud and express our concerns about the tutoring sessions. I feel that, in this conversation, we both agreed that we cared enough about each other and about learning to make the tutoring relationship work.

That we had better rapport seemed clear in our next session. Allison brought with her a copy of the paper topic, her rough-draft thesis, and a short outline. When she talked about the paper, she spoke very quickly, her words showering the session like rain falling from the sky. I needed mental buckets to hold all her ideas!

Allison's personal involvement in the topic she wrote about enabled her to take a clear stand. She could recognize, easily analyze, and support her examples. For instance, she pulled out the book as she was talking and began to search for a passage. She wanted to show me an example of a particular character's frustration. She chose a scene where a black doctor compared his expectations of his children with his expectations of the entire black race. Allison described the doctor's strong belief and pride in his people, and then added her own opinion. "I understand where the character is coming from because I'm black, and I'm proud of it, too."

Her ability to support the text as well as to present her own beliefs was evident when she announced, "Guess what? I even spoke in class!"

I smiled and asked, "What did you say?" She began a lengthy description of the boy who sits next to her and how he told the class that he didn't understand why this particular character seemed frustrated. When she finished the story, she covered her face with her hands for a moment. "I was so nervous," she said. "I thought I would shake. But I didn't." "I'm sure some people in the class were thinking, 'So that's what her voice sounds like!'"

I am not saying that just because Allison and I had one talk, she gained self-confidence and can write perfectly. However, I can say that the turning point in our relationship coincided with Allison's own personal turning point in her journey to become a better writer and more expressive student. With the help of the video, I could actually see our session as it went on and didn't have to struggle afterward trying to remember all the details. After the video, the new, more comfortable atmosphere that permeated our sessions prompted Allison to tell me exactly what happened in class. She understood how much I wanted to help her and to be the best tutor possible. Her understanding plus a topic that she was interested in writing about motivated her to begin to help herself.

DISCUSSION QUESTIONS

If you don't have a video camera, what other ways might you learn about your tutoring errors—like crowding the student, asking too many questions, or trying too hard?

I Have Been Meaning to Write for Some Time
Judith Wolochow

> Students who are repeating the basic writing course have two problems—overcoming their writing deficiencies and rebuilding their confidence.

Tracy came to me one third of the way through the semester. When he told me he was a sophomore repeating Subject A, many thoughts ran through my mind: Was he unmotivated? lazy? dumb? or, maybe, he merely had a bad day on the final exam and now, having gone through it all before, would easily pass the course. I was wrong on both counts. Tracy was a hard worker, but the grammatical and structural problems that he had not cured in high school were still haunting him and lowering his performance. Tracy provided me with an incredibly challenging tutorial experience. Honestly, I felt burdened at times with the responsibility for either his success or his premature departure from Cal. Yet I then realized that he was also feeling pressure and needed my support. I became sensitive to his repeater status, and our friendship and successful teamwork evolved from acknowledging him as a fellow student, writer, and person.

We spent our first session getting to know each other. I inquired about his other classes and how things were going. Tracy gave me the impression that he was keeping his head above water despite commuting everyday and having an unaccommodating job. I sensed that he was a relatively adaptable person. Tracy also offered me some insight about what it was like being an affirmative action student and dealing with all the added pressures of proving himself that the university environment creates. Once I had a grasp on Tracy's student status, I turned my attention to his writing.

Tracy informed me that he had gotten D's on his first two papers and had failed his first midterm. I tried not to panic. He assured me, though, that he liked his teacher better this semester and would work harder. He then said, with a smile, "Anyway, I can only do better." I admired his attitude. Tracy knew that he had a lot to work on if he wanted to succeed this semester, but regardless, he always seemed positive. I do not think he realized how much I appreciated that.

When he showed me his first paper, it was full of repetitious sentences, modification, spelling, capitalization and punctuation errors, run-together sentences, improper subject-verb agreements . . . . I instinctively wanted to take my pen and just start fixing all the cosmetic errors but realized that they might heal themselves if we concentrated on construction and reworked his ideas. I assumed (and I later learned from Tracy never to assume anything) that his errors were due to sloppiness because when I asked him what was wrong with certain sentences, he recognized the mistakes immediately. Great, I thought, he understands. However, when those same errors appeared on his next paper, I began to doubt my initial judgment. Admittedly, I gave him too much credit and should have had him do grammar exercises earlier. However, I had assumed once more that he would feel humiliated if I forced him to do the grammar exercises that he probably had done last semester. I was wrong. After working on the exercises, Tracy both improved his skills and was really grateful to me for clarifying his basic grammatical uncertainties.

When discussing his paper topics, Tracy articulated his thoughts very well but could not transcribe those same thoughts onto the page. Although this is not an unusual problem, it particularly alienated Tracy from his work because he felt he was an isolated case. Normally after discussing his topic I would say, "OK, write that down." Tracy would usually look at me as if he had seen a ghost. His defeat last semester had bred tremendous insecurities that were now interfering with his ability to make thoughts come through on paper. "OK, Judith," I would say to myself, "do something. Inspire him. Let him know that you have faith in him." He had the potential, but I needed to find a successful method to reintroduce Tracy to writing.

Timed writings were a successful starting point. They gave him writing practice while I was able to observe what was hindering him. I discovered the basic problem was that Tracy was not giving himself time to think and was stifling himself with his pen. His repetitious, vague statements evolved from his anxiousness to get the writing over with. Tracy also never reread what he wrote. I talked to him about the possibly overrated but important thinking process that precedes writing. I suggested that he write down notes to help keep his thoughts straight and then, after writing, go through and ask himself questions imitative of the ones I might ask him. His next timed writing was better. We were getting somewhere.

Ah, but there was one more major obstacle: thesis development. Tracy could explain the ABC method taught in the Subject A class, but he could not apply it to his own writing. I told him that a strong thesis refines the topic and makes writing much easier. That was all he needed to hear, and after an hour or so, he had composed his first complete thesis sentence. Tracy can really apply himself when he understands what he needs to do. Seeing his own words in the thesis formula he had described clarified it for him. He still struggles with his thesis on each paper, but at least now he knows what he is struggling for.

My efforts were not always successful, and oftentimes they were frustrating. We would go through Tracy's many rewrites carefully, and I would help him with the various troubled sections. He was usually receptive to my suggestions and had a lot of personal input, but then when he would bring his papers back to me, the errors we corrected either still existed or the corrections were awkwardly inserted with no real coherence. What went wrong? When I talked to his teacher about this problem, she felt he was merely lazy and had not put in time outside of our session to make the corrections work for his paper. I agreed to some extent, but I also felt as if I had not given clear explanations and was blinded by his enthusiastic, agreeable nod. Or maybe I had just wanted him to understand so badly. I realized that if he did not understand what was wrong in the first place, how could he make appropriate corrections?

With only a month to go, Tracy became very inconsistent. Often a very productive, innovative session was followed by a cancellation. Then he would come to the next session unprepared, appearing uninterested in me and his work. He had failed his second midterm and realized that he might fail the class. This was difficult for both of us to accept. While I got more eager and enthusiastic, he withdrew somewhat. His outward calmness stemmed from his attitude that if he did not work hard and failed, he could say, "Well, I just didn't try." Instead of forging ahead and giving his all, Tracy was protecting his pride from another possible failure. This horrified me. I entirely understood but there was no time for sympathy. I told Tracy that his teacher and I had total confidence in him and then, I said with a smile, "Anyway, I hear the female English 1A instructors are beautiful." Tracy smiled, and at the end of the session, he asked for some practice writing assignments. I felt that his shattered confidence was on the road to renewal.

Tracy's story is not over. He might fail; he might pass. However, I have seen his writing improve, and he has gotten a lot out of the readings. I honestly hope he passes Subject A, not only so he can remain at UC Berkeley but also so that his confidence in writing and, more importantly, in himself, will improve. There is hope, for he came back to tell me he passed his last paper!

DISCUSSION QUESTIONS

1. Why do you think the tutor tended to ignore Tracy's grammatical mistakes during the first session?
2. Describe Tracy's attitude toward failing. Can you think of any way to help students with this attitude?
3. What do you think caused this to be a successful tutoring case?

On the Level
George Durgerian

> Is it possible to make a student so overconfident that he forgets he has more to learn?

When I read all the case studies that they fed me in the first weeks of my how-to-be-a-tutor class (English 310 at Berkeley), I realized they all said the same thing: "Teach the student to solve problems by himself or herself," which translates to "Shut your mouth, and instead of dominating the session, listen to what the student has to say." I knew that if I hadn't read those studies, I'd have fallen into the same trap, but I had read them, so now what? I mean, now that I know how to keep my mouth shut and not give the answers, what should I do? I was on my own, and I knew it. What I needed back then, in addition to those (sincerely helpful) readings, was a little help in the mental methods of tutoring—how to give a little confidence to an obviously bright student who'd just failed the Subject A test, a student who'd always had top grades and now suddenly doubted his writing ability. Now that I'm ending my first semester as a tutor, I've realized that by building his confidence and putting the student on my level, I learned more about tutoring from Aesop and my freshman-year Psych. 1 class than from anywhere else.

Steve George is a freshman at UC Berkeley, a tall, lank, basketball fanatic who always seems to be armed with a ball and gym shorts, ready for a game. Coming from an upper middle-class neighborhood in sunny San Diego, Steve had significantly more to adjust to here than the always overbearing intellectual climate. As an affirmative action student, Steve also had to deal with the "you're not smart enough to be here" mentality that results from misconceptions about AA. When I first met Steve, he seemed to have met these challenges and come away unscathed except for a mild but visible culture shock. It was the third week of the semester, and Steve had come in because his instructor suggested it after reading his paper. The first thing that went through my head when I heard this was "Wow, I probably would have taken that pretty hard," but Steve seemed to take it well and was ready to get started right now.

The first thing I noticed about Steve's paper was that it was a lot better than I'd expected. After reading some of the examples I'd seen in preparation for tutoring, I was expecting some pretty bad stuff. For the first of many times this semester, I was wrong. Steve's writing showed intelligent thoughts and good development, along with a rather extensive vocabulary. His main writing problems were no big deal—a reliance on passive voice and a nagging tendency to use cliches and simple sentences. His main personal problem, however, was quite a big deal—insecurity.

Steve, like most Cal students, had breezed through high school, never questioning his ability to write a decent essay. Now, not only had he failed the Subject A examination (which, if passed, allows students to skip the course), but his instructor had told him that he'd better get a tutor if he wanted to pass the course at all. Steve's confidence was badly shaken, and he told me about it. He was hurt and angry at himself for failing the initial test, and even more upset that he was failing a remedial course. I learned the most important lesson of the semester right there—I learned to put Steve on my level instead of thinking of him as my student, instead of putting up a teacher-pupil barrier. I realized that he was a student just like me, with intelligence and ability and insecurities and frustrations, just like I had. I'd been just as frustrated with my first college writing class, coming in confident, then being slapped with a D+ . I knew what I needed that day, and now I know what Steve needs.

I looked over Steve's paper and told him what I thought of it— how I'd been impressed with his vocabulary, thought process, and development and that I'd honestly been surprised at how good his writing was. He knew I was sincere, and he believed what I'd told him. I then said he needed to work on passive voice; his dry, cliche-ridden introductory sentences; and some grammar problems. Subject A, I continued, was one very tough class but one he'd pass with no problem and probably get a good grade. Steve relaxed and seemed to regain some of his confidence.

Soon Steve had all of his old confidence and more. He was earning a B– average and was ahead of most of the class. He came into sessions with an attitude that said, "Hey, George, I'm a great writer, and I can't improve any more." I'd created the proverbial monster with my confidence-building scheme, but that wasn't the main problem. Steve had overcome his old problems and he'd started to develop his own style, but the structure and development of his papers were terrible. I couldn't believe it; in my eagerness to help him improve, I'd completely missed his structural problems and seen only the minor flaws. My confidence in his abilities obstructed my view of his problems. We had to start over, reviewing the basics of structure: the thesis, topic sentences, development of ideas, and the conclusion.

Steve learned it all quickly, dropping his overconfidence (though not in the way I would have wanted him to), and came out on the top of his class on the next midterm. His instructor said he'd probably end up with an A−, a considerable improvement over his first D grade. I couldn't help feeling, though, that I'd robbed Steve, denying him the potential he could have achieved if I hadn't been so careless.

Steve and I both learned something this semester, and though I'd expected a lesson, I didn't expect it to be as harsh on either of us as it turned out to be. Steve not only learned to believe in himself and his ability but also to keep a level head and not become overconfident. He learned the hard way to take academic opinions with a grain of salt and not to place anyone's judgment on a pedestal. I came away with the knowledge that self-esteem and confidence were two keys to improved writing and, unfortunately, that a careless, gung-ho attitude might seem effective at the beginning but leads to confusion and wasted time. Maybe I had been too successful, not only in raising Steve's confidence but also my own sense of infallibility.

DISCUSSION QUESTIONS

1. During the early tutoring sessions, what was George concentrating on most? Do you think he was doing the right thing?
2. How did George respond to Steve's attitude change as Steve's composition grades improved?
3. Do you agree with Steve's assessment of what the tutor and student each learned from this tutoring experience, or do you feel that the tutor was being too pessimistic? Explain.
4. How would you have handled this situation (i.e., when a student seems to be overconfident)?

Avoiding Tutor Dependency
Karin Michele Cintron

What do you do when a desperate student calls you at night and begs you to meet her and help her with a paper that's due tomorrow? Karin has fallen into this trap before and suggests ways to handle it.

The telephone's ringing startles me. It's almost 8:30 on a Thursday night, and I have just settled down with Joseph Conrad's *The Secret*

Sharer. I am very comfortable beneath the warm covers of my bed. Since none of my roommates are home, I must get up to answer the phone.

"This is Tammy," the voice from the other end of the line booms. "I need help. I'm totally stressed. I don't know what to do."

"What is it?" I ask. Tammy is a first-year student in English 1A. I have been tutoring her for nine weeks now, and during that time we have developed an excellent rapport. It could even be called a friendship. We discuss far more than her papers; we talk about roommate problems, housing problems, and relationship problems. Now, I can hear the tension in her voice.

"This paper is due tomorrow, the one on *Emile*, and I feel like it's getting nowhere. I can barely remember what I wanted to say, anything we talked about, and what I do remember I can't keep organized. I need help desperately. Are you going to study somewhere? I was wondering if you would please, please meet me. We could go to a café. I promise you'll study too."

Tammy knows I like studying at cafés. Several times before we have met for late tutoring sessions at cafés. I could read *The Secret Sharer* just as easily there as here. What do I say?

In my journal entry following our first session together, I had written,

> Tammy's writing skills are strong. She demonstrates sophisticated word usage, and a clear understanding of concepts. I'm surprised that she even thinks she needs a tutor. I think my main goal in working with Tammy this semester should be to help her develop a sense of independence. She has the ability but not the confidence.

More often than not over the nine previous weeks, I told Tammy, "Yes, sure I'll meet you." What were the larger issues of Tammy's asking me for last-minute help, and of my acquiescence? In this paper I will discuss what I now recognize to be the larger issues. I will describe my emotions, analyze the techniques I used in dealing with Tammy's requests, and offer some alternative approaches. Mainly, my tutoring experience with Tammy has made me realize the need to beware of tutor dependence. In retrospect, I realize there are a number of things I could and should have done differently throughout the course of this semester. I offer these insights and my own experience to future tutors, so they may recognize some of the signs of tutor dependency and act before it is too late.

I know that by meeting with Tammy I was only fostering her dependency on me; moreover, I was aware of the initial goal I had set for our tutoring sessions, which I also realized that I had refused to confront. However, being aware of this did little to change my attitude; I felt an obligation to help Tammy, and considering the urgency of her requests, it was difficult for me to see that it would be more helpful to allow her to write the paper without my assistance. In retrospect, however, I realize that agreeing to alleviate Tammy's last minute academic crises did little to accomplish my original goal. If I had it to do over, I would force myself to recognize the detrimental consequences of my actions, and I would take the time to discuss my feelings with Tammy. Clark (1988, 149) advises, "In general, honesty with a student about whatever is on your mind can help clear the air. It also helps the students see you as a real human being, neither a convenience to be taken for granted nor a god to cringe before."

As a first semester tutor, I was especially susceptible to Tammy's late night pleas. After all, I wanted my students to like working with me, and I wanted to help them as much as possible. Thom Hawkins (1980, 66) notes that in peer tutoring, "tasks are accomplished because there is a mutual effort between friends, a situation of closeness, not distance, that fosters a sense of community. . . ." As a true believer in this theory, I found it extremely difficult to refuse my students help. This situation raises several questions. We were told in tutoring seminars that sometimes less help is more. Working on this premise, it is obvious to me now that by accommodating Tammy's immediate needs I was jeopardizing her ability to act independently of me. Perhaps Tammy's real problem was procrastination, not her dependence. Had Tammy worked on her paper earlier, she would not have required emergency assistance.

In her book *Talking About Writing*, Clark (1988, 139) notes that "many students know they're supposed to start writing a paper long before it's due, but they keep procrastinating anyway. They dash it off at the last minute. They expect you to tutor them at the last second." Although Tammy and I set goals for particular tutoring sessions, we should have spent more time on establishing overall goals for each assignment. Rather than just ending a session with, "OK, have most of it written by Tuesday," I would change the way we set our goals. If I were still tutoring her, I would spend at least five minutes at the end of each session developing a time-table for each assignment when she receives it. This process could be very simple:

1. Formulate thesis, Tuesday day
2. Write introduction, Tuesday night
3. Outline for paper, Wednesday
4. Relevant quotes from text, Wednesday
5. Write body, Thursday and Friday
6. Write conclusion, Saturday
7. Proofread and revise, Saturday and Sunday

Making a chart would emphasize the importance of adhering to our original goals. By writing goals down, they become tangible and, more importantly, manageable assignments, not just mental clutter on the "things I should do" list. Also, for many people, keeping a written list, even one that is this simple, provides its own moti-vation. You know that after finishing each miniscule task, you get to cross it off.

To be sure, there are other techniques that might be used to encourage diligence in the procrastinating student. As an ultima-tum, some tutors refuse to meet with students who consistently come unprepared to tutoring sessions. Personally, I find this method excessive and rather dictatorial. Instead, I would suggest using the hour as preparation time for the student, perhaps by giving him or her ten minutes to brainstorm for ideas that you can discuss together. Or have the student write something such as an intro-duction to get the process started.

Students often refuse to put an adequate amount of time into an essay because they fear failure. The reasoning goes something like this: if students write their papers the night before they are due and receive a grade of C, they can blame their lower grade on waiting until the last minute to write their paper. However, if they spend a great deal of time and effort working on a paper and it still receives a C, then the grade is a direct reflection of their writing ability. Luckily, tutoring can prove a solution for this problem by allowing tutors to discuss these fears with students and work with them on the specific problems that led them to a C grade.

I feel I should have spent more time with Tammy helping her develop a strong sense of her personal worth by underscoring the strong points of her writing, which, truthfully, were many. Richard Beery (1975, 203) goes as far as to suggest, "The personal worth of each individual is not contingent on ability, or for that matter, on performance." Whether this is true or not, a good dose of confidence can remedy much of a student's anxiety.

Ultimately, students must write their own papers. Although tutors can be excellent sources of support and direction, the final responsibility for completing an assignment rests with the student. Perhaps if this were recognized and verbalized early in the tutoring relationship, the results would be more definitive in cases like Tammy's. When collaboration ends, the student's liberation begins. As tutors, we should remember that that is our primary goal.

DISCUSSION QUESTIONS

1. Karin doesn't directly state whether she gave in to Tammy's last minute demand for help and met her at a café. What do you think happened?
2. Why do you think Karin never confronted Tammy's procrastination problem directly?
3. One solution that Karin proposes for helping students who procrastinate on writing assignments is to write down goals, tasks, and deadlines. What might be a problem with this approach as Karin describes it?
4. Can you think of situations where setting ultimatums and denying tutoring appointments for students who come unprepared could benefit students? Have you tried this? If so, how did it work?
5. Do you think that Karin was just being softhearted when she said she could never deny a tutoring appointment to a student who wasn't prepared? What other reasons might she have to say this? Explain.

6. What one word would you use to describe Tammy in this situation?

Getting to Know You: Building Relationships as a Tutor
Karen Castellucci

> Because she spent her early years in Taiwan, Leanne felt her English was limited and she'd never write well. Through tutoring she learned that it was confidence, not skill, that she needed.

Get to know your student before you begin any work. It will be easier for you, they said. OK. So here I sit across from my first tutee. We have conversed now for seven minutes. I know that her name is Leanne and that she is an Economics major. Her family is in New York, where she has spent the last several years of her life. Leanne wants to pass English 1A, take English 1B next semester, and then never set foot in another English class. She says she does not "care for" the subject. I've exhausted all the getting-to-know-you questions in seven minutes. We are still perfect strangers. I don't know what to say, and yet I feel sure that we have not reached a level of familiarity that will be comfortable for the tutoring situation. What is that level, and why is it important to tutoring?

Writing is primarily a personal activity; it can be difficult, at times painfully embarrassing, to speak without inhibitions to a complete stranger (even a complete stranger who might help you significantly improve your grade!). Having a bond of mutual trust between tutor and tutee can do much to increase the success of the tutoring experiences. Tutoring is different from teaching in that it involves a collaborative effort between both students, who agree that writing is a process improved by feedback. A tutor and tutee who have built up a relationship of trust will be friends. They will be friends in the sense that the tutor cares about the tutee as a person. The tutor will recognize that the tutee has needs and concerns beyond the paper in front of them. The tutor must view the tutee as a person. It would be easy to gain a misconception of this kind of friendship. The tutoring relationship has not failed if the pair do not end up going out to pizza and a movie every weekend. This is not the kind of friendship necessary to tutoring. In fact, this extreme will also make tutoring less effective. Our best buddies rarely feel comfortable giving us honest opinions about a piece of writing. The tutor needs to fall into a category somewhere in the middle—someone with whom the tutee can comfortably share her ideas and who is reciprocally comfortable enough to give constructive help.

It is difficult to pinpoint the exact steps to building a trusting, working relationship. By looking at the evolution of my relationship with Leanne I can suggest a few ideas. My first day with Leanne, I felt I did all that I was supposed to. I asked her what her major was and where she was from. I asked her about her background in English and her expectations for 1A. She, in turn, asked me some pertinent questions that seemed more related to my qualifications as a tutor than any curiosity on her part about me particularly. This cursory exchange did not make me feel very comfortable with Leanne on our first day. I wanted to be this great resource for my freshman tutees to seek out whenever they were struggling with anything related to their new college life. Leanne wanted someone to proofread her papers. I wanted to discuss challenging questions with her and help her express herself with literary prowess. Leanne wanted a proofreader. I wanted to be a friend. Leanne didn't need a friend. Our agendas were different—probably equally skewed—and we needed to discover a happy medium.

The second time Leanne and I met, she had received an assignment and had a rough draft completed. The paper asked her to write about an episode in her childhood which affected her significantly and to discuss its implications for her adult life. When Leanne showed me the assignment, I smiled inside, wondering what this session would be like. The topic was somewhat personal, and Leanne and I were not on a personal basis. Besides that, she seemed very reluctant to show me her draft.

"I'm not a good writer. You probably will not understand this paper," she told me. "Maybe I need to explain myself a little. I came to this country from Taiwan when I was eight. English was a new language for me. Even now, ten years later, I still make many mistakes. This paper talks about my first year. I was teased a lot for my accent and my looks—I just didn't fit in." She slid the paper in front of me and leaned back in her chair. I slid it back.

"Why don't you read it to me?" I prompted. Leanne's eyes grew wide, and she just stared at me. After a moment, when she had convinced herself that I was serious about this sadistic suggestion, she began to read.

I listened to Leanne's soft voice as I read over her shoulder. The story that was unfolding was a surprise. Not only was it written in a charming voice with a broad vocabulary, but the message was touching. I wanted Leanne to know that I truly liked her paper. She kept giggling nervously when she reached emotionally charged passages or stumbled over words. I knew she didn't like sharing it with me.

"This is a terrific paper," I said. "I like the voice you use to tell the story, and you allow your feelings to be transparent. What is your favorite part, something you would like to include in another paper, some technique that you feel works well?" Leanne gave me a blank stare. Clearly she did not see tutoring as a collaborative effort. In fact, she hadn't planned on talking much at all.

"I don't know. It's got some problems. What do you think?" she asked me with a shrug.

At this point I realized that Leanne misunderstood the object of tutoring. She didn't want to get into a personal discussion. In fact, she didn't want to discuss anything period. Leanne had hoped that I would take this paper, make any necessary changes, and give it back. I decided I would have to model this kind of exchange for her, so I chose one passage that I found a bit cryptic.

"Here, Leanne, I just don't quite understand you. I feel like you need to explain more what you are thinking because this is essentially a story and the reader needs to have more details to follow it." I pushed the paper over to Leanne and pointed to the paragraph I was talking about. She made no move. "Well, how could you change it to make the idea clearer?"

"Hmm, I'm not sure. What don't you understand about it?" Leanne asked. At least she had asked an interactional question. I continued to probe her to get at the main idea of the paragraph. We eventually got into something that resembled a dialogue, but Leanne was noticeably uncomfortable. I assumed that this was going to be a long semester.

I was wrong. Leanne's instructor had structured her whole course around the question, "Who are we, and how do we define our identity once we have discovered it?'' Every author and work had been chosen to deal with this issue. Leanne admitted to me that she had never really pondered the problem before. At first the readings were very difficult for her.

One day very early on when we had been going over the essay topics, Leanne put the reader down in frustration and said, "I just don't understand it at all. Can you please help me?" This frankness was new for her. She had traditionally sat quietly during our sessions, only answering my direct questions. I told her that when I'm reading difficult books I find it helpful to sit down with other students and toss around ideas. So she asked me to read the book. Well, I really don't have the time to read everything my tutees are assigned, although I wish I did. I made an alternative suggestion that Leanne try to explain as much as she could and I would read one chapter. This worked well for us. I found that Leanne had many good ideas and that she felt insecure discussing them because of her language barrier. She always felt that she must have missed some crucial angle because of her limited English. The truth was Leanne lacked confidence. When we got into conversations together, she often had insights that I hadn't even considered.

Leanne recognized that I cared about her success, and she began to feel more relaxed. Several weeks into the semester she asked if we could meet twice a week instead of once. She began to see our times together as a chance to clarify her thinking and bounce off her ideas. She grew less afraid of telling me her thoughts. The transition from storytelling (her first paper) to critical analysis became easier because Leanne trusted me and knew I genuinely cared about her work. She felt safe telling me when she was confused or discouraged. I knew she understood the idea of tutoring when Leanne started doing all her writing and revising at home so we could spend all our time discussing the larger concepts.

Leanne just turned in her final paper yesterday. She chose to write an extra credit assignment summarizing all the authors read in the course and discussing her own method of defining the self in reference to their methods. Her last five papers have all received very high marks. I feel that after fifteen weeks Leanne no longer needs me. She has made me obsolete as a Mr. Fix-it. Leanne doesn't want a proofreader anymore. She has asked me to be her tutor next semester for English 1B. Leanne understands that tutoring is for everybody, not just for those who struggle with writing. She says it would be good for us to meet together again because "we already know how to talk about this kind of stuff together." Leanne also understands that a relationship built on trust makes the writing experience better. Today, I found a card in my box from Leanne. She wanted to wish me a Merry Christmas and thank me for all my help. What help? Leanne learned this semester that tutoring is just guided talking—and that she already knew how to write.

When I look back on my semester with Leanne, I'm not sure exactly what made us click. I tried to show Leanne that I cared about her and saw her as a fellow student. I asked her about other classes, her boyfriend, her family. I took note of her assignments so I knew what we should be working on and when. All these elements assisted in communicating that I was interested in helping. But Leanne actually learned to trust me through our exchanges about literature and her writing. She learned to trust my opinions, suggestions, and questions, not because I am some expert in the field. Some of the essays Leanne produced were admittedly better than most of my work. Leanne learned to trust me because we are both students. She is writing to communicate her ideas to an audience like me. I can show her where I understand clearly and where I do not. Together we make her writing clear. Leanne knows that I do not want to judge, evaluate, or grade her work. I only want to help her make it better. And now that she's had a successful semester and has discovered that she really can write, that's what Leanne wants too.

DISCUSSION QUESTIONS

1. How would you react if a student said to you, "If I pass this course, I'll never set foot in another English class again?"
2. How did Leanne and the tutor differ in their expectations about tutoring? How did the tutor help Leanne become more realistic about her responsibility in the tutoring situation?
3. What do you think of the way the tutor handled the situation when Leanne asked her to read her book?
4. What signaled that Leanne had finally understood what tutoring was all about?

Connecting Clauses
Lisa Armstrong

> Does it take an earthquake to make one aware of the nature of collaborative learning? Lisa goes beyond her role as tutor when she volunteers to replace Luke at the Red Cross so he can study for exams.

I began to see the nature of collaborative learning and its key role in the educational process shortly after the earthquake. It took me a long time to return to some semblance of normality, and I'm told to give up trying to reach absolute normalcy. The strange sluggishness of the week following Tuesday, October 17, affected everyone and induced in me a wave of unproductiveness compared to what I normally expect of myself.

"How's what reading going? Oh, I'm on page 35. I have been for twenty minutes. What do you suppose Dr. Lindemann is saying here?" I certainly had no clue.

My tutorials related only superficially to writing this week, and I have only a vague recollection of what transpired at all.

Well, let's see if that semicolon is correct. Are the two clauses grammatically complete? Are they joined by a conjunction? Is the resulting sentence complete? What does the Strunk and White book say? You've got it! Have you gotten in touch with your family? No, me neither, the lines are still down. How's the physics going?

We were connecting clauses with one hand and reconnecting lives with the other.

However, the memory of one tutorial is less nebulous than that of the others, and that of the resulting phone call clearer still. The conversation was not about the tutorial at all, but I feel it captured the feeling of collaborative learning perfectly.

I had been concerned about Luke since our first session, but not necessarily about his writing. He's been in this country only three years, and his prose is beautiful, alive, and passionate. I'm concerned about his health, and he's beginning to be also. Luke averages only four or five hours of sleep per night and has lost a significant amount of weight since the beginning of the semester, bringing him down to less than 118 pounds for his more than six-foot stature. He drives himself extremely hard; yet, in spite of his own concerns, he took time away from his sixteen-unit course load to address a need in the larger community. The Saturday night following the earthquake, Luke worked an eight-hour shift at the Red Cross, keying in damage assessment statistics. He was planning to do the same the next weekend but realized he couldn't afford the time away from preparing for the upcoming chemistry and physics midterms. I offered to take his shift for him.

When Luke called to give me the shift information, our conversation lasted an hour. He expressed his concern about pouring so much energy into his classes and getting unsatisfactory results. Not only is he not getting A's, in some classes he's rehashing what he learned in high school. He recognized that he needed time to refocus and perhaps talk to a counselor. I said,

Unfortunately, Luke, some lower division courses do feel like mandatory review sessions, and it is hard to stay focused when you're frustrated, exhausted, and relatively unexcited about the material. But you are extremely competent and dedicated. Give yourself a little time to adjust to Berkeley. I work with a woman up at the health service who counsels in stress management. She's very approachable, so why don't you give her a call?

I think Luke and I approach our studies in a similar way and expect similar things from the learning experience; we don't want trivia. We want to feel as though the information we receive somehow changes the way we perceive our world, and we want to know that we aren't alone in our struggle to connect those clauses of information with some degree of cohesion.

What transpired that night was, to my mind, collaborative learning. It was a process of sharing experiences, discovering resources, and encouraging continued learning. The circumstantial activities of the tutorials applies this definition specifically in the writing process, but the spirit of that definition is essential not only to academic growth but to personal growth, and one cannot occur without the other.

DISCUSSION QUESTIONS

1. Compare and contrast Lisa's definition of collaborative learning with that implied in Dina Fayer's vignette?
2. What were some of the things that Lisa learned about David during the phone call? Do you think she would have learned as much during a tutoring session? Would it have been as easy to refer him for counseling in a normal tutoring session? What do you think?
3. Do you think that Lisa's volunteering to take David's job so he could study was an appropriate act for a tutor?

Fear and Loathing in the Videotaping Room, or You Oughtta Be in Pictures
Elizabeth Abrams

> Elizabeth suggests some ways to reduce the anxiety of your first videotaping session.

The first time I went through a videotaping session with one of my students, the question echoing in my mind was, "What the hell am *I* doing here?" That question stayed with me as we sat side by side in the taping room and sweated it out. To be perfectly honest, I sweated it out; my student was calm, organized, and goal oriented, all qualities that left me as soon as the taping began.

Anxiety is a common reaction to your first videotaping session. A certain amount of nervousness is natural, but the paralyzing, sweaty reaction I went through need not be a universal experience for new tutors. Here are a few things to remember about videotaping before you start:

1. Videotaping is a learning tool. It is designed to help you evaluate your own performance. It is not a punitive measure structured to catch your most embarrassing tutoring session on tape.

2. Videotapes are for limited viewing. Only you and your senior tutor will see the tape. Tapes are not copied and made available for home entertainment.

3. The tutoring session that takes place on tape need be neither your best session nor your worst. Think of it as a day like any other.

These items undoubtedly are not new to you, but they deserve further discussion.

Learning Tool

Several fellow tutors told me how intensely they disliked being filmed. They noted, however, that they had learned enough from their taped sessions to make the experience worthwhile. Now this is good for a start, but going into the taping room with the attitude that, "Someday I'll be thankful I did this," is not an optimal situation. To capture your most typical reactions on tape for future perusal, it might help to demystify the process. Call the camera a name (no, not that kind of name!), perhaps that of the senior tutor who will watch the tape with you later on. Respond to the camera rather than trying to ignore it. Become familiar with the room, or try conducting a tutoring session sitting side by side prior to the scheduled date of taping. In other words, try a dress rehearsal. These are ploys, some silly sounding but effective, that let part of the anxiety drain away and help the taped session become a more accurate portrayal of your everyday meetings with students.

Limited Viewing

After your taping session, you will view the tape once by yourself and once more with your senior tutor. The first time around will allow you to become familiar with how you look and sound and how you performed. It allows you to develop a subjective view of your technique, interaction with the student, and general poise (not to mention the opportunity it gives you to evaluate your possibilities as a movie star). You can also pick out the parts of the tape you want your senior tutor to respond to, since there might not be enough time to watch the whole tape together.

The tape viewing with the senior tutor becomes much more objective. In my case, at least, I felt very reassured after our joint viewing—my senior tutor was constructive, honest, and kind. By watching the tape with her, I was able to recognize the good things I did as well as those areas that I needed to improve.

Picking and Planning the Session

Consider the taping session as just another tutoring session. It's best not to start taping with the expectation of having a banner day of progress with your student. Speaking about the student, try to pick the one with whom you are most comfortable for your first taping session. Why set yourself up for a difficult time? Don't do anything different on this day than you would any other day. Remember that this is a tool to learn about your tutoring technique. If your student needs to free-write, have her free-write. If she needs to discuss grammar, do so. But what if your student forgets to bring everything you had planned to work on? (That happened to me.) As in any tutoring session, it is not a good idea to have the entire taping session prestructured and too many goals set. However, it is always helpful to have some alternatives planned beforehand—a short essay question to outline, sample reading to paraphrase, anything. But don't panic if neither you nor the student have anything prepared; it is not the accomplishments you record but the communication.

I believe that if you keep these few suggestions in mind, your first videotaping session will be a little easier than it otherwise could be. And it will be more enjoyable if you can relax and stop thinking about the final results or analyzing your every move. Tutoring can be fun, videotaped or not.

4   Cultural Diversity

The Journey Continues
Vincent Harris

> An experienced African-American tutor explains how he feels about racial issues and continues to tutor to better understand the barriers to inclusiveness.

Why am I a tutor? Over the past semesters, many incidents and comments have influenced and changed my perceptions on tutoring. These incidents and comments are part of my journey; this journey's goal is to answer the above question. Some of the reasons I tutor are clear and obvious, such as wanting to help others and improve my own writing. However, other reasons are more complex and confusing, such as acknowledging a part of myself and understanding a little more about people in general. The journey is difficult because it is an emotional and a personal one. I don't have much of an idea where this journey leads, but I do know where it started.

I entered the first semester of tutoring full of idealism. After completing extremely useful writing workshops in English 1A and 1B and hearing about a shortage of writing tutors, I decided that becoming a tutor might be an interesting and challenging assignment. I would get a chance to develop much needed interpersonal skills, and the students and I would work together to develop essays and improve our writing skills. Our sessions would be totally professional; few, if any, outside interests would inhibit us for that hour or two hours a week that we met. And yet, as the sessions started, I began to see other purposes that I could serve as a tutor.

I started to share parts of my University of California experience. Depending on the student's major, we discussed classes, instructors, and other relevant topics like scheduling, commuting, and dorm life. In terms of classes, I always highlighted the fact that the Golden Bear Student Learning Center sponsors study groups in most introductory courses and that most people found them useful. Also, I shared the fact that the study groups provided an opportunity for students to make friends. Tutoring, though, remained a very objective experience; I never did much self-examination, but as I now think more about it, there are more subjective and personal reasons why I became and remain a tutor.

Maybe it was the first time that I noticed the cultural and racial divisions in the Golden Bear that forced me to reconsider my role as a tutor. It amazes me that the white tutors, for the most part, hang out together, and that the minority tutors, for the most part, hang out together, and it appears that there is little informal cross-communication between the two groups. This seems expected and accepted by most people in the center. Given that a substantial number of Golden Bear customers are students of color, it looks strange that this polarity between the races would exist; this realization irks me because it reminds me of classes like Math 16A, History 4B, and Physics 10 that I've taken here at Cal. I remember too clearly how the races, for the most part, polarized themselves. For some reason, I thought that the Golden Bear was different, but it too is infected with the same ethnocentrism as the rest of the campus.

When I spoke with a few white tutors, they expressed a sincere desire to help and empower their students. And yet, if on an informal basis white tutors feel uncomfortable with students of color, then I wonder how they feel interacting with their tutees of color. Also, when I spoke with a few African-American tutors, they too expressed a strong desire to empower their students but seem to prefer hanging out with other African-Americans. This scenario goes against the pseudoliberal idealism that brings some students to Cal and breeds a great deal of cynicism. Given that this ethnocentrism exists on both sides, I wonder how many people acknowledge it. This realization irks me not only because it represents something disturbing but also because it forces me to deal with my own ethnocentric feelings and, for good or bad, how the Golden Bear itself reflects and perpetuates some of the exclusive attitudes on campus. As a tutor, I must strive to understand these attitudes and how they affect me in tutoring.

A study group leader's comment made me aware of another role of a tutor. This leader asked me why I was always in the Golden Bear and when I told her that I was a writing tutor she expressed surprise—she actually told me that she thought that I was being tutored all those times when I was sitting at a table. Those types of comments made me angry, upset, and frustrated. Her comment angers me because it is extremely disempowering. Her reaction suggested that somehow because I was going to her study group for one class, I couldn't be proficient in another. This reflects one of the greatest negative stereotypes about seeking help—if you need it for even one class, then you must be dumb. I was upset that this leader somehow saw my study group attendance as a sign of weakness and not one of trying to get ahead, because that's why I was there. One thing that I definitely try to do as a tutor is maintain the assumption that my students are coming to sessions to get ahead.

The Affirmative Action meeting also reinforced another role of a tutor. As we discussed issues of race and the person-of-color experience at Cal, an anger that first erupted freshman year was now resurfacing. This rage centers on the fact that white tutors and minority tutors have different frames of reference. It is difficult for a minority tutor to appreciate the white student's experience at Cal and for the white student to appreciate the person of color's experience at Cal. For example, there is no question that racism is still a problem today; however, a white tutor might not agree or even see my point. The emotional charge of these issues makes it difficult for me to acknowledge or even express their importance. When a white social science tutor expressed his need to show his students how much he knows about the subject in their first session, I wanted to rip his head off. How could he take such a paternalistic attitude toward his students? I hoped that none of his students were persons of color. At a campus where a significant number of people consider minorities academically inferior, you don't need some insecure tutor further perpetuating this stereotype and untruth. As a tutor, I now see that I must be sensitive to my attitudes regarding these issues and accept their existence.

The change in the ethnic makeup of my students also enhanced my understanding of the tutoring process. The first semester, my students were Hispanic and Asian. This semester they are all

African-American. At first, I didn't think that this would matter, and yet it does—I am quite pleased. I appreciate the chance to help another African-American student. This is strange for me because I've never thought of myself as being ethnocentric, though I've always been sensitive to racial issues. I guess I never expected this feeling to demonstrate itself in such an obvious manner. Having all African-American students makes it easier for me to think about my own experience though I'm still mega-uncomfortable discussing it. As I talk with students, I gain an appreciation for the "Black" student experience at Cal and not just the "student" experience at Cal. As a tutor, I am now more willing to acknowledge this experience, though I've just done so two times this semester. First, I shared with students a 1983 *Daily Cal* article on the Black experience at Cal. Second, as a student and I worked on an essay on Dr. King, I discovered a sentence where the student referred to the 1960's society as Dr. King's society. For a quick moment, I thought about what progress and lack of it there's been in race relations; and then I asked the student to change "his" society to "our" society to highlight that the battles Dr. King fought years ago are still raging today—are still raging in me.

My reasons for tutoring are much more complex than I first realized. Wanting to help others is always meaningful, but I stay for more subjective reasons. The idealism is still very strong; however, it is also complemented by a firm sense of reality. I remain at the Golden Bear because every day I'm forced to deal with issues of race. True, the ultimate goal of all tutors regardless of race is the same—the empowerment of our students to become better writers, but we cannot say that race doesn't matter. We must be willing to admit and accept differences of opinion, experience, and attitude. The challenge is not for all of us to see each other as being alike; rather, the challenge is for all of us to examine, appreciate, and respect our differences. We must strive for inclusiveness, not sameness. The Golden Bear is at the forefront of a timeless tension—race relations. The Student Learning Center is one of the few places on campus that openly strives to achieve some understanding of this complex and dense issue. I stay to comprehend these relations and how and why they affect me. I stay because this journey is a difficult, challenging, rewarding, and personal one. I'm not here to accuse or attack, but I wonder how many others are on the same journey.

DISCUSSION QUESTIONS

1. How would you describe Vincent's journey and his goals?
2. How did his observation of the cultural and ethnic divisions in the Student Learning Center affect his perception of his tutoring role?
3. Vincent seems to be saying that the ultimate outcome of his experience as a student and tutor in a multicultural institution is the enhancement of his own commitment to helping students from his own ethnic background. Do you think that this is an inevitable result of experiences like he had?

Monocultural Blinders
Brian Hebert

> Brian realizes that good grades and a "privileged" preparatory education are not the only elements necessary for some students to learn and appreciate the different perspectives that UC Berkeley offers.

Since I first started tutoring for the Student Learning Center, I've helped students from a wide variety of cultural backgrounds. I've tutored students from Greece, Taiwan, Korea, Guam, and the USSR as well as English as a second language (ESL) students whose first languages are Spanish, Greek, Korean, Hebrew, Russian, and Chinese. This experience has been valuable for me as a potential teacher in California's multicultural classrooms. I've learned a lot about the difficult questions of cultural hegemony and minority culture assimilation in education. I've seen firsthand the special difficulties experienced by students from multicultural backgrounds who are trying to learn in a monocultural environment and must simultaneously learn the culture and the curriculum. What I hadn't seen until recently, and really hadn't expected, was the educational disadvantage of being a part of the homogeneous dominant culture.

Let me explain. This semester I began tutoring Mark, a white male, nineteen years old, from a wealthy family. He grew up in an exclusive and culturally homogeneous suburb on the Peninsula. He attended a well-funded, crime-free high school where his teachers bent over backward to see that he succeeded. He was enrolled in a college prep course and received excellent grades. However, I'm now tutoring Mark in Subject A—basic composition.

My other Subject A student this term is Kim, a young Korean student from Guam. Since Guam is under the sphere of American culture, her transition to the United States doesn't seem to have been too difficult. Her English is very good, but it still gives her some trouble.

Since both Mark and Kim are taking Subject A, I thought they would have similar problems. Boy, was I wrong! Mark's biggest problem was not his ability to use English (which he has a good command of) but his willingness to use his brain and his ability to see beyond his monocultural expectations. Mark, it seems to me, is so much a part of the dominant forces in this society and has been so isolated among people who act, think, and are exactly like him that he hasn't developed any skills for dealing with novelty—and now he lives in a fraternity! When confronted with ideas that don't fit his deeply entrenched orientation, he just shrugs them off. Nothing new seems to sink in.

Kim, on the other hand, has her greatest difficulties with language and argument. She struggles with her compositions on the sentence, paragraph, and argument level. But at least she does struggle. She comes from a very heterogeneous environment, and every moment in her life has reinforced the notion that there is diversity in the world—diversity of cultures and diversity of ideas. She herself has moved between these various realms, associating with Koreans, Taiwanese, Americans, and native Guamanians in high school and migrating halfway around the world to go to school in Berkeley. And she lives, not in a homogeneous enclave of her own people, but in the relatively heterogeneous diversity of the dorms. When confronted with new ideas, she grapples with them, testing them, and, if they make sense, integrating them into her view of the world.

Since all Subject A students were required to read Margaret Atwood's *The Handmaid's Tale* this semester, I was able to compare Mark and Kim's reactions to this provocative novel. Kim's reaction was complex and sincere. She found the book "disturbing" and felt that reading it had made her more aware of the seriousness of sexism and social conformity. The paper that she wrote for the class, though plagued with problems of organization and grammar, was an interesting exploration of the importance of self and society in the formation of individual identity. Her reaction to this book and her studies in general was summed up by this remark: "There's so much I didn't know about before; I'm really learning a lot."

Mark, on the other hand, didn't see anything disturbing in the book, which depicts a religious-totalitarian social order based on the absolute subjugation of women. When it came time for him to come up with a paper topic—he was considering an assignment on the operation of language as an instrument of control in the novel— he rolled his eyes and said, "What if I don't agree with any of this?" I asked him if he thought women ought to be dependent on men. "I think they ought to stay at home and clean," he replied. I asked him if he thought that was the idea behind Atwood's text, He retorted, "Why does a book have to have a meaning anyway? Why can't it just be a story?"

With every challenge that came up, Mark and Kim's reactions were predictable. Kim would think hard about new ideas, struggling to grasp them and work them into her understanding of the world. Mark would play golf.

Although Mark's personal laziness and ideological rigidity cannot serve as a typical model for his class, I think the general lesson I drew from observing him is valid. It seems that despite the difficulties multicultural students face, they have one significant advantage over their more privileged peers. Because they don't see their own culture as the dominant one and they don't see their own prejudices and assumptions reflected back at them by all the institutions of society and all their friends and relations, multicultural students grow up with some sense of the subjectivity of their views. When a person understands that there are many ways of looking at things, that other ideas exist, she or he is better able to deal with new situations and is better able to learn.

DISCUSSION QUESTIONS

1. Can you think of any techniques that Brian might have used to change Mark's attitude toward literature and writing?

2. Might there be other explanations for Mark's comments and behavior than the ones Brian gives? If so, give some examples.
3. Brian does not describe his own background. Should we assume that he comes from a white, middle-class family?
4. How do you think Mark feels about Brian?
5. Do you think that Brian is aware of his own bias?
6. Brian does not discuss the grades his two students were getting in their composition course. What do you think they might have been? Do you think Mark will flunk the course? Why or why not?
7. Discuss how well this paper supports Brian's premise that people who grow up in a multicultural society are aware of their prejudices and are better able to learn. What evidence does he give to support his point? Is the evidence sufficient or do we need to know more about the students to draw the same conclusion?
8. Do you think it is fair to say that Brian's concern with his students' personal characteristics seems to overwhelm any consideration of their writing problems? Compare his attitudes with those of Helen Woo in her essay, "On Crossing the Tutor-Tutee Line: Toward a New Kind of Relationship."

Langston Hughes Takes on Tutoring
Jessamy Town

> Jessamy discovered a new world of meaning when she asked her African-American student to read a poem orally. This insight led her to question the cultural and ethnic constraints we place on writing.

The University of California, Berkeley, heralds its student body for its "excellence through diversity." However, some questions have been raised about how much students from various cultural and ethnic backgrounds really do interact in the university community since most students tend to gravitate to their own cultural and ethnic groups for support and socializing. While sitting at the tutor recruitment table on Sproul Plaza with a fellow writing tutor, we noticed that we could not anticipate the type of person who would be interested in our information. People from every walk of life asked for an application or wanted to know how much we were paid or what were our hours. A middle-aged woman with a child, an African-American man wearing a T-shirt with Greek letters, a Caucasian girl in a turban, and a six-and-a-half-foot-tall Samoan man in a Cal crew sweatshirt asked about tutoring at the Student Learning Center. I was sure we'd been set up for a UC Berkeley recruiting video.

The experience at the recruiting table led me to think about a recent tutoring session that left me feeling exhilarated because I felt my student and I had shared meaning in working together on Langston Hughes' "Theme for English 1B" and in doing so had transcended racial and ethnic differences. I left this tutoring session feeling that not only had Sheila made progress on the structure of her paper but that I too had begun to understand how tutoring writing is a form of communication that allows individuals to explore ethnic and cultural differences constructively.

Neither Sheila nor I had read Hughes' poem before, so we each read it silently. Then I suggested that she read it aloud so that we could get a firmer grasp of its meaning. As she read, I realized that her intonations and rhythms were completely different than those I had imagined in my own mind. Reading the poem on my own, without her voice, was not the same experience. Her oral version did not highlight our racial and ethnic differences as barriers, rather it represented a sharing of new insights instead.

Sheila and I then discussed Hughes' situation in the poem as an African-American man at an all white university. Hughes had written the poem as an assignment for his white English professor, and both Sheila and I began to question the effect of race on writing, just as Hughes did. He asks, "Will my page be colored that I write?/ Being me, it will not be white." The idea that words had color had not occurred to either Sheila or me before. We wondered, "Do words reflect a person's race or gender? If so, then what color and sex defines the 'standard' paper-writing voice? Is it a standard set by a white male history of literature, or is it writing without race or gender, or does using a white male standard take our race and sex away?" I felt horrified at these thoughts, and even more horrified that I had never questioned the standard before.

If white male writing is the standard, is every other person's writing a divergence? Why do people describe Alice Walker as an African-American woman writer and Maxine Hong as an Asian-American writer? Why not just a writer? Also, here at UC Berkeley, are students of color considered to have a nonstandard voice when their papers are graded? Can Sheila or I feel free to write in a female or an African-American voice, or have we been trained to edit, to cut and paste, to erase, and to drain our own warm real voices of any sexual or cultural identity? Also, how do these questions relate to tutoring? Are we as tutors aiding the denial of cultural identity in writing, or is writing, in fact, devoid of gender or culture?

Ironically, other students on campus were protesting the university's unequal policies concerning the ethnic studies and women's studies departments while Sheila and I sat quietly discussing the issues posed by "Theme for English 1B" in the Student Learning Center. Although I can't say I have found answers to the questions the poem raised, I think the answer lies in the questioning itself. I do know that I left the session resolved to be aware of my own choices about editing my voice when I write and to be aware of any suggestions I might make to my students to edit theirs.

Hughes' poem, "Theme for English IB," embodies the ideals and possibilities of good tutoring as it left me with many questions. But it also left me with a renewed admiration of literature's power to communicate through barriers and differences. Hughes showed that words are the keys to all of the protests, politics, and differences in Berkeley. Words stir up questions and awareness; they communicate over place, time, and solitude. With words, everyone can choose to solve a problem in exactly their own way.

DISCUSSION QUESTIONS

1. What happened that made Jessamy realize how different her interpretation of the poem was from Sheila's?
2. Do you agree with Jessamy's statement that in college writing you learn to edit out your own voice? If so, give some examples.
3. Do you think that most college professors would accept papers written in your own voice reflecting your cultural and gender identity? What does Jessamy suggest as the solution? Do you agree with her position?

Supervisor's Comments

When students begin their academic careers at UC Berkeley, they are not only being initiated into an academic community, but also meeting and confronting new ideas and new people. Jessy relates how two individuals from different backgrounds are inspired by an assigned poem to explore the issue of who has the power to validate a particular kind of writing. In any tutorial relationship, there always exists a power dynamic that must be acknowledged and understood. For instance, the tutor has the power to nurture and develop a student's sense of identity, a delicate endeavor. Tutors like Jessy are able to gently push their students to better understand how ethnic identity influences writing. Students need to critically examine the canon and the history of the university so that they can choose how they will interact with it.

All educators will have to decide how to provide the skills, tools, and knowledge that linguistic, ethnic, and other minorities need to participate actively in the educational system. I have heard well-intentioned people argue that educators are wrong in addressing these differences. They argue that we are all part of the human race and that discrimination will end when we all accept this argument. To those advocates, I argue that the sentiment is nice but it falls short of remedying any of the problems facing minorities. It is foolish to think that we all come to the task of tutoring and writing with identical historical and political experiences. To deny this would destroy the wealth of perspectives and images that come from being different. One of the more fascinating elements of writing and tutoring is that when students write and talk about their writing, they expose the many influences that have shaped their identities.

—Rosaisela Rodriguez

A Little Enlightenment in the Golden Bear
Susanna Spiro

A Caucasian tutor feels isolated working with an African-American student in a setting where the tutor is in the minority, and the student is among friends. However, by conveying a feeling of warmth and concern, the tutor soon finds herself more comfortable as the student begins to accept and confide in her.

Marie, a young black woman taking Subject A for the second time, was assigned to me, a young white woman tutoring for the first time. Despite all the preparation, despite my general optimism and confidence in my abilities, I found myself deeply unsure of what

I was doing. It was not that I had forgotten how to write essays; it was that I didn't know what to do with the gap between Marie and me. Socially, educationally, and personally, we had completely different backgrounds. I supposed I could just go ahead and start tutoring; we did have in common the desire to improve her writing. But for me there was no ignoring the social and personal aspects of a tutoring session, and I felt uneasy with her. She knew many more people in the Student Learning Center than I did, and I was impressed by the friendliness that prevailed inside the building; but I myself did not feel entirely comfortable, being so new here, being a racial minority here, and being faced with the task of fusing a relationship with someone so unlike myself. It was from the general, friendly sorts of questions I asked her that I learned her background; but sometimes I did not even understand her answers, because her speech was unclear to me. It wasn't a question of dialect; she slurred her words and often did not look at me, directing the sound off somewhere else. What was she thinking—what did she think of me?

It was a simple act of waving—Marie waving at me when I came into the Golden Bear—that made me begin to feel better. Her friends smiled at me sometimes. Marie began telling anecdotes about her home life, which were extremely interesting. With unexpected speed, we created a very satisfactory relationship. But what was this relationship? It could not be called intimate since, although it was a friendship of sorts, it was artificially structured and had boundaries. Nor was it purely professional, that is, although it was our purpose to discuss Marie's writing, I did not consider the writing aspect to be the most important part of our relationship. On the contrary, I found myself thinking about Marie a great deal, but not about her writing. I didn't wish to neglect her writing, of course, but I felt that something else more important than just that was happening.

It would have been impossible to address Marie's needs simply in terms of paper writing. I was learning to recognize the more complex needs of a first-year student who not only was having academic difficulties but also seemed disoriented and unaware of the demands of the school. Marie had failed Subject A once, and her instructor suggested to me that she might indeed fail again. At this point, I by no means resigned myself to the certainty of failure; but neither did I feel that a superhuman effort toward passing was appropriate. We would continue our work together and achieve what we could. But other issues filled the picture, too.

Certain small events allowed me to feel that I had a place in her experience. One day after tutoring, Marie asked me in an offhand way what services the hospital offered. I was slightly alarmed, because I thought something might be wrong but was quite sure Marie would not tell me what. I did not rely on her straightforwardness. A certain lack of directness was one thing that helped to characterize for me Marie's not-quite-complete transition from high school to college. I got the distinct impression that a lot of her reactions were governed by high school–type expectations. For example, if she missed an appointment, she would later swear that she had left me a note that had somehow gotten lost or that she had shown up and I hadn't—assertions that showed a transparent effort to avoid getting in trouble with me. I apparently occupied the standard teacher role in her mind. I kept wishing she would realize that such covering up wasn't necessary, that I only wanted her to take a little responsibility for her actions rather than resist an equal, honest relationship with me. These small indications of her concept of how to deal with responsibilities on campus worried me. At any rate, I offered to take her up to Cowell Hospital and show her around, and she was glad to go with me. I felt somewhat more free with her outside the Student Learning Center, because our walking somewhere together was a positive sign that we had some relationship outside tutoring. In fact, after our little tour of Cowell, during which Marie was happy and thanked me but offered me no information, I felt that despite her basically withdrawn attitude, she did trust me on some level that was important to me.

I tried to help Marie become acquainted with some other methods of helping herself. When I found out that she hadn't started her anthropology project and was intimidated by her teaching assistant, I got in touch with the TA and talked with him a little about Marie's situation. He was interested but still failed to be particularly responsive: he wasn't available during his office hours and never attempted to talk with Marie. At that point, I got in touch with a friend of mine who was also an anthro TA. I thought Marie would feel more comfortable with her. After one of our sessions, I told

Marie that this TA was having office hours at that very moment and that I would take her up there to meet my friend and talk about her project. Marie was unsure about this, and I felt a little pushy. But I also knew that without some guidance, Marie would not get through this ten-page research paper (which she should have begun a month earlier), and I wasn't in a position to tell Marie the specifics of the project. So I sort of insisted, knowing that Marie didn't have class or other commitments then. We walked up to the anthro building, and I introduced the two and left. A few minutes later, I walked by the door and they seemed quite engaged in their conference. When Marie called me and told me she liked the new TA and was going to meet with her and show her an outline of her project, I had a warm feeling of success. Marie had been missing tutoring, forgetting her drafts and books, and generally discouraging me; but in the midst of this, she had learned how to approach a TA for help, and that's an important skill.

I kept coming back to the feeling that even if Marie did not stay afloat at Berkeley, she was gaining knowledge that would never be wasted. I reassured myself with this, and then scolded myself for thinking negatively about her possibilities here. But then again, there are also realities of failure.

I am convinced that I learned more from Marie than she has learned from me. I had a lengthy one-to-one relationship with a woman whose past and present (and probably future) differed from mine greatly, whose family experience was alien to me, and whose educational experience was far different from mine. Without that artificial friendship created by tutoring, I would probably never have gotten to know Marie; the social opportunities for such relationships are rare on campus. If I was able to help her, I think I mainly helped her by doing her some small, more personal services that showed attention to her specific needs, without confining myself to the boundaries of the Student Learning Center. She has been part of the process of coming to terms with some of my intimidation in the Golden Bear—an intimidation I was able to reduce by getting used to surroundings I would not normally encounter. Racial tensions are carefully measured in the Golden Bear, and recognizing those tensions has been an important part of my tutoring experience. As I found with Marie, racial hostility is soothed and replaced by general good will in the Golden Bear; but it is in just these surroundings that awareness of differences peaks.

Postscript

The concealed element in Marie's emotional life, which was no doubt a major cause of her increasing distraction, turned out to be a pregnancy. She was due to have a baby the following semester and eventually decided that it was unrealistic to try to stay in school at this point. She withdrew during the last week of classes and told me she intended to come back after a year. All this news had quite an impact on me. I realized I could not possibly have fully assessed Marie's needs, no matter how attentive I had been, without knowing this essential information. And I was struck again, and harder, with the intensity of the gap in experience which separated us. This eighteen-year-old woman was about to enter a world of which I knew nothing. Yet both of us had sat together for hours, looking at passages and going over grammar—for a time we were both students. Part of me fears that Marie might not come back to school, or perhaps not for many years. She'll have a lot to contend with in her new life (it certainly must be a new life, although Marie seemed inordinately calm about it). But am I really in a position to fear for Marie's future? In thinking this way, maybe I am only saying that I, were I in her shoes, would fear for mine. But we are two different people.

DISCUSSION QUESTIONS

1. Recognizing that hindsight is always clearer than foresight, are there other things that the tutor might have done to help Marie? Do you think that Susanna might have been a bit overprotective of Marie? If so, explain why.
2. Do you think you would have been able to ask Marie more direct questions about her health when she asked about the hospital?
3. What effect do you think the fact that Marie was among friends when she came in for tutoring had on her tutoring?
4. What were some indications that Marie was beginning to trust Susanna?

Prejudice and Power Plays
Rachel B. Levin

> What happens when a student picks a vulnerable female tutor whom
> he proceeds to harass and dominate? In this case, tutoring became a
> power struggle.

I had to reschedule my first meeting with Ali, and when I called
him, a bit nervous about my position as a student who would be
influencing another student's writing, I was very surprised by his
response.

"OK, so I'll meet you Monday at nine," I said.

"Great, Rachel, but could you describe yourself to me so I know
what you look like and who to look for?"

I felt somewhat uncomfortable about his request but told him
anyway. However, he interrupted me saying, "Oh, I'm just kidding.
I know what you look like."

Considering I had never met this person—I had not even known
by the name if he would be male or female—I was thrown off
guard. It turned out that Ali had seen me learning how to be a
tutor and had picked me when he signed up for tutoring like a
patriarch picks a member of his harem.

My tutoring relationship with Ali that developed throughout the
semester forced me to recognize problems with power related to
gender and religion. Gender played a large part in this power play,
and I believe that the reason he chose me as his tutor was because
I was female. He must have had difficulty admitting to himself
that he needed a writing tutor and took this as a personal deficiency. Thus, to regain control, he picked someone whom he could
dominate—a woman. Working with Ali forced me to deal with prejudice and stereotypes in a way that I never expected to have to
do in a tutoring situation. The problem continued throughout the
semester, getting worse around midterm, and finally becoming a
bit more equitable, though still unpleasant relationship at the close.

So when we started, I knew that Ali had picked me out of a
crowd, and I wasn't sure why. Our first session went well, but
looking back (since hindsight is always 20/20), I spent too much
time apologizing to myself for the things he said and did, in an
effort to make the session positive, productive, and successful. It

was my first tutoring session, and I wanted it to be good, no matter what. Thus I dismissed his touching my arm and his odd, slightly directive and patronizing questions as just being a way to get used to each other while, in truth, they reflected his personality.

Even his writing seemed to reflect the way he interacted. His major problems, issues we worked on almost every session, included a limited way of thinking through and developing ideas, repetition, and verbosity—in short, saying the same things over and over in the most pompous and complex way possible without going deeper into the issue. Similarly, he treated me as the audience to whom he addressed his papers, someone who was inferior to him. He refused to look beyond my gender and my religion. He would remark that people in certain religions talk more with their hands. Racial epithets like that allowed him to fit me into a cultural stereotype. He reduced me to a simple formula, and after two or three sessions, his personality began to have a very negative effect on me.

In beginning to write this case study, I felt I might have over-reacted—that I misread his actions and blew them out of proportion. However, when I look at examples of what he said and did, I realize that I was not just imagining things.

Whenever Ali brought in a new paper, I'd read it to him so he could hear how it sounded. This technique, I felt, helped him pick out overcomplicated sentence structure, poor word choice, and repetitions. He would stop me and make a mark in the margin for us to return to later. But instead of pointing out the error directly and immediately himself, he would ask me as if he were testing to see if I were competent enough to see the problem. He tested me and patronized me throughout the semester, and the relationship reached a low point around midterms. That was when he walked into our appointment ten minutes late, holding the paper we had worked on the week before.

"Bad news," he said, "guess what we got on this paper? B−." I was dumbfounded. "We? It's your paper," I wanted to say, but no words came out, I was so speechless. The way he phrased these salutary remarks made me feel like I was at fault, that he didn't do as well as he deserved because I am a bad tutor. I felt like I failed. His placing the blame on me might have been unconscious, but I think he needed to deny his deficiency and place me in the inferior position by discrediting me and hurting my feelings. This was an even more personal blow than discrediting my religion or my gender.

After the initial shock, the session continued to go downhill. We did not even work on the B− paper that he felt was my fault; instead, he wanted to work on his application to the business school. But the session was unproductive because I felt hostile and angry toward him, and everything I suggested he would twist to make it sound like I was wrong again. For example, I pointed to two sentences and asked him what he thought about them, and he admitted that they both said the same thing. So I asked him to say it in one sentence, but he wouldn't make the corrections on the paper. So I asked him, "Don't you like these changes we're discussing? Is that why you're not writing them down?"

"Oh no," he retaliated, "I'm just thinking about them, Rachel," and he touched my arm in a way that made me both uncomfortable and revolted at the same time.

After that incident, I really wanted to drop him, but I felt that our problems were unresolved and that I had not dealt with the situation in a completely sound way. I also wanted to prove to him that I was, in fact, a smart person and a capable tutor, even if I was female. So I met him again and gave him one more chance, and miraculously the session went relatively well. I tried to distance myself physically (I sat farther away) and psychologically. But the main reason that this session worked was because I got a chance to prove myself intellectually. He had neatly categorized me as one of those female English major types, like his instructor, about whom he voiced much disrespect. Once he had done that, it was very easy for him to think of me as an inferior, even when he was coming to me for help. However, the paper he brought in for this session discussed American economics, a subject I knew something about since I had taken a course in it. (He is an economics major.) Once I was able to show him that I knew something else besides English, he seemed to view me differently, and I seemed to rise in his esteem.

Situations in which gender and religion become major stumbling blocks can never be pleasant and productive atmospheres for tutoring. My personal situation with Ali became bearable only when I was able to distance myself from the remarks he was making and concentrate more intensely on his writing. I knew that I would never be able to change the way he fixated on power, the way he tried to put me down, and I didn't even want to try. I just wanted to help him on his papers. I did that, and now it's over, and I don't want to find myself in a similar situation although I know that I might have to deal with overt or subtle prejudice for the rest of my life.

DISCUSSION QUESTIONS

1. Do you think Rachel was aware of how she contributed to the power struggle she had with Ali? What was it that she seemed to be determined to prove?
2. What were some of the things that Rachel did that might have made her relationship with Ali worse?
3. Why do you think Rachel felt Ali was biased against her religion?
4. In your opinion, would it have made a difference in their relationship if Ali were from a Moslem country? or if he were an African-American?
5. Can you think of any reasons why Rachel did not ask her supervisor to change Ali to another tutor early in the term?

Supervisor's Comment

Rachel had the option, should she have wished to exercise it, to ask her supervisor to find another tutor for Ali. Every semester a few tutors and students request a change. Changes can be made without blaming either party; not every pairing is a good match.

—Thom Hawkins

Close Encounters with Feminist Ideology:
A Case Study
Linda Irvine

> We are not always aware of how our personal biases intrude in our tutoring. Occasionally students invest a lot of effort in trying to please their tutors only to find that it's to their detriment.

As a student in the English Department, I make it my job to think deeply and thoroughly about literature. This has both helped and hindered me in my work as a writing tutor. On the one hand, I am eager to discuss literature paper topics with my tutees; on the other, I come to our sessions with a lot of theoretical baggage, with fifty ways to interpret *Hamlet,* when they don't even have one. I am often tempted to launch into an explanation of my interpretations, when I am supposed to be helping my tutees articulate their own ideas. Although I have learned to bite my tongue and control my enthusiasm for my own ideas, I can never contain my feelings completely. In fact, my attitudes come across loud and clear: I flinch involuntarily at ideas I dislike; I nod my head wildly when the student feeds me a line I like.

Why do I feel so strongly about literature? I feel that there is a lot at stake in how students learn to look at literature. Any interpretation of literature carries with it a perspective that extends far beyond the paper, to affect how the student interacts with his or her world. In my own life, I have found that a feminist approach to literature has given me a new outlook and made me question things in the world that I previously took for granted. As a new tutor, I was looking forward to talking with students about women's issues and perhaps changing their approach to literature and to life.

Brian was more familiar with the tutoring process than I. He had had a tutor for English 1A; now he was back for more help, in English 1B. His goals were clear: he wanted to work on generating ideas and making his papers more meaty, and he wanted to reduce his many mistakes in articles and idiom. It seemed to me that his grammar wasn't the problem. Rather, he had a larger problem. He didn't understand the point of studying literature. He approached each text as a cut and dried piece of evidence that pointed to one truth, and his papers retold that truth. They were not arguments, but statements of fact. No wonder he found English class boring, useless, and of little importance compared to his Economics classes. I should have been tipped off at the start, when he told me that he didn't use a word processor because he planned never to need one after this class was over. As a sophomore Econ major, he would pass this English course and never write another paper in his life.

At our first writing session, I was excited to see that he had chosen to write about "Edna's rebellion against societal expectations" in Kate Chopin's *The Awakening.* Here, I thought, was a student with an interest in women's issues and a sensitivity to gender differences. I was relieved, as I had dreaded an uncomfortable confrontation with a male chauvinist. Instead, we would have wonderfully frank discussions of women's issues. I must admit, I was more interested in Brian's topic than I was in his actual paper. I hoped that in the process of helping him define a topic and write his paper, I would learn vicariously about this founding text of feminism. We plunged into a discussion of Edna and her rebellion against society. Our discussion was rather vague; Brian could point to instances of Edna's oppression in the novel, but he didn't seem to connect them in any pattern beyond the limited instances in the novel. I wanted to know, "Why did Edna rebel? What was wrong with society? Why did Edna's rebellion fail? Were there any successful rebels in the novel?" When we got to a discussion of Edna's affair with a young man, Brian turned red and laughed but didn't want to go into details. I was dissatisfied with the discussion, but I thought he was on the right track. At least he had chosen an interesting topic, I reasoned.

His paper came out quite mechanical and matter of fact. It was plot summary with a bit of social theory thrown in for effect. I wanted to ascribe this less-than-successful effort to bad luck; everyone sooner or later has a paper that misses the mark—you are so intent on proving your thesis that you forget to evaluate whether that thesis is worth proving. But this was just the first of Brian's uninspired, unconvincing papers. In his next paper, he chose to examine the role of the mother in a short story by Sherwood Anderson. I was again excited by his choice of topic, and we spent two sessions discussing the paper. In our discussion, I was struck by his confusion of the author's position and reality. He tended to see them as one and the same. Anderson portrayed the mother as an oppressive, ambitious, destructive woman who brought ruin to her family through her attempt to dictate their lives. Brian started making statements like, "The mother is responsible for the fall of the family." He had picked up the misogynist tendencies of the author without recognizing them as such. I asked him if the author's portrayal of the mother might be the expression of a man who felt threatened by women. He immediately agreed with me that the author might have been threatened by women, but he didn't incorporate any critique of the author's view in his paper. I was beginning to suspect that there was some critical gap between Brian's choice of paper topics and his true interests.

We proceeded through other painful papers; I could never quite grasp his point, yet his topic choices indicated a sustained interest in women's issues. I wasn't forcing him to write about women (or so I thought), for he always had a general topic chosen by the time he came to our session. Finally, he came to a session without any preconceived ideas. He said he was supposed to write on *As You Like It*. I asked him what grabbed him most in the play. He said it was a scene in which Rosalind disguises herself as a man and convinces her unsuspecting lover Orlando to treat her [the "man"] as if she were Rosalind. Innocent Orlando agrees to treat this strange "man" as Rosalind, to practice wooing her. Brian said that this scene struck him as "true." He saw that Orlando was uncomfortable talking to a women and could talk freely to Rosalind only when he thought that she was a man. As Brian grew more and more eloquent about the virtues of man-to-man conversation, it dawned on me that I was irremediably not a man. If he identified so strongly with Orlando, did he prefer to talk about personal things (such as interpretations of literature) with a man? I asked him if he felt more comfortable talking to men than to women. He admitted that there were a lot of things that he couldn't talk about with women; women couldn't understand certain things, and other topics were just plain improper to mention to women. I could only guess what they were because he was not about to throw off his inhibitions right there and talk to me man-to-man.

The session left me both dismayed and delighted. At last, Brian had a topic that he felt strongly about. His insights were keen, his ideas were interesting, and he could talk about them from personal experience. On the other hand, I thought, how could we ever have a meaningful conversation if he felt inhibited by my femaleness? I had been mistaken about his feminist sensitivity. How could I have assumed that his choice to write on women's issues was proof of some acceptance of the feminist project? I felt guilty for channeling his papers into an area he neither believed nor understood.

But how could I be guilty? Wasn't I just following his cues, trying to get him to develop ideas that he suggested? In retrospect, I realized that I had showed enough enthusiasm in our first meeting for Brian to realize that I ascribed to a feminist school of thought.

He had also picked up enough cues from his instructor to know that he would appreciate papers that addressed women's issues. I had been blind to the extent to which Brian had detected my ideological slant and had chosen his topic to please me rather than himself. He had picked up some of the vocabulary of feminism, but he had not accepted it as practice in his own life. In his feminist papers, he was going through the motions without believing in his ideas, and his writing suffered from his lack of conviction and failure to understand his topic.

I am not suggesting that he was wrong to feel more comfortable talking to a man. That is acceptable as long as he can understand and confront the issues that underlie that discomfort. Does he think women are somehow sacred or too dumb, too ladylike, too bossy, too domineering to engage in frank conversation? Is he aware that women have been painted in these negative ways throughout literary history and that it is up to us as readers to point out the tendency and examine it in our own lives?

When my initial dismay passed, I realized that I had to work out two issues with Brian. First, I explained that he shouldn't ever write to please his tutor because his ideas were much more important than mine. Then I asked him whether he felt uncomfortable talking to me because I was a woman. This question made him uncomfortable; obviously, he *did*. We had a discussion of why he felt uncomfortable and how we could change our sessions. We didn't resolve anything, but we did get the issue on the table, and we still come back to it from time to time in our sessions. Brian might not be as comfortable talking to women as he is talking to men, but at least he is comfortable enough to be honest about his interests in paper topics. He doesn't try to please my feminist views; he is currently happily writing on the virtues of Hemingway's code of ethics. His writing is not perfect, but it has an enthusiasm that was lacking in his feminist papers.

DISCUSSION QUESTIONS

1. Do you have any strong feelings or biases about the subject you tutor? If so, what? Are you able to control your enthusiasm or like Linda, do you give your students clues about how you feel?

2. Linda describes a situation where a male student feels uncomfortable talking with a woman tutor. Might the same sort of problem occur for a male tutor working with a female student whose assumptions were being challenged?
3. How did Linda overcome her student's discomfort? Do you think you might have handled things differently? If so, how?

A Minority Writing Tutor at the Golden Bear
Eduardo Muñoz

What happens when a tutor finds himself playing cultural role model for a new student?

When I went through the application process for a position as a writing tutor at the Golden Bear, I believed that my relationship with my students would be strictly dictated by their questions and problems with writing. My expectations were based on my personal experience with the Golden Bear as a tutee two years ago. My relationship with my tutor, Bill, a graduate student working on his Ph.D. in political science, was friendly yet detached. Although the differences in our cultural heritages—his Jewish and mine Mexican— provided us with the potential for entering interesting discussions, there existed between us a "professional distance" that neither of us attempted to shorten. He was the tutor, I the student. Where the tutor application asked for my preferences with respect to course subjects and student ethnicity, I marked Chicano studies as the subject and Chicano students after some reflection. I had noticed a scarcity of Chicano tutors in the Golden Bear, so I thought I would benefit those students who preferred a writing tutor with a similar cultural background. However, at the time I really had no clear idea how any of these students would benefit from our shared ethnicity. In fact, even with these students, I believed that my relationship would be similar to the one I had experienced with Bill. When my tutoring sessions got underway, my relationship with one of my students, Alex, shattered my initial expectations and helped me define my role as a minority tutor. Our relationship also moved me to dwell on the ramifications of getting intellectually and psychologically involved with a tutee in areas other than writing.

I remember clearly my first impressions of Alex when we met

for our first tutorial session. A sophomore here at Cal, he came across as friendly, ambitious, and with a keen sense of how he wanted to utilize our sessions. After sharing a few minutes of superficial details about ourselves, I was impressed by his articulation and reasoning. During that first session, he had me look over a copy of his first paper, in which he stated his reasons for taking Chicano Studies 1B. Alex's essay was well structured, and my comments were limited to nitpicking those few areas which either were awkward or needed elaboration. But for my purposes here, the form of his essay was not important; it was the content. In his essay, Alex expressed a deep and sincere desire to familiarize himself with his Mexican heritage. He wrote how, as a second generation Mexican-American raised in an affluent and predominately white neighborhood, he felt ignorant of the issues concerning Chicanos in the United States. He thirsted for a familiarity with his ancestral, historical, and cultural heritage, as well as with present day Chicano politics.

As our tutorial sessions continued, I could read between the lines of his essays a sincere attempt to assess his relationship with Mexico. One of his essay assignments was to describe and analyze a social event. He chose to describe an annual fiesta that his family participates in every time they travel to Mexicali to visit relatives. The purpose of the fiesta is to celebrate the annual reunion between the two families. As I read the essay, I noticed a tone of condescension in his descriptions; it was as if I was reading an anthropological report or an article from a 1920s *National Geographic* magazine. I remember the following line from his essay: "When we reached our destination, I noticed the indigenous natives performing their afternoon chores in preparation for the quickly approaching evening meal." At that line, I turned my face quickly to hide a chuckle. Alex, however, took notice and inquired about the source of my smile. I honestly told him that he was describing the scene as if he were in a stage coach, holding a teacup with his fingertips as he looked out the window. He looked at me with incredulity and remarked with bewilderment that his professor did not at all appreciate the tone of the paper. And he was right. His professor had crossed out "indigenous natives" and suggested "relatives," advising him to instead use a more familiar phrase and tone. He asked me to explain her dislike for his style of expression.

I looked at his face intently and realized that perhaps Alex was only vaguely aware of the attitudes and feelings of other Chicanos when it came to the issue of cultural roots and heritage. I began to realize that Alex was perhaps unfamiliar with the concept of selling out, or Pocho (a Mexican term with a derogatory meaning used to describe those Mexican-Americans who had forsaken or consciously chosen to ignore their heritage out of the desire to assimilate into American society). I explained to him that one of the underlying objectives of some Chicano studies courses is to instill within students a pride for their heritage in an effort to strengthen their self-esteem. Some professors in the department, and Chicanos in general, I elaborated, frown on those Mexican-Americans who refuse to acknowledge a tie with their heritage and, much worse, those who feel ashamed about it. I told him that this was strictly off the record and that my explanations were based on my personal experiences with the department.

To relate my explanation to the comment on his paper, I proceeded to explain to him that his professor perhaps did not appreciate the tone of his paper because it seemed to side with those Mexican-Americans who had chosen to look down on their heritage. I looked at him and could see behind his eyes a mind vigorously at work, attempting to digest everything that I had said. He explained to me that he did not look down on the people in Mexicali, nor on his relatives, but instead loved and respected them very much. After some hesitancy, he also said that he described the scenes the way he did because he liked to exercise his vocabulary. (I concluded that he simply liked to sound scholarly and educated. Indeed, throughout the semester, he worked hard to achieve that effect in all his essays.) He rewrote the paper and made the changes reluctantly. The ramifications of my explanation, however, were to be felt throughout the rest of our tutorials.

After our next meeting he invited me out to coffee. I was reluctant at first, but only out of exhaustion. He persisted and I finally capitulated. As we sipped our mochas in "Sufficient Grounds," he unleashed thousands of questions. His questions slowly elicited autobiographical information from his tutor. He found out that I was raised in East Los Angeles and had transferred out of the local junior college there and that on my arrival to Berkeley, I had joined a fraternity where I was the only person of color. When he inquired about my girlfriend, he was surprised to discover that she was raised in Santa Cruz and not of pure Mexican descent (she's half French). Throughout our conversation, I realized that he was trying to determine where it was that I stood. However, I decided not to reveal my politics but instead to help him come to his own conclusions. I believed that my politics, given my position as a peer tutor, had too much potential to influence his own private quest for cultural knowledge and self possession. I questioned him about his feelings about assimilation and asked him to focus on how he felt about those Chicanos who completely ignored their roots and those who fervently tried to sustain them. I asked him to look into the implications of both choices. Our discussions even led him to look for a position somewhere in between. With that I suggested that he read *Hunger of Memory: The Autobiography of Richard Rodriguez*, a very controversial book because its Chicano author argues against affirmative action and bilingual education. I recommended Rodriguez's book because he captures his upward movement in American society and culture with both a critical eye and eloquent tongue. I didn't tell Alex any of this, asking that he read the book both critically and with an open mind.

Our tutoring sessions were proceeding well, and we continued to discuss the concerns he had about assimilation as he walked me home or followed me to the library immediately after our sessions. He told me that he saw Rodriguez's autobiography like a mirror reflection of his own life. He quoted passages where Rodriguez argued that his upward social and educational movement served to separate him from his parent's culture. He empathized with Rodriguez, who one day returned home for a break from his graduate studies at Berkeley only to discover that he had no words to say to his mother; he felt nothing culturally in common with her. Alex's face really came to life when he related to me how the subject of Rodriguez had come up in his Chicano studies course and how he was amazed at the animosity that almost the entire class (including the professor) had toward Rodriguez. And then he really got excited when he related to me how he strove to defend Rodriguez's position. He attempted to explain to the class why Rodriquez chose to repress any nostalgia he had for his heritage and concentrate on assimilation. Rodriguez simply believed that for a Mexican-American to try and recover his or her cultural heritage is both foolish and regressive. Alex then looked at me with downcast eyes when he told me that the professor interrupted him to exclaim, "But you must realize that the decision to reject one's cultural heritage is a conscious one!" I asked him how he felt about that. He said he was disappointed with the way the professor seemed to single him out with a harsh tone and glare as she delivered her opinion and that he was still somewhat confused and uncertain about some of Rodriguez's conclusions, which he found both disturbing and contradictory. As I went to sleep that night, I thought about how I myself, in some respects, am still confused about the issue of assimilation and the retention of one's cultural heritage. I couldn't help but empathize with Alex's confusion and inner strife and feel ambivalence about the wheel of cultural self-consciousness that I had helped to accelerate. What I did feel strongly that night was a special bond with Alex, and I soon realized that my relationship with him as a tutor had assumed an unexpected dimension, one that gave our sessions an added incentive and energy. Good writing, Alex quickly learned, was not only a valuable asset for academic projects but also a powerful vehicle for self-discovery and self-possession.

Alex's last assignment for the course is to write an autobiographical essay. Although we have yet to discuss the essay in depth, we agreed that it has the potential to magnificently end the course by enclosing all of his previous essays with one that contains a resolution to his desire for cultural self-possession and identity mentioned in the first. I told him that in it he will have an excellent opportunity to make some preliminary, if not firm, conclusions about how he feels about his ancestral connection with Mexico, his *own* feelings and beliefs about assimilation into American culture, and the implications his stance will have within the Chicano community (and whether or not that should even matter). When I asked him what he thought he would entitle his essay, he replied with a half smile that implied facetiousness, "Hunger of Memory." Even now as he works on his essay, I ponder my involvement with Alex. I realize now that it was foolish of me to anticipate a similar relationship with Alex to the one I shared with Bill, especially given the nature of the course material and objectives of Chicano Studies 1B. I also learned to place a high premium on my personal experiences as a minority. I realized that Alex's cultural dilemma called for some level of participation on my part that drew on my academic and personal cultural experience. As a result of my sincere interest in his problem over personal identity, I cultivated a trust that facilitated our tutoring sessions in many ways. The sessions, for the both of us, took on an astounding dimension of energetic enthusiasm. In a final analysis, Alex found not only a writing tutor at the Golden Bear but, more importantly, a friend and cultural peer.

DISCUSSION QUESTIONS

1. How does Eduardo contrast the relationship he had when he had been tutored by Bill with his present role as tutor to Alex?
2. How did Eduardo react when Alex described how he couldn't understand why his teacher and his class put him down when he supported "Rodriguez's desire to suppress any nostalgia he had for his culture and concentrate on assimilation"?
3. What do you think Alex and Eduardo each gained from the tutoring relationship? Cite examples to support your answer.

How I Spent My Ethnic Semester
Patricia Chui

> Patricia tries to apply the ideas she learns in her ethnic studies courses to understanding her students, who, in turn, help Patricia understand her own cultural traits.

At the beginning of this semester, I told people that this was shaping up to be my cultural semester. In retrospect, I suppose that I really meant ethnic, for my course load emphasized how differences between ethnic groups lead to important cultural differences and issues. These courses, including Ethnic Studies 142: Race, Gender, and Ethnicity in the Hollywood Film, and English 139: Cultures of English (focusing on Mexican American and Asian American literature), represent part of a gradual and growing process; in my three years here, UC Berkeley has worked its magic on me, and I have started to wonder about my cultural background and the cultural background of others. As a third-generation Asian American from a conservative Southern California suburb, I grew up not really caring about my ethnicity or ethnic issues, not really thinking about how ethnic and cultural differences might affect the way people act and interact. Slowly but surely, Berkeley has changed all that. This semester in particular proved truly ethnic for me as I found myself, to my surprise, confronting with my students the very issues I studied in my classes. I feel that with such experiences I strengthened my skills as a tutor and realized a lot about myself and about how I have changed while at college.

This semester, like last semester, all my students were of color. A few years ago, such a thought might have intimidated me. Two Asians and two Mexican Americans? Heaven forbid! Where were the, well, the "normal" students? How would I ever relate? I had heard of Berkeley's famed diversity, but I originally came to this university to broaden my mind intellectually, not politically. Of course, by this semester, having experienced the diverse environment for two and a half years, I now thought almost nothing of my students' ethnic makeup. I barely even noticed their color. And I never dreamed that their ethnic backgrounds would, or should, make any difference in our tutorials. I would eventually see things differently.

My first student, Julie, was a bright, talkative freshman in Native American Studies 1B. A second generation Chinese American, she seemed as assimilated as I. Yet one day we began talking about the upcoming Chinese New Year, which for me and many other Chinese Americans usually represented only an opportunity to receive money. (This year I, the dutiful and opportunistic daughter, called home to say "Gung Hay Fat Choy," one of the few Chinese phrases I know, and was duly rewarded by the arrival of a cherished, money-laden, red envelope in the mail.) Julie mentioned that she would attend the Chinese New Year parade, and we drifted into talking about how Asian, or non-Asian, she and her family are in terms of maintaining Chinese culture. I decided to test out a new theory of mine, despite my relative lack of connection to Chinese culture.

I had recently come to realize that certain aspects of my upbringing and, consequently, of myself were Asian in nature. To test my idea I began to discuss these aspects with Julie. "You know," I ventured, "I never thought I was very Chinese, but actually I've discovered that I act in certain ways because I was brought up in a certain way, and a lot of other Asians were too. For example, a friend of mine said I was 'too nice'. But if you're Asian, you're brought up to always offer things to others, even if you don't want to, and to refuse to let others do things for you, even if you're dying for them to do it." As I went on, Julie began laughing, her eyes widening in surprise and her head nodding emphatically in agreement. "That's totally true," she exclaimed. We shared experiences and discovered that we did share a link that went beyond mere race. By the end of the session, not only had we grown closer, but we had managed to relate the subject of cultural traditions to her work in Native American Studies. We both found that parts of a culture can permeate one's everyday life and carry on to the next generation. They are naturally preserved despite the individual's attempts to discard them.

Discovering an ethnic link with Julie did not take much effort; we were simply talking about a subject we both found interesting and even amusing. I encountered a different sort of cultural issue with her classmate, Carrie. Carrie, a freshman, was a fourth-generation Mexican American who could not pronounce her last name correctly. I saw a lot of myself in her, not only because she admitted to feeling distanced from her ethnicity but also because of a linguistic tie. My parents were born in Peru, so having grown up surrounded by the Spanish language, I have always felt a kind of kinship with people of Latino as well as Asian background. But like Carrie, I remain monolingual because my parents have always addressed me in English. I did feel on first meeting Carrie that she thought even less about ethnic issues and her ethnic background than I did, and I attributed this to her fourth-generation status, but I was soon to discover that our attitudes differed because I had changed.

Carrie's assignment for her Native American Studies 1B class instructed her to write a "trickster" tale. She had decided that her trickster, a "country bumpkin" character, would arrive in Berkeley and adapt to the strange, new environment by tricking some threatening homeless people out of their money. In this way she would demonstrate how one should adapt to his or her situation. I thought that the idea of stealing money from homeless people seemed a bit . . . unsympathetic, to say the least, but I held my tongue and helped Carrie develop her idea. She turned the paper in without my getting a chance to see it, but a few weeks later she showed me the returned, graded paper. As we went over it, I couldn't help but notice her consistent references to the homeless people as "six black bums." I again said nothing, but when we read her teacher's comments, Carrie seemed incredulous that her teacher had written, "I wondered why you would make your group of homeless people all Black, given the diversity in Berkeley . . . I found this quite racist."

Carrie did not see her depiction as racist or even related to race at all and was frankly offended that her teacher would call her racist. I, too, was shocked at the teacher's charge, but I did understand the sentiment, and it now fell to me to try to calm an increasingly agitated student. Carrie's defense was that the assignment suggested the students use actual experiences as material for their essays and that this situation had actually happened to her—she and some friends had been accosted by six Black homeless men. I tried to explain that even if the incident had actually happened, it might present a harmful depiction to the reader. A reader not knowing anything about the homeless might be led to believe that all homeless people are Black. To correct this, Carrie could have added a line or two indicating that she understood that such uniformity of race was unusual, or she might have changed the racial mix of the group slightly so as not to offend or misinform anyone. I also pointed out that the word *bum* could be construed as derogatory, giving a negative impression either of homeless people or of African Americans, or both. To my relief and gratification, Carrie, at first resistant to my suggestions, began to nod her head in agreement and to voice understanding of what the teacher had meant by her comment.

What surprised me the most about the session was not Carrie's reaction to the comment but my own. I remembered my freshman year, when I had just begun to hear the term *politically correct* and wasn't exactly sure I liked the sound of it. Living in the residence halls, I found myself inundated with advice and explanations (from well-meaning but insistent resident assistants) about what I should or should not say. And like many other overwhelmed freshmen, I exhibited an equal and opposite reaction—I rebelled. "Who has the right," I complained, "to tell me to say *Asian* instead of *Oriental?* Shouldn't *I* be the one to make that decision?" I thought that *African American* sounded ridiculous, and no one really used it, anyway. And why couldn't I say *girls* instead of *women* if my friends didn't mind? We certainly didn't feel that we were women yet. My freshman self, and even my sophomore self, crossed the diversity boycott lines, and I argued vehemently against affirmative action and political correctness.

But although I fought it, kicking and struggling, UC Berkeley's politically correct attitude somehow wormed its way into my consciousness until I suddenly found myself staunchly upholding the very principles I had previously disdained. I practically had to stop and pinch myself while talking to Carrie, and I told her so. "Two years ago I wouldn't have been telling you all this," I said. "But in Berkeley you're so surrounded by this environment of diversity and political correctness that you can't help but eventually be affected by it." For even though I still believe that the whole PC (politically correct) movement has gone overboard, and though I still occasionally refer to myself or other college students as *girls*, I do watch my language more carefully and use "politically correct" terminology more often. I understand that language has power and effect, whether we intend it or not, and that we should be aware of the sensibilities of others, no matter from what racial, ethnic, or cultural background they might come. It doesn't cease to amuse me that I never really wanted to think this way—I fought against it, but I changed anyway. And I hope that by addressing the issue with Carrie, I helped her think about ethnic sensitivity in a less hostile and more open way than I once did.

In terms of hostility, however, Carrie could not compare with my Subject A student, Allison. At our first meeting, Allison, a Vietnamese first-semester student who had been in the United States for eight years, declared that she hated her class, she hated her teacher, and she didn't think she belonged in Subject A. "The people in there are so dumb," she said. I spent half our first session trying to convince her to give the class a chance. One day, I experienced more of her hostility when I gave her a timed writing exercise, giving her fifteen minutes to come up with a thesis and outline for the topic "Berkeley."

When she finished, she had one part of her outline on homeless people. I asked her to elaborate, and she said, "Well, they make Berkeley ugly. They ask me for change, and I never give it to them. They should just get jobs or something and quit asking for money."

"Wow," I thought, "she sure hasn't been in Berkeley long. What a freshman—that attitude isn't going to last." I kept my opinions to myself, however, and we went on.

Toward the end of the semester something occurred that shed new light for me into why Allison held the opinions she did. She was reading a book, *The Dispatcher* (which she hated, of course), about the Vietnam War. Of all the topics we had ever discussed, I found that this sparked her attention most because she had more personal interest in the subject. She animatedly told me why she thought the United States should have stayed out of Vietnam and what the war did to her country. One reason that she gave was that the economic status of the haves and have-nots evened out more. I, as a firm believer in equality, asked Allison why this constituted a problem, and I gradually learned from her answer that her family had held considerable influence in prewar Vietnam. Her father had been part of the government, and the war left her family stripped of its previous wealth and power. Through our conversation, I gathered that Allison had little sympathy for poor people; and if she had power in Vietnam, she would feel little obligation to them beyond seeing that they got an education. Beyond that, she said, if they really deserved to succeed, they would through simple hard work. Allison herself lusted after a life of power, wealth, and high society.

This conversation with Allison fascinated me. Suddenly, I felt I understood a lot more about Allison's views toward many things. Having grown up treated as privileged and elite, she tended to maintain that attitude toward new situations and people. This helped explain her disdain for Subject A, her opinion of homeless people, and her general dislike of Berkeley's diversity. I don't mean to say that Allison acted like a snob. But her background, which I previously had regarded as relatively unimportant, played a large role in helping me understand her as a person and as a student. It was wrong and hasty of me to assume that she held certain positions simply because she had not lived in Berkeley long enough to know better; cultural factors and socioeconomic background can never be summarily disregarded. Although I did try to point out certain social issues she might not have thought about, I realized that not only do attitudes not change overnight, but her attitudes would change more slowly because of their deep cultural basis.

As I think back on the semester, numerous other ethnic encounters occur to me, but my final session with Carrie best sums up my approach to ethnicity and culture. She was writing a paper on what she felt she had learned in her Native American Studies class, and as she struggled to think of a unifying theme, she had a burst of insight. Maybe, she reasoned, she could write about how the course material related to her personally, since she feels the same divisiveness that the Native Americans do. We began to discuss this, and Carrie revealed that she had begun to wonder about her cultural background. She was thinking about taking a class in Spanish, and she wanted to find out more about Mexican traditions, "just so I could be aware of my background." I asked when she had started to feel that way, and her answer made me smile. "Since I came to college," she said. "I didn't really care that much before, but here people attack you and say, 'Why aren't you interested?'" I felt like I was watching a protégé take her first toddling steps toward ethnic and cultural awareness. I have a long way to go before reaching full awareness myself, but this university has given me a mighty shove in that direction, for which I will be eternally grateful. When I look back on this semester, I will remember it as the semester when I opened my eyes to the ethnic issues surrounding me.

DISCUSSION QUESTIONS

1. How did Julie help Patricia work through some of her feeling about how her Chinese background affected her behavior?
2. Explain how working with Carrie helped Patricia recognize that her own attitudes about ethnic diversity had changed since she started college? What evidence does Patricia give that Carrie was far removed from her ethnic roots?
3. Do you think her instructor was correct in labeling Carrie's paper "racist"? Why or why not? In your opinion, were Patricia's suggestions to Carrie about softening her remarks to improve her paper appropriate?
4. Do you think Patricia's explanation of Allison's attitudes was correct? Can you think of any other reasons for Allison's negative attitudes toward school and street people? What do you think

the chances are that Allison will change her attitudes if she stays at UC Berkeley?

5. Patricia often bites her tongue in working with her students. Do you think she didn't make comments because she was trying to be sensitive to their opinions, or was she playing her cultural role of being too nice?

5 Check Your Assumptions at the Door

Session from Hell: The Dark Side of Collaborative Learning
Jason Buchalter

> Often we never really learn what underlies a student's passivity and helplessness. The tutor in this story, driven frantic by his student's "I don't knows," finally tells her to take some responsibility for the sessions or not come back.

"Hi, how's it going?" I asked Lisa, my tutee, as she rushed into the Golden Bear, huffing and puffing and out of breath, late as usual. "What do you feel like going over? Did you prepare that draft we talked about last session?"

"No."

"Well, OK, is there something else you want to go over?"

"I don't know."

Hiding my frustration, I forced a weak, sickly smile, and, like I do with all my other tutees, cheerfully asked, "Well, what do you feel like working on during our session today?"

"Well, uh, I don't know."

I tasted the sickly sweet taste of blood as I bit the inside of my lip, trying to restrain myself from reaching over and smacking her. I felt a dark, evil tide rising up within me, compelling me to grab her and shake her and ask her the question I have been dying to ask her since we first started working together, five weeks ago: "Is there anything you do know?" I've longed to grab her and scream at her until she comes to understand that she is at Cal, goddamnit, and if she doesn't start showing some goddamn initiative and take control of her own goddamn education, she is going to be out of this university faster than a bat out of hell. But remembering my training seminar, where we were taught to make friends with our tutees and act like collaborators, not instructors or drill sergeants, I continued with my valiant but vain attempts to collaborate. However, in the back of my mind, I felt the dark, evil forces gathering strength, urging me to reach out and beat some sense into her.

So at this point, after regretfully eliminating corporal punishment from my rather sparse collection of pedagogical techniques and strategies, I decided to divide our time between going over her last essay and generating ideas and a thesis for her upcoming assignment. Since she didn't disagree to this agenda, we began going over her paper.

By now, since we had been working together for five weeks, I assumed she was familiar with our tutoring routine. First, the tutee would read her draft aloud, without any interruptions, and then she and I would take turns reading and analyzing specific paragraphs and passages. All my other tutees would come in, sit down, take out a draft, and start reading aloud, all before I even had the chance to open my mouth. But no, not Lisa.

Lisa and I sat and stared blankly at the essay. Actually, I looked at the essay, and she watched my trusty Citizen, patiently ticking off the minutes until the dreadful hour expired and she could leave. After a moment or two of pained silence, she asked, "You want me to read it aloud???" Her tone of voice gave the impression that reading the paper aloud was an activity akin to popping the frog from her biology lab out of the bottle, stuffing it into her mouth, and washing it down with a healthy swallow or two of formaldehyde.

"Yes, please," I demurely requested. All the while biting my lip, gripping the edge of the table with white knuckles, and suppressing the urge to calmly scream, "What in the hell do you think? Haven't we been doing this same routine twice a week for the last five goddamn weeks? Jesus, is it that hard to read your paper aloud? After all, I don't get any sadistic pleasure out of making you suffer. My god. Like maybe you haven't caught on, reading your own work serves to decontextualize your prose, not only giving you incredible insights into the stylistic dimension of the writing process but also illuminating the flow of your argument, your thesis statement, your major premises, and the evidence you use to support each premise."

After she finished reading the paper, I asked her how she felt about it, if there were any changes she would like to make.

"I don't know."

"Well, did you like it? How do you think you could of, um, presented your argument in a clearer, more precise manner?"

"I don't know."

"All right, well, uh, do you want to go over the logic behind your argument or concentrate on sentence level stuff, like subordination? I noticed your instructor, Ms. Ruger, wrote you need to work on developing subordination and coordination skills. That might be good."

"Let's do the logic of my argument."

"Sounds good. OK, uh, what's the, um, thesis of this paper?"

"I don't know."

"All right, well, what's the main idea of the paper? What, in other words, are you trying to convince or tell the reader?"

"Charged language is used in all forms of discourse and makes speech more graphic, illustrative, and colorful."

This sure sounded like a thesis statement and was written in the introductory paragraph, where the thesis usually is, but there was something fishy about it. It just didn't sound like Lisa's literary voice. Going on a hunch, I asked to see her assignment sheet. As I suspected, there it was: "Ques. #3. Do we use charged language in all forms of discourse? Does charged language serve to make our speech more graphic, illustrative, and colorful?" I knew it; my hunch was right. Lisa just lifted the question from the assignment sheet, instead of developing an actual thesis of her own. Deciding not to comment, I continued collaborating.

"OK," I said, "Sounds good. Now that we have your thesis, what are the main points you use to prove your thesis?"

"I don't know."

My inner voice screams, "Jesus, you should know, it's your stupid essay!" Of course, I restrain myself, which is taking more and more effort as the session wears on, and patiently ask, "What examples of charged language do you use to illustrate your thesis?"

"I don't know."

"Look carefully at your outline and try to figure out what each paragraph is trying to prove."

"Well, uh, it's about charged language and how people use it all the time and stuff."

"Great, now what is charged language? Before you can write an essay, you have to have a solid understanding of your topic. First, why don't you define charged language in your own works. OK?"

"I don't know."

By now, after suffering for forty-five minutes, I was wholly frustrated and decided to quit talking, hoping the silence would spur Lisa into volunteering information. We embarked on our special version of collaborative learning: the pained silence. Seven whole minutes without uttering a word. Usually, at least with my other tutees, silence meant the gears in their brains were churning away. With Lisa, however, the only gears churning, I fear, were those inside my watch, which she kept staring at.

I finally said to hell with this and asked her not to come back until she was ready to collaborate. "After all," I said, "half of the tutoring job must be done by the tutee. No tutor, no matter how skilled, experienced, or enthusiastic can help a student who doesn't want to help herself. You gotta do your part and at least meet me half way. Please. Look, when you finish the draft of your next paper, call me to set up an appointment to go over it. But listen, you gotta be willing to take some responsibility for these sessions. OK? No, um, the ball is in your court, and I am not going to be calling you. If you want to make this thing work, you are going to have to take responsibility for improving your own writing. When you're ready, and have a serious draft you want me to help you with and are willing to let me help you improve it, call me and schedule an appointment."

Lisa never called.

DISCUSSION QUESTIONS

1. Can you think of three different ways to explain Lisa's behavior?
2. Were there other things you might have suggested to Jason to draw Lisa out before he gave up?
3. Do you think there's any reason to suspect that Jason's expectations influenced Lisa's behavior?

4. Can you think of statements that Jason could have made early on that might have averted the final showdown?

Coping with a Learning Disability
Robert F. Derham, Jr.

> His teacher believed that Arthur couldn't improve because his writing problems were the result of his disability. His tutor accepted this at first but then found a way to communicate with Arthur as he learned it's not wise to stereotype disabled students.

How would you cope in a highly competitive university if you had a learning disability? This was the question I continually had to ask myself while I tutored Arthur Smith last spring, my first semester as a writing tutor. Arthur was a Subject A repeat. He had taken the summer course but failed. Needless to say, it was my job to help him raise his writing skills to a passing level, but this, I initially felt, was beyond my capabilities as a writing tutor, mainly because Arthur has a neurological deficiency known as cerebral palsy, a condition that impairs one's motor coordination.

Our first meeting left me with little encouragement as his writing samples revealed some very serious writing faults. For example, he had trouble organizing his ideas; consequently, his arguments would digress rather than progress. He would often introduce completely irrelevant topics midway through and draw conclusions only remotely related to his original thesis—that is, of course, if his thesis could be determined, for he seemed to write without any well-formed thesis. In other words, his papers essentially displayed no clear or consistent controling ideas. It became apparent to me that he lacked a firm understanding of just how a successful essay could be written. In short, I was perplexed. I did not know where to start with Arthur. His writing seemed to present some insurmountable problems.

I consider myself to be a tenacious person. I don't generally throw in the towel when it looks as though things are getting too nasty and difficult. And not to commend myself individually, I know that most of us by the time we reach Cal have developed a sense of discipline that compels us to succeed and achieve our best. We are fighters, but Arthur, unfortunate as he appeared to me, was losing a battle for which he was inadequately equipped to fight. Granted, like many Subject A students, he had the usual difficulty developing and subordinating his ideas effectively for the construction of a satisfactory essay. In addition, he suffered from poor grammar, but so did many of my other Subject A students. What made Arthur Smith different, however, was that he appeared to be more handicapped than the others. After working with him for a few weeks, I came to a conclusion that I had tried to avoid, that his writing problems were directly related to his palsy. That is, I assumed that somehow his mind could not operate at the level of spoken and written language that the university requires for most passing undergraduate written work, or even for Subject A.

Arthur has trouble speaking. His speech is very slow, his words poorly pronounced, and his spoken sentences are for the most part fragmentary and frequently incoherent. I often had difficulty discerning what he was trying to say, as he had poor control of his lips and tongue, which greatly diminished the clarity of his speech. In addition to being slow, he generally spoke as little as possible. There was a communication barrier between us. I felt I had to coax words and ideas out of his mind as he often could not fully express his thoughts. I found myself finishing his spoken sentences when it looked to me as though he couldn't. As a result, I did most of the talking.

I began to assume that these deficiencies in his spoken language caused his writing problems. If he could not speak clearly, I thought, how could he write clearly? I was overwhelmed by his cerebral palsy. His condition, in addition to hampering his ability to communicate verbally, was such that the very act of handwriting itself was extremely challenging as well as exhausting. He explained to me that during grammar school he needed to wear some kind of hand brace to facilitate his penmanship. And today, his handwriting is barely legible, despite his painstaking effort to slowly write carefully formed letters. What does this mean in an academic sense? My theory is that he probably never really learned how to write well in the first place because of his debilitating neuromuscular limitation. I feel that the act of writing has always discouraged him. Think about it. If you had great difficulty writing words down, then writing a complete essay, or even just a single sentence, would be just that more arduous and even discouraging.

In short, the whole practice of writing for Arthur was (and still is) an extremely strenuous and demoralizing experience. For example, he has to rely on other students' in-class notes to supplement his own, which are usually sketchy and unreadable. As for in-class exams, he has to make special arrangements for a take-home option.

During the seventh week of the semester, I talked with Arthur's TA for the third time. His TA once again suggested that Arthur's writing problem was essentially a learning disability compounded by his physical disability. Initially, I agreed with him on this, but when his prognosis for Arthur's passing Subject A looked grim, I asked myself, "Does this mean that Arthur will never be capable of writing satisfactorily for this class?" After all, he was passing all his other subjects, which included Math 1A and Chem 1A, both classic "weeder" courses. I never questioned Arthur's intelligence, as he often impressed me with his incredible mathematical ability. He differentiated almost every integral I placed before him. And it has always been my understanding that intelligence is a transmutable trait. If Arthur is intelligent enough to glide through calculus, why can't he use his intelligence to improve his writing? Obviously, he needs to learn what he has not mastered. In other words, I realized that maybe he would never be able to write well, but perhaps he had always been reluctant to even attempt to improve his writing skills due to the inhibiting nature of his handicap.

I began to focus on his writing problems as writing problems without worrying about how his cerebral palsy might prevent the improvement of his writing. The first problem I tried to eliminate was our communication barrier. I needed to find some way to allow him to talk to me, instead of me always talking to him. I could talk to him, but I wanted him to talk back. As I explained earlier, he cannot speak too clearly. He can, however, type words with a surprising degree of efficiency. Then it occurred to me that a word processor would be an ideal aid. I set him up on a word processor, and this alleviated many of his physical difficulties, allowing him to write with greater ease, and instead of illegible manuscripts, we could read his writing on crisp computer print-outs. This made things a lot less messy and complicated for both of us. At least now, I no longer had to squint. I know that using this machine helped Arthur talk to me. If he couldn't say something, which was more often the rule than the exception, he could just type his message on the screen. Now that we were finally able to communicate in a more precise manner, we could begin to work on his writing.

Essentially, I gave Arthur a crash writing course of my own design. Because he had such difficulty in developing a logical argument, I put him through a series of what I call cogency exercises. That is, I would make him write for fifteen minutes on a single subject that we would agree on beforehand. In this way, I encouraged him to think about restricting and organizing what would turn out to be a minicomposition.

In all these exercises, I emphasized the importance of his strategy, that his purpose was not so much to inform us of what he thinks about his subject but to convince the reader what he thinks is true. I tried to instill in Arthur a sense of how a writer's argument could be effectively conducted. In a nutshell, these little exercises were based on a conventional question-answer system. Once he chose to write about marriage. The basis question was, Why get married? His initial answer was "insecurity," but I then asked him a more precise question, "Why do we need someone?" He responded, "sex" as a partial answer and "companionship" as a second partial answer. Then I posed a final, more precise question, "Why make one friend so significant?" His final answer, "so that we don't have to endure hardships alone." His progression of thought (with my assistance) could be diagramed like this:

Sentences 1–2	Basic question: Why get married?
Sentences 3–4	Initial answer: Need
Sentence 5	That answer inadequate: Does not explain need
Sentence 6	More precise question: What do we need?
Sentence 7	First possible answer: Sex
Sentence 8	That answer inadequate: Evidence of other animals
Sentence 9	Second possible answer: Companionship
Sentence 10	That answer inadequate: Many friends can supply companionship
Sentence 11	Final, most precise phrasing of question: Why is one friend extraordinarily important?

Sentences 12–14   Need for someone to help endure
hardships, to share life with, possibly
raise children, etc.

Of course, I coached Arthur through each step. As he would answer each question, I would ask how effective his answers were. If they were not effective, or reasonably convincing to me, I would tell him so, and then he would try to figure out why. Basically, I wanted to introduce to Arthur a method of approaching his topic that would require him to ask a series of relevant questions before he would even begin to write. This technique I felt helped him get acquainted with his topic by encouraging him to focus his ideas in a logical way, such that they could be developed and expanded later into a miniessay that I would then have him write for about fifteen minutes. When we proceeded through these cogency exercises, both he and I could observe his writing in progress, and this was important because we could make immediate corrections.

Perhaps the most useful aspect of the initial cogency exercise was that it gave Arthur a clearer idea of how a thesis can be formulated. He would often use for his thesis in the follow-up essay the very last and most effectively phrased answer to the question posed in the cogency exercise. For example, his follow-up essay for the topic, Why get married? had for a thesis statement, "People get married because they need someone to share their lives with." Then, I would make certain that his follow-up essay formed a complete, logical argument. I would make him rewrite it until every sentence linked together under his thesis statement.

I think doing these exercises over a period of time helped Arthur immensely in his regularly assigned papers. His essays began to wander less because he not only learned how to formulate a supportable thesis but learned how to support it through the duration of his essay as well. I conditioned him through these exercises so that he could develop a consistent train of thought through the course of just a few thoughtful sentences. His completed mini essay would look something like the following:

People marry because they need someone to share their lives with. Life without a long-term partner would somehow be incomplete, unfulfilling, and very lonely. Anthropologists say that humans thrive on each other's support and companionship. Marriage can provide these comforts in a permanent, life-long way. And besides, the Bible says that it is not good for man to live alone. (Genesis)

He then used this skill in writing the longer two- and four-page assignments for his class. Looking back, what Arthur needed most was to learn the process of writing an essay at the most elementary level. I found that once he discovered a way to organize his ideas within a logical structure of an overall argument or theme statement, the more he would write. His earlier papers were often too short, suffering from incomplete development. I encouraged him to use as much concrete detail as possible, as this lays the foundation material for a strong, supportive argument. Later on, he began writing at greater length and detail. Some of his later papers incorporated an impressive use of evidence, whereas before he would have never thought to use such embellishment, mostly because he did not know how to incorporate it within the context of his overall argument. Yet the more confident he became in writing successful arguments, the more he was able to strengthen his essays with pertinent, enlightening, and supportive detail. I will never forget his essay on Orwell's *Nineteen Eighty-Four*. I actually forgot that I was reading a Subject A paper because this one presented such an impressive array of relevant quotations, all of which he carefully included within the context of his argument. That is, he didn't just drop a large block of quoted material, as many Subject A students are in the habit of doing, and refer back to it in some sort of vague way. No. His argument accounted for every quote. In other words, nothing dangled precariously.

I have been using these cogency exercises for quite some time now. It seems to be a key device in prompting students to think more critically about their writing. In Arthur's case, I know that this method proved effective as his paper grades climbed steadily from the low D range to a solid C+ level. But even more important, I am convinced that he will continue to think about his writing process. When we worked together, I emphasized the importance of connecting sentences logically in well-ordered paragraphs. If I were to select just one concept to characterize what I taught Arthur, it would have to be ''compositional logic.'' His early papers failed because they didn't make sense. They were unconvincing because their arguments were flawed or incomplete. But then his papers started making sense because his arguments had become more fluid. "An essay," I used to say to him often, "is like a jigsaw puzzle where there is a place for every piece; but naturally, if the pieces are jammed in the wrong positions, the resulting image will be unreadable or unrecognizable. Similarly, in an essay, the sentences should follow a logical sequence to ultimately create a kind of coherent mental image or train of thought." This, it seems, is the basis of all writing, a concept that I think Arthur began to grasp by the end of our time together.

I was initially discouraged by Arthur, but he surprised me in the end. Despite his disability, he put up a fair fight and won. I won't hesitate to say that Arthur's success was due largely to the quality of our relationship. He cooperated with my suggestions, my cogency exercises, largely because he felt accountable to me. I became optimistic. I was able to make him believe that he could write in a better way, and he in turn fulfilled my expectation. There's something truly beneficial about a positive attitude, especially when one is working with a disabled person. I challenged him. When something about his writing "stunk," I let him know. Of course, I would always tell him why I thought so, as well as suggest a means by which to correct the fault. I would never praise anything he had written unless I felt that it was truly praiseworthy. Honesty pays in the long run. But he always knew I really cared, and that was important. I gained his respect. He never once blew me off. It is hard to say who learned more from the experience. For my part, I realized that success in tutoring is closely linked to one's attitude. If you stand to help someone salvage his or her academic future, you sure as hell better have one heck of a dedicated, serious commitment to helping this person. For Arthur's part, perhaps he has become less skeptical of his own abilities. I am very pleased with his success in passing Subject A.

DISCUSSION QUESTIONS

1. In your opinion, would tutoring Arthur have turned out differently if the tutor had consulted with a learning disabilities counselor at the beginning of tutoring?

2. What marked the turning point in the tutor's work with Arthur? Was it his change in attitude or the discovery that Arthur could use a word processor?
3. At the end, what did the tutor attribute Arthur's writing problems to?
4. Can you think of other types of students who might respond well to these cogency exercises?

Before Ideas: The Preliminaries of the Student-Tutor Relationship
Jennifer Fondbertasse Royal

> The tutor learns that sometimes students have other problems that impinge on their academic performance.

We first-semester tutors at the Student Learning Center learn quickly that there are fundamental principles in tutoring, and our education is helped by a variety of assigned readings covering all aspects of the peer tutoring process. We learn such exciting terminology as *collaborative learning, catalyst for change,* and *organic relationship between thought and conversation.* Yet, with my head full of scholarly theory, I tutored Roberto, a Rhetoric 1B student, with utter failure. This is not the fault of the principles, or even my ability to apply them. We never got that far. I did not discover, until after many sessions, the barriers that were between Roberto and his work, and Roberto and his success at UCB.

I approached my first sessions with Roberto hoping to inspire him. I was hoping to draw out his ideas and, by my enthusiasm, bring him to run with them, so to speak. In his work, I sought out the points where I could see his interest, for most of his paper showed only his boredom, and I asked him to talk to me about them. However, Roberto would only hesitatingly look at my confident, open expression. He seemed to be blocked somewhere, and I could not determine if he simply could not recall what he had written, or if he was thinking about something else, or if he just wasn't interested. He would make a self-deprecating laugh and say, "I guess I don't know what I mean." What to do? At that point, I imagined he was boggled by his own lack of organization. Roberto affirmed this when he said he did not use an outline and did not really know what he was supposed to do in his paper. However, time spent discussing how to create an outline to help organize his thoughts only brought insecure approval from Roberto.

In the next few sessions, I reorganized how I worked with Roberto. I was determined to increase his confidence about writing. I thought I was being too abstract for him. Perhaps he was more visually oriented? I brought in several books of rhetoric instruction and highlighted sections defining his problem areas. This concrete approach seemed to have an impact on Roberto, and I thought I could see him making mental connections. What a relief! Yet, false elation—the immediate result seemed hopeful, but by the next session and the next draft, he showed no progress. I thought once again how his lack of confidence must have frustrated his writing.

I could not imagine what to do next. I turned to outside resources—my senior tutor, my supervisor, my seminar group—and I concluded that I should continue with a concrete approach (i.e., using reference materials and motivating Roberto to bring in hard drafts). Roberto seemed enthusiastic, and in the next session, he brought a draft of a paper. We worked through it using his notebook to jot down ideas for changes. This yielded some good results, even though the instructor was unable to see his progress. I could see that Roberto had developed the wrong part of his thesis sentence. Instead of fighting for his ideas, he spent the paper retelling what the author said. In other words, in the thesis he stated first the author's intent and then his own opinion, which should have been the thrust of his paper, but instead of fighting for his argument, he spent the entire paper explaining what the author had to say— like a book report. At least the paper tried to follow the thesis, where before there was neither a thesis nor a coherent structure.

This was about as far as Roberto and I got together. The next week, he canceled our appointment, and the following week, he appeared, to my great annoyance and exasperation, without any desire to work and without having turned in his midterm paper. He laughed cynically and tried to act as if he didn't care. He seemed to have convinced himself that because several others in the class had done the same thing that it was the fault of the instructor for giving an incomprehensible assignment. At the time, I believed that he really did not care, and I spent twenty minutes pushing him to imagine what kind of career he could picture for himself if he did not know how to write. I also explained that upper division courses, besides English, would all require effective communication in papers. And I was worried, thinking he could be considering dropping out. I told him bluntly that it was up to him, and I wanted to help, but success at UCB required more devotion than he appeared willing to give. Then, as I paused to see his shocked expression, I felt guilty in such a sudden condemnation. To give us both some relief from the tension I had created, I gave him an article on "No Sweat Writing" and left to hunt up some effective student rhetoric papers to use as guidelines. During this time, we both cooled off. However, he left with less resolve to improve than I would have liked. I felt there was nothing more I could do.

We met together one last time a week later. The lecture of the previous session, as uncomfortable as it was for both of us, did help him. He had completed the paper and, although he did not bring a copy with him, he said he felt good about it. But the best part of that previous session was that it released the tension between us. I realized, by virtue of his new ease with me, that he had perhaps felt intimidated by me, my being an English major, my being older than he. I had also come to this session after voicing my concern about Roberto to my supervisor and was made aware that perhaps Roberto's problems were not with writing but that something outside could be undermining his ability to concentrate and succeed. I took instantly to the suggestion that Roberto might do well to see a counselor. And suggesting this to Roberto helped him to open up to me. He said his mother had been giving him a lot of trouble and wanted him to come home. He was divided between obligations. Also, he was from a home where his native language was Chinese, but the spoken language of his town was Spanish. He was dealing with three languages! And on top of all that, he was afraid he didn't belong at such a large school but was also afraid to admit failure. Essentially, Roberto was torn in so many different directions that he could not hold himself together.

I found this moment, when Roberto began to talk about who he was, the most rewarding experience of our relationship. All I did was listen and encourage him not to give up. But I could not help thinking that if we had only opened up this ground earlier, we might have released all that tension between us. We might even have made progress with his writing. I just did not consider all that went on behind the writing process for Roberto—all that was preventing him from feeling capable of success.

The student-tutor relationship involves more than just the intellect. Students bring their frustration and enthusiasm and feelings of self-worth into the session with them, and it is up to the tutor to promote the best possible results by *first* encouraging openness and trust.

DISCUSSION QUESTIONS

1. Can you think of ways the tutor might have learned more about Roberto's problems earlier in the tutoring relationship?
2. Do you agree with Jennifer's statement that she "tutored Roberto . . . with utter failure"? Explain your answer.
3. Are there other things you might have tried if you had been tutoring Roberto?

Supervisor's Comments

The most successful writers honor their version of the truth by exploring it and writing it down for an audience. However, at any point that the writer lets something other than his or her truth control the piece, it loses its authenticity and in many cases its focus. That something can include a tutor if she doesn't continuously evaluate and modify her approach. Tutors make assumptions about themselves, their students, and the nature of tutoring in general. Jennifer assumed she could inspire her student, and, in so doing, took responsibility for his successes and failures without looking for the underlying cause. She had ignored the truth of Roberto's life, and his essays had nothing of Roberto in them. By constantly reexamining her approach and seeking outside resources, she was able finally to discover the true Roberto. Naturally, tutors make mistakes, but your willingness to ask for help and to change your point of view will make you much more likely to find solutions that fit each individual student.

—Anya Booker

Fire, Grapes, Guns, and Water
Jennifer Markley

> An over-anxious tutor finds her student guiding the sessions and
> waiting for her to give him the answers. She learns that to work
> productively, she must overcome her nervousness and become
> comfortable with silence.

"Hi, you have reached 555-8149. Carlos and Steve cannot come to
the phone now. Please leave a message. We'll get back to you as
soon as we can. BEEP . . ."

"Hello, ahh, this is a message for, ahh, Juan. Hi Juan, this is
your writing tutor, Jennifer Markley. Ummm, I hope I have the
right number, but I just wanted to call and remind you of our first
meeting tomorrow. Oh, and, ahhh, bring a recent writing sample
and call me back about tomorrow and, umm, let me know if I got
the right number." Click.

"Oh great!" I thought to myself. "He's going to think I'm a total
dimwit now. I don't know his name, and I can't even talk to an
answering machine. How am I going to talk to him in person? Maybe
I got the wrong number."

Quickly I dialed again and got the same message. Click.

"Dammit! Oh well. Maybe his roommate will get the message
for him and erase it. Or, maybe he'll cancel tutoring after hearing
it. Yeah, then I can start again with someone else!"

RING! It was Juan, or should I say, Carlos. He called me right
back, having just got in, to tell me he'd be there for our first
meeting.

"I look forward to it," he said. "I'll bring my writing sample. Sor-
ry my recording confused you. I go by Carlos most of the time. See
you tomorrow, Jennifer—that is, if I have the right number . . . "

"What a great guy," I thought to myself. "Kind of a smart ass,
but that's OK. Imagine that! He's excited about tutoring and doesn't
think I'm a dimwit . . . I hope."

This was how our first few sessions started out: Carlos, excited;
me, scared to death. Gradually, though, Carlos, with his easy-going
disposition, calmed me down.

"OK, Carlos. Do you have your paper? What did you work on?
When is this due? What should we do today? What did you think

of your last paper? Do you still need to reschedule this week? Is this chair OK? Do you want to sit somewhere else? Can I feed you grapes and wait on you hand and foot?"

Well, that's the way it went. Not quite, but almost. I'd hit him with an explosion of nervous questions, determined to get us off to a good start, even if I wasn't sure what it was.

"Wait! Slow down, Jennifer. Take a deep breath. OK? Here's my paper. You told me to diagram each paragraph into topic sentences and supporting points. It worked pretty well, but I couldn't do it for these paragraphs. I don't know what happened . . . "

In this manner, Carlos got our first few meetings on track. He sensed immediately the direction our sessions should take. As an overambitious and underconfident beginning writing tutor, I was bursting with new ideas and goals but unsure how to implement them. Instead of establishing a steady, organized discussion of topics introduced instinctively and insightfully, I blurted out everything I planned to cover in a session within the first fifteen minutes. I needed a system of pacing and deliberate silence. I needed to trust my own inclinations and think about my student, instead of dwelling on my own approach. After all, it was as much his session as it was mine—perhaps it was a little more his.

So I let go. I let Carlos calm my stressful interrogations with his instinctive and methodical concerns and responded to him as each situation called for. I became confident in my role, letting thoughts and ideas flow naturally into the conversation, pacing my questions, and giving answers only as they became necessary.

I guess you could say I was no longer an exploding, underconfident tutor. My raging fire was stomped down by Carlos. However, this is not to say that the flames were entirely extinguished. It's true that the stress that caused me to blurt out everything at once was subdued as I began to adapt to the sessions.

"Should I rewrite my paper on murder in the bay area, or the one on race and ethnicity? I got the same grade on both."

"Which one would you prefer to do?"

"Murder."

"OK, let's do that."

But still my overanxiousness had not completely subsided. I felt like I was no longer a raging fire but a series of low-burning, controlled flames. I still became uncomfortable during the silences and ignited them with information, encouraging Carlos to take off on my little cues:

"How could you support this point, Carlos?"

Pause, pause, pause.

"Why should I care about this serial killer? What if I was killed by him? What would you look for first?"

"Another tutor." Pause, pause, pause.

"OK, good thinking. But what common evidence relates all these murder cases?"

"Oh, I see . . ."

That wasn't good thinking but rather clever responding on his part. As I continued to fill up the silences, Carlos continued to lie in wait, silent and ready to react on cue. He became the hunter and I the hunted.

"I'm trying to decide whether to develop this paragraph more, or link another paragraph to it." Pause, pause, pause. He hid in the grass awaiting my response.

"What do you think of developing it more?" I responded. BANG! I was shot in cold blood, blown away by my answer.

After the session, I reflected on the brutal killing: "If only I had rephrased the question! If only I had shut up during the silence!" But it was too late. Carlos was stalking for the kill. He became dependent on the effect of the silences, and when I stopped filling them in, he lost confidence in his own ability to answer.

"Does this example justify your thesis, your main argument?"

Pause, pause, pause. "Umm, yes?"

"How does it support it?"

Pause, pause, pause. "Because it makes my argument stronger? More believable? No? Is that right?"

Carlos was no longer a discussion participant, he was a hunter for the right answer. Collaborative thinking was lost, and my life was in danger, or at least our tutoring sessions were. Although he had calmed my rage of flames at first, easing me into self-assurance, now Carlos was playing with that fire, using it for his own immediate needs but not for any long-term good. Without my approval for his every statement, he was lost.

"Is this right? Does this sound OK? Should I write this? Could you feed me grapes and wait on me hand and foot? Do I have the right number?''

Now who lacked self-assurance? Who was the raging fire in need of a douse of water?

"Wait! Slow down, Carlos. Take a deep breath. OK? Now, I see a lot of ideas in this paper and feel there are tons more in your head. I haven't got the right answer, because there isn't one. Don't be afraid of the silences. They're time for both of us to think. I really want to hear what you have to say. I'm counting on you as much as you are on me.''

That day I saved my life and our tutoring sessions, burned up his hunting license, and ignited collaborative thinking between the two of us. We stopped exploding during the silences. Instead, we let them fuel our ambitious minds.

"You know what? I'm not going to rewrite the paper on murder in the bay area. I'm going to rewrite the one on race and ethnicity.''

"Why did you switch?''

Pause, pause, pause.

" I don't know. I just don't think I could shoot my tutor.''

"Ohhh, that's kind of you.''

Pause, pause, pause. "No, really, I switched because I couldn't find any support for my argument, but I thought of a bunch of things I could add to the race and ethnicity paper.''

Finally, we both had reached the right number.

DISCUSSION QUESTIONS

1. Jennifer describes how she burst out with an explosion of nervous questions when she first met with Carlos and how his calmness got them both on track. What insights did she gain about tutoring that enabled her to slow down?
2. Jennifer says she turned Carlos into a "hunter for right answers" rather than a collaborator. Do you agree with her assessment? If so, what were some of the things that she did that led him to behave like that?
3. What were some of the factors that led them to a true collaborative learning situation at the end?

4. What did Jennifer mean when she used the expression, "Can I feed you grapes and wait on you hand and foot?"

Notes on Being Prepared
Cordelia C. Leoncio

> Cordelia found herself at a loss when it came to predicting what her students would do and felt she should have been better prepared to deal with the unexpected.

I realize it's impossible not to have certain expectations of students and of how they will behave in tutoring, and in many ways my expectations helped me to prepare myself as a tutor, but the shortcomings of my expectations often came as a shock. After all, some of the experiences I had during two semesters of tutoring, I think, went beyond what anyone might expect. Certainly, they went beyond my expectations, for better and for worse.

During my first semester as a tutor, I saw Susan. Maybe there were ways I could have been better prepared to deal with someone like her, but I'm not sure how. Sure, I could have been a little harder on her by not putting up with the no-shows, her lack of preparation, and her failure to keep me informed about her basic writing courses. I could have dropped her, but I kept her because her instructor asked me to. She felt that Susan needed extra help in understanding the writing process. Or I could have passed her on to another, more experienced tutor, but I kept her as a favor to her instructor. We both agreed that it was a little late for that anyway. I could have spent more time with her instructor, but we could only accomplish so much if Susan was not making much commitment to our tutoring sessions. But I admit there might have been ways I could have done more to help her by being better prepared.

But there were also things that Susan did that I can't imagine anyone being prepared for. Like the day she took it on herself to introduce me to her new pet and let it roam about the table. I tried to engage her in a discussion about her instructor's comments on her last paper as the rat crawled into my backpack and stayed there. Then there was the problem of keeping her awake during a session. I would slam my hand down on the table once her head started bobbing, but this only worked while sitting in the learning center. Nothing in my orientation or readings about tutoring showed me how to wake up a student who has fallen asleep in the main library during a mock final—that she requested!

So now I come to my second semester as a writing tutor. You'd better believe that I was going to do what I could to prevent no-shows and unproductive sessions this time around. Enter Richard, the perfect student. Or so I thought. For our first meeting, I pulled out the "How to Get the Most out of Tutoring" sheet and all the notes I'd made for myself to prepare for the first session. I asked Richard for every bit of information I thought could make our sessions productive. As we went over the information, I explained that it was to act as an agreement to do our best and be considerate of one another's time. I thought the first session went well enough, despite the fact that Richard never offered a hint of a smile. But that was all right; I'd gotten through all the preparatory, precautionary things I'd wanted to say and ask.

When the next few sessions with Richard turned out to be too good to be true, I was sure my efforts were paying off. Even though he told me he didn't have any paper assignments to work on, he never showed up empty handed. In fact, he would bring self-assigned papers, complete with carefully highlighted reading material, sheets of brainstorming, and an outline.

But as time went by, my thoughts went from "Yay!" and "What does this person need a tutor for?" to "There's something very suspicious about his not talking about his writing course." I was having trouble coping with the fact that I really didn't trust this very diligent student and that I really had no control over the sessions. What a switch! I'm usually trying to get my students more involved in contributing to and planning the tutorials. Here I was trying to keep myself more involved.

Since I was getting sick of not knowing what was going on, I finally did what I should have done in the first place. I went to his instructor's office hour. Somehow Richard kept failing to remember his instructor's name and office hours during those first few sessions. So I got his instructor's name from the receptionist and went to her office. She told me that Richard had not been in class for quite a while. He must have dropped it. Amazing! Richard went from being the perfect student to being the student from the Twilight Zone.

Beyond having a commitment to students in writing courses (the reason I gave Richard), I simply couldn't keep tutoring someone whom I didn't trust (the reason I kept to myself). Should I have known to keep asking whether he was still enrolled in a writing class? Was this a lesson I skimmed over too quickly in the first semester's reading assignments? Did I miss that day in seminar? I doubt it. It took these weird situations to teach me a very basic lesson—I can only be partly prepared for what might be coming my way. Being prepared means more than taking precautions. It means knowing that I might have to adapt to situations that can be neither predicted nor controlled.

Maybe I blew it more than once. I can either sit here and say, "forget it," crawl into a hole, and not deal with anything, or I can think back on what I didn't do and look forward to what I can do differently. After all, I'll be graduating soon. That means leaving Berkeley, looking for a job, meeting and talking to more people, and all the while running the risk of getting into new and improved weird situations.

Maybe it shouldn't have taken these strange situations to teach me what being prepared means. But I'm glad I learned it. Before going out in that real world anyway. In fact, I realized just how glad I am about it when a friend said to me the other day, "I think you just attract weird situations." I guess that's another good thing to know.

DISCUSSION QUESTIONS

1. Would you have let Susan's pet rat wander around in your backpack during the tutoring hour? What might you have said to Susan about the rat?
2. In your opinion should Cordelia have discussed Susan's habit of falling asleep with her?
3. What does the story tell you about Cordelia? Do you think she was being unjustifiably hard on herself when she said she felt she should be better prepared for the eccentricities of these

students? Or do you think that she asked for some of the problems she got?

4. Should Cordelia have told Richard that she couldn't keep tutoring him because she couldn't trust him? What might have happened if she had talked to him about her feelings?

5. Can you ever really be prepared for the unexpected?

Getting Real

Holly Holdrege

> Some people would be more successful in college if, when they moved in the dorms, they'd remembered to bring a tape recording of mom or dad yelling at them to study. Here the tutor gets carried away building rapport with a cute and funny student who uses her social skills to hide her lack of effort. Fortunately, the tutor is able to help. (If Nora Ephron had been a tutor, her memoirs might read like these.)

I remember preparing for my first ever tutoring session. Over and over I read the handouts and relevant articles that had been bestowed on me, the Xerox tomes providing the Right and True Way toward Higher Tutoring Consciousness. Among the truisms they offered: collaborate, don't evaluate; keep in mind you are a peer tutor; talk on a student-to-student level to inspire confidence and comradeship. I eagerly interpreted these words to mean, these poor, frightened freshmen already have enough professors, TAs, and voices of authority oppressing their neophyte writing instincts. Far be it for you, cocky tutor, to scare them further. Be a pal, someone with whom they can open up and feel comfortable. Reach across those chasms of writer's block and dangling modifiers and clasp their trembling hands in friendship.

Therefore, that spring, when I met my three tutees for the first time, I spent a good portion of the hour getting to know them. Place of origin, date of birth, current housing situation, and favorite TV show—all these topics were bandied about in the hopes of putting them at ease, letting them know I was cool, establishing that crucial rapport. And it worked. The idle chatter and resultant laughter loosened up their shy, studious spirits, and we were able to comfortably settle into William Blake and the mysteries of clauses. At the end of the term, they had improved as writers and passed their classes with ease. As I cheerfully waved the last one out the door, I leaned back, smiled contentedly, and reflected, "Peer tutoring. Yeah. I've got it knocked."

It was a good tutoring term, that spring. But, in that cyclical way of life, this fall, my second semester, has been its direct opposite. Everything connected with the Student Learning Center seemed to go wrong. Whereas the first time around I'd had to beat potential tutees off with a stick, this time absolutely no one deemed it necessary to appear at appointments; apparently their names on my scheduling sheet would set up a mystic connection between us, and I could tutor them without actually ever meeting them. One, and only one, showed up at all. That was Kristi.

Unlike the previous tutees I'd had, Kristi was bubbly and gregarious. Establishing rapport, which had been an excruciatingly delicate process before, happened instantaneously, thanks to Kristi's effusive nature. Hesitatingly, I pulled out the sheet explaining "What Your Tutor Expects of You," which, to my mind, condemned the innocent and obstructed the relationship with its foregone conclusions of flakiness. I quickly and shamefully skimmed the "rules" with her, careful to add the right touch of antiauthoritarian sarcasm to my voice, so as to let her know I had to do this, it was sort of dumb, she shouldn't get offended. To further establish my peerhood, I explained I was no stickler about fixed appointments; we could move our times around weekly at her convenience; if she really had to cancel, I wouldn't rat. Once the bureaucratic stuff was taken care of, I launched into my cocktail party bit and picked up her personal history, hanging intently on every word so she would have no doubt I was her friend.

Our conversations about the writing process were much the same. "Sometimes I just can't think of what to say, and I wait until the last minute to write it," she would complain.

"Oh, I totally know what you mean," I admitted truthfully. "I'm the queen of the last-minute paper; first draft, hot off the typewriter, into the professor's hands."

"Yeah, and sometimes I think the essay topics are really stupid anyway," she continued, invigorated by my confessions of ineptitude.

I'd chuckle sympathetically. "Well, no one's perfect, not even Sub A instructors. Sometimes," I'd agree, "the questions can be a little lame."

And so it went. Kristi appeared faithfully, twice a week. For at least ten or fifteen minutes, she'd ramble about how tired she was, problems with her boyfriend back home, her dumb job, and what a total bummer it was that she had to go to Poli Sci when the sun was so amazingly situated for prime tanning.

She was cute and funny, and I'd listen and laugh at her problems, although I finally started to get a little anxious that we were spending so much time debating the merits of the frozen yogurt at Yogurt Park versus that at Christopher's. "So," I'd sneak in, "do you have a rough draft for us to work on?"

"Oh, well, I turned in a paper on the computer this morning, so we just have to talk about my next one. I need," she'd invariably wheedle, "a thesis."

Once we'd get down to business, our meetings were nearly always about the ideas she'd be discussing for upcoming papers. Her training in high school left her critical thinking skills somewhere short of finely honed, so I didn't object to abstract discussions instead of grammar tune-ups. Sometimes she would bring me the skeleton of a thesis or an introduction, but by the eighth week I still had not seen a rough draft anywhere close to completion. For that matter, I hadn't seen a returned essay with her instructor's comments and grade. I asked her to bring in her graded papers so I could gauge her process. "Um, okay," she said, but seemed reluctant. Just shy about her writing, I figured. "Next week. I'll bring them Monday."

Monday arrived, a Monday so what-else-can-go-wrong. It was poetic. I trudged into the Learning Center, shook the rain out of my hair (no umbrella, of course) and deflated into a chair at the table where Kristi sat smiling brightly. "Hi!" she beamed. "Guess what? I talked to my boyfriend this weekend, and he fully apologized for being a jerk, and everything's so good now, and we're going to Texas in June, and—"

"Kristi," I cut her off a bit moodily. "Did you bring your papers today?"

She bit her lip. "Oh," she hedged. "Actually, you see, basically, I haven't really actually turned any papers in yet."

I opened my mouth. I shut my mouth. I shut my eyes. I opened them again. "What?" I asked, not loudly, as I was momentarily stunned. "Nothing?"

"Well, that first thing, you know, that first week thing. Basically, actually I might not try to pass the class," she spit out.

"You might not try to pass the class," I stated. She smiled again, shook her fluffy little head.

"You want," I continued, getting a little louder, as the shock was wearing off and being replaced by lividity, "to take Subject A OVER AGAIN? You, who are perfectly capable, who have passed the midterms, simply are not handing in your papers, and you want to take this class from hell OVER AGAIN?"

She looked struck. I'd done it. I'd crossed the fragile line. The friend and buddy had retreated, replaced by the combination of responsible student and latent teacher inside. It all added up to authority figure, but I couldn't help it. I was off and running.

"Kristi!" I yelped. "Why on Earth . . ." I trailed off. Touches of mother there. "What have we been doing for the past eight weeks then? If you don't care about wasting your time, I certainly care about wasting my time! This is important to me, and I don't do it for the pleasure of spinning my wheels! But beyond that, I don't know why you'd do that to yourself! You've got all kinds of good ideas, and I know from your midterms that you're far from hopeless as a writer. In fact, I never dreamed you wouldn't pass. You're the passing kind!"

She rubbed her finger over a scratch in the desk, back and fourth, looking down. "Yeah," she said, "I just, I don't know."

I paused a minute. All her breeziness, all her giggly manner and delight in small talk—could it be that she was simply stalling? Had I been so busy sealing our friendship that I'd missed what was probably a deep insecurity about writing? After all, they'd told her she was deficient; she was in Cal's equivalent of remedial English.

"Kristi," I repeated, calm again and aiming for understanding, "I'm not kidding you. I know you can pass this class. I've tutored enough to know who's capable of it. You are, beyond a doubt." She looked at me. "All you need to do is write the papers. I know you can do it. I know you can."

Now I was beginning to feel like a football coach, but she seemed to respect me enough to believe me. "OK," she said simply.

"OK," I answered. "Now, if we work out a thesis today, can you bring a paper on Thursday?" She nodded.

And she did. When she finally brought a paper to me, I couldn't believe what I read. Brilliant prose, sophisticated ideas, clever and elegant argument—I think I've discovered the next Joan Didion. She might be published soon, and all she needed was a little encouragement.

No, not really. She's no threat to Didion quite yet. But she did bring a paper Thursday. And the week after that. Since my mini-explosion, she has not only been keeping up with the class schedule but going back to complete everything she'd missed. One more paper, and she'll have done all the work. And, as a C+/B− student, she'll pass. I leave it to her English 1A tutor to refine her hidden talent.

And now, the moral: true, every freshman has teachers, TAs, and authority figures. They also have friends, who will offer them gossip, praise whether deserved or not, and complete commiseration. As tutors, we have to maintain a stable balance between the two poles. It's a hard niche to fit into, but it's the one we belong in.

And the tutor-tutee relationship needn't exclude personal friendship. When last heard from, Kristi was fighting with her boyfriend again . . .

DISCUSSION QUESTIONS

1. How do you think Kristi felt after the tutor's miniexplosion?
2. Does this story suggest that tutors should avoid spending time socializing with their students?

Whose Problem Is It?
Monique San Martin

> If you've ever felt like strangling a student out of frustration, you'll sympathize with Monique's dilemma—how to convince herself that it was his problem, not hers.

"Well, how did your essay turn out?" I asked George as I approached the table at which he was sitting. "Do you feel confident about it?"

"Uh, it's OK. I mean I don't think it's great or anything cuz I had some problems with it."

"What problems? I thought we covered everything that you were

having trouble with? When I left you last week you said you were
ready to whip the paper out. After all, we spent the past two
weeks developing the paper," I exclaimed. "At least you're done
with it." As these final words spilled out of my mouth, his facial
expression changed just ever so slightly. Then I realized it. I could
feel that all too familiar feeling of nausea rising in me. I knew
what was coming. How could I not when it was the same stunt
George had pulled all semester.

"You know what my problem is?" he said.

I didn't even bother to answer him. I just stared silently at him
and then thought to myself, here it comes—the excuse.

"I just can't get motivated. You know how when you write a
paper you like, you get a feel for it. It's like you know the paper.
And other times you just write but you really don't ever get a
feeling for it. Well, I just couldn't get a feeling for this paper," and
as he stressed this, he squeezed his eyes and clenched his fists. "I
just couldn't get into it, man."

If I could have bet money on this student's inability to "get into"
anything, I would be a rich woman today. The feeling of nausea
continued to grow in me. "You didn't write it."

"No, I wrote it. It's just not ready to be turned in. I need a little
help," he quietly said as he pulled out two handwritten pages from
his notebook. This was the almost complete six- to eight-page, typed
paper that was due weeks ago with which he needed just a little
help. A little help!

I wanted to drop my head on the table and cry. I didn't want
to strangle him out of anger but out of frustration. Frustration that
stemmed from this scenario happening all the time instead of just
once in a while. I felt so useless as a tutor. Here I was supposed
to help this student improve his writing skills, but no matter what
I tried I couldn't even get him to write his papers. Didn't he realize
it was the eleventh week and he had not turned in a single assignment in this class? Didn't he understand that to learn how to
write, he had to do it once in a while? Did the idea that his professor
might not pass him fail to enter his mind? But, most importantly,
did he honestly believe he was pulling the wool over my eyes and
I couldn't see what he was doing?

Or maybe the whole object was to drive me crazy. Maybe God
sent down this angel in disguise to test me, and I was falling for

it. At this point, I wanted to believe anything except what was really happening. George couldn't be that irresponsible. This had to be a joke. I was sure that someone in the Student Learning Center had a hidden camera. However, the person who was supposed to pop out and say, "You're on Candid Camera!" must have fallen asleep.

George and I started working together shortly after the semester began. When I first met him, he was already behind in his class, but he said he would get caught up if it was the last thing he did. We developed a practical schedule that would allow him to catch up with everything in a reasonably short period of time. George acted motivated and eager to work with me and do well in his class. He spoke with such enthusiasm that all I could do was thank the Almighty for sending me such a perfect student. Of course, this was before I got to know George.

I quickly learned that George had the best of intentions, but that was all he had. He lacked the motivation, planning skills, and focus he needed to accomplish any of the things he spoke of so often. George and I would work on papers until I thought it was just a matter of typing it into the good ol' computer and printing it out. We would brainstorm, develop theses, write outlines, and find specific evidence for all his points. Sometimes he would even write sections of the paper during a session. But somehow George never made it to the good ol' computer from our sessions. The results were always the same. Either he would lose interest in the paper we were working on and become dedicated to starting another paper he had not turned in, or he would discover another current assignment that was much more important.

The funny thing was that it was I, not George, who got gray hair over what was happening. I began to dread our sessions in fear of what George was going to spring on me next. "Well, this paper was due last semester, but I didn't get inspired to do it until this week, so how about it? Better late than never, right!" I couldn't understand how he could keep pulling this and not have a nervous breakdown or develop a twitch in his left eye. I think it bothered me so much because I took George's actions to heart, as if they were happening to me, by me. I would forget that I was sitting across from George and was not his mirror. I also interpreted George's writing performance as an evaluation of my performance as a tutor. I wanted George to succeed for him and for me. If George didn't succeed, neither did I. It took me quite a while to finally realize that my talents as a tutor were not directly linked to George's academic performance. He was not my ultimate critic, and I was not his. I finally decided that if I kept equating my adequacy as a tutor with George's behavior, I would have to quit being a tutor.

So every time George would start off with one of his excuses—"I just wanted to relax and not worry about school. I mean it was spring break and all. Plus the paper was already two weeks overdue, so why does it matter when I get it in now?"—ideas of murder would dance in my head, I would remind myself that he was not me. The person sitting across from me made his own choices. I could try to influence those choices and lead them in a productive direction, but ultimately the choices were his and so were the consequences. I learned how to separate myself from what was happening to George by realizing that I needed to help him in the best way I could and then go on with my own life.

I decided to get tough with George. My last alternative was to be totally straight with him, so my comments from that point on were blunt and honest. I told him exactly what was wrong with his papers and no longer debated him on trivial matters. I also told him what would happen to him if he didn't get on the ball. I stopped listening to his excuses and began setting limits on how much time we'd spend on a single paper. After the time limit was up, he was on his own. I ceased meeting him at any time and day and taking his calls at home. I began to take full control of our agenda by making the decisions on what we were going to work on, based on his syllabus. I also demanded that he assume complete responsibility for his work (or lack of work in most cases).

I can't say George liked me as much toward the end of the semester as he did at the start, but he did take me more seriously. I don't think that George ever lacked respect for me, but he was trying to pull me into his fantasy world. I'm not saying that I don't occasionally escape from reality myself, but I have never played pretend for a whole semester.

I never lost hope in George. Once in a while I would panic and revert to my mother role. I would try once again to explain nicely what the situation was and what he needed to do. But I stopped praying for a miracle that George would be completely transformed. I realized that you can talk until you're blue in the face about what should be done, and you can lead the person step by step until you get close to the goal, but you can't make him do it. He'll do it when he's good and ready. And there is no reason for you to pull your hair out, because there is nothing else you can do. Thank goodness George did improve by the end of the semester. He even turned in some papers on time.

I am proud of the progress I made with George regardless of how small it might be. I am also proud of myself because I did some growing too. I learned that I am not superhuman, that I shouldn't look for myself in all my students, and that even the smallest improvements are successes.

DISCUSSION QUESTIONS

1. Monique describes George as having an uncanny ability to drive a tutor crazy. What were some of the things he did that made her feel that way? Do you think you would feel the same way if you were George's tutor?
2. Do you think that George realized that he was getting to Monique? If so, do you think he really wanted her to help him keep up the fantasy?
3. What were the conditions that led Monique to decide to get tough with George? Do you think things might have been better if she had decided to get tough earlier? Explain.

Dealing with a Touchy Subject
Po-Sun Chen

> What can a tutor do when his student can't keep her hands off him? Po keeps his sense of humor while he desperately tries different strategies to avoid her hands.

Imagine you've been tutoring Alice Entoyo for over half a semester now. She is a very confident and outgoing individual, but she has lived in the United States for about three years, and her English is a bit rough. She came in for tutoring to tighten up her grammar, spelling, and overall writing skills. She's outgoing and you're outgoing and the two of you get along marvelously. However, Alice has a habit of being a little touchy, not in the sense of being overly sensitive to certain things but rather because she is used to demonstrative language. Whenever she greets you, she really enjoys touching your hair, or coming up behind you and putting her arms around your neck. But what really starts to irk you is that she puts her hand on your arm whenever you say something funny—in fact, she even does it when she says something she thinks is funny! In addition, whenever you try to give her advice on her paper, she starts to stare at you. You don't really get the feeling that Alice is coming on to you; in fact, that really isn't the issue. You've already tried everything from sitting on opposite sides of the desk to jumping up and yelping when she puts her hand on yours, but nothing works and you know that this simply cannot continue. What would you do? Jump higher? Yelp louder? Say you have a rash? Heaven forbid, you wouldn't actually talk about it openly with her, would you? Unfortunately as with many other tutoring dilemmas, there is no one best answer to this question. But perhaps by examining this case a little closer we can come up with some possible solutions.

People like Alice are naturally very comfortable with a lot of physical contact. So you have to be sensitive and find a way of dealing with their discomfiting behavior without dismissing their touchiness as some sort of character flaw. As I mentioned before, I tried several tactics. The first, sitting opposite her at the desk, did not work for me because it was just too difficult going over papers together; invariably, one of us would get so cramped trying to read upside down or turning our heads at some obtuse angle that we couldn't pay attention to the paper. Photocopying the paper or having two copies printed by the computer could solve the problem. That would make it less likely that your student would grab your arm, since she would have to reach across the table to do so.

On a less serious note, the second tactic, jumping up and yelping whenever the student gets touchy, probably could work, but there are several obvious reasons not to do it. First of all, it makes a lot of commotion in the tutoring area, and you probably wouldn't want your supervisor to hear of your reputation for jumping up and yelping. I never tried this technique because I felt Alice might erupt in hearty laughter. That really wasn't the direction I wanted things to take.

A third technique that I haven't mentioned was the one that worked most effectively with Alice. My initial reaction to Alice when she first started touching me was to look in every direction but hers. I was trying to avoid dealing with my own feelings about being stared at, poked at, and whatever else she felt like doing. Thus, she began grabbing my arm and staring at me even more to make sure that I was listening to what she was saying. Eventually, she began to verbalize her concern about my attention span—"Are you listening to me, Po?"—and she even became annoyed at times. In effect, my unconscious reaction to her touchiness evoked in her an even greater desire to touch me and get my attention. I found that when I acknowledged her complaints and began listening to her very attentively and initiating a lot of eye contact, she backed off without our sessions losing any effectiveness. In fact, since I now was more comfortable because she wasn't touching me and she was more comfortable because of my increased attentiveness, our sessions became more productive than ever.

There is no single textbook solution to this problem, and most certainly the three I propose are not the only ones. I merely wish to illustrate the development of my own reactions to Alice as well as the subsequent—and fortunately pleasant—resolution of the problem. A case like Alice doesn't come along too often, but when it does, it makes you pray for a miracle. So the next time you come across one of those "huggie-wuggie" students that surprise you by playing with your hair or grabbing you from behind, don't be instantly critical of him or her, but examine your own feelings and react accordingly. You'll usually emerge a better tutor.

DISCUSSION QUESTIONS

1. Why do you think Po avoided talking directly with Alice about how he felt when she touched him? What might have happened had he done so?
2. How did Po explain Alice's need to touch him? Do you agree with his assessment, or do you think that there might be other reasons for her behavior?
3. What factors were involved in finding a solution to this problem

so that tutoring could proceed? Do you think Po's solution might work for you if you found yourself in a similar situation?

4. If this situation arose between a female tutor and a male student who constantly touched her, do you think Po's strategy would work, or might another approach be needed? Discuss.

6 Tutors Learn from Tutoring Too

Using Your Intuition: Hearing Your Inner Voice
May V. Espeña

> May reveals what is going on in her mind when she listens to
> students and tries to figure out how best to communicate with them.

I've often experienced a strange sort of anxiety as a tutor. It's a
phenomenon that occurs when a slightly nervous, cautious, and
inexperienced tutor faces tutoring for the first time: the inner dialogue. It's the voice in your head that is telling you, *You're doing
fine . . . hope he doesn't ask about grammar! He's going to write
ten pages on that! Is there a nice way to tell him to start over?* The
peculiarity of this stream of consciousness is that it is rarely syn-
chronized with the words coming out of my mouth. But throughout
the semester I have learned to listen to the voice inside of me that
is not the infallible, objective tutor. Learning to trust my own
intuition and abilities has helped me help my students. Developing
that trust, however, demanded a continuing, conscious effort on
my part. In having my worst critic and my best coach both conveniently located in my head, the constant dialogue with myself
developed into a welcome, often helpful aspect of my tutoring.

My inner voice was at its harshest during my first tutoring session. I felt extremely unprepared, and I was hoping my student
did not see through my front:

"Carrie? Hi, I'm May. How are you?" *Stay cool! This isn't so
bad. She's not that scary. I can do it. Got my questions. Make sure
to ask the questions! Get to know her. Talk about the good stuff, the
questions! Ask her the damn . . .*

"So what do you want to do today?" *I missed the questions.*

Can't go back. Stupid! This isn't the way the book says to do it. Now what? Why am I here? I'm the one who needs tutoring. Should I tell her I've never tutored before? Can she tell?

"So your teacher wants you to write on the kind of material you want to read this semester, and you said you wanted to read about political issues?" *Politics? She doesn't really want to read about politics, does she?* "Okay that's great. Do you want to read your essay out loud?" *What would I do if I were to write about that? Literature? Morrison would be cool. She wants to read about politics because it's important? That's her thesis? Nah, it couldn't be. It is her thesis. Uh-oh, crisis.*

"That was pretty good, you brought up a lot of important points. You talked about different international issues and why we need to be more aware, but I'm still confused about your thesis." *Jeez, I sound like a book. Why did she have to go and pick politics? Couldn't she have picked something else like her favorite author or something?* "Let's try and flesh it out some more. Let's see, can you tell me where your thesis is?" *Too broad, way too broad. What about politics does she like? Yeah.*

"So, Carrie, what about politics do you like?" *OK good, get her to talk. Ask plenty of questions.* "I mean, what makes you *really* want to read about it?" *Play dumb . . . do the dot thing, the dot thing!*

"You like to read about it because it's important? It is important." *She's not getting it. What about?* "Can you tell me three reasons you like reading about politics?"

"You don't know why you like politics—oh, hm . . ." *This is frustrating. Be nice. Don't make her feel bad. Beware of your tone.* "Girl, you wrote four pages and you still don't know why? Well you must know something if you got four pages on it!" *Good, she's laughing. Let's try something else.*

Looking back on that first session, I don't think I perceived that inner voice as something helpful. On the contrary, I thought of it as a hindrance, something that got in the way of tutoring. My inner voice caused me to question my abilities as a tutor and plagued me with self-doubt. I was under the mistaken impression that all sessions should flow smoothly and naturally. That first experience at tutoring should have indicated to me that none of my future sessions would ever take place without that inner dialogue. I would later realize that talking to myself during sessions was like tutoring myself. *How am I going to make him realize that his paper is going in ten different directions? How am I going to get her to understand the difference between explication and analysis? How am I going to help her map out an outline without doing her paper for her? Bubble diagrams? Charts?* When I first began, this kind of rapid-fire dialogue ran through my head. Getting over the first-session jitters was difficult, but trying to stay one step ahead of my students proved more problematic.

I had a student named Amy who needed help with an essay on Samuel Beckett's *Waiting for Godot.* I had never read the play, but I knew enough about it to know I didn't want to have to explain it to her. Amy complained, "How am I supposed to think of a topic when I can't even understand this play?" Having experienced that kind of frustration myself, I empathized and asked her to give me a quick synopsis:

"So, it's about two guys who are waiting for a guy named Godot. That's it?" *Uh-oh, that can't be it. I don't want that brief a summary.*

"Well, what do they do while they're waiting? Nothing? Oh." *What a dumb assignment! How is she going to do this? Brainstorm ideas? Bubble thing? Nah, those are weird. WEIRD!*

"What's the weirdest thing about this text? I see. So because they're so bored, they try and find ways to kill time." *Oh Jeez, this situation is not improving!* "They even try to kill themselves because they can't find anything better to do? Hm . . ." *That's weird, not getting anywhere with the plot, so style! Ask her about style!*

"What do you think about Beckett's writing style?" (Silence.) *I think I'll just flip through the book while she's thinking . . . still thinking . . . still flipping. She's stumped. One, two, three . . .* "Was there anything in the writing style that jumped out at you?" *OK, she looks confused still—four, five, six—OK, hint.* "Why do you think Beckett uses so much repetition?" *Maybe we'd better try something else.*

All sessions can't sound like the plucky little conversations in the tutor handbook. Many times, some of the brilliant ways I think of to engage my students fizzle and dry up. Talking the tutoring session through with myself helps me figure out which direction would be best for the student. Ideally, the student will take that cue and run with it. As a tutor, I've learned that many sessions do not flow like they do in Teri the Tutor's session. With Amy, I had to keep trying to find the thing that intrigued her enough to write five pages of analysis. The old method of trial and error still applies when you are trying to draw things out of a student.

As the semester progressed and I was gaining confidence in my role as a tutor, I was reminded that my students were actually *students*—that is, people who make a study of something. Once again my inner voice, who had formerly exclusively checked only my tutoring strategy, reminded me that someone had to listen to all of my introspection. Listening to my intuition and trying to stay a few steps ahead of my students sometimes resulted in my getting caught up in my own head.

I had one student, Mike, whose biggest problem was writing clearly. In an attempt to state his ideas powerfully, he often used big and unfamiliar words and lots of prepositional phrases in his essays. Although I commended him for expanding his vocabulary, his unfamiliarity with usage made his writing confusing for the reader. I told Mike I was glad he was varying his sentence structure, diverting from the usual subject, verb, object construction, but his lengthy sentences often obscured his points.

"So, Mike, do you understand what I'm trying to say? You don't have to use big words to get your point across. A lot of my teachers appreciate clear, concise writing instead of wordiness. Powerful writing can also mean writing simply." *What? Why is he writing that down? Oh no, he'll hold me accountable for that. What if I've stunted his growth as a writer? What if he throws that back in my face later on and I won't be able to defend myself? Don't write that down! Quit it. I don't want to be blamed for anything I've told you. Now it's recorded that I've given you a rule, not an alternative. I don't think I'm allowed to do that.*

That moment made me truly realize that tutoring was not just about me fretting over what and how I'm supposed to say things. I realized that, if I've done well, students will go home and think about what I said and apply it to their own writing. Remembering what I felt when I witnessed him write down something I had said brought home the idea that tutoring was not a personal exercise on how I organize my thoughts. I had forgotten that someone was really listening to me. My being satisfied when I thought I was being clear was not enough. I became aware of the student's position in this whole process. Suddenly tutoring became a lesson not only in speaking but in listening.

My inner voice is no longer the only voice I listen to when I tutor. I remember my student's personal involvement in writing and pay close attention. It's still there; I still talk to myself all the time. My inner voice keeps me on my toes. It reminds me that I have much to learn from my students.

DISCUSSION QUESTIONS

1. Compare and contrast May's story about her inner voice and Mary O'Connell's story, "Ignoring the Voices." How are their inner voices similar? different?
2. What was the incident that alerted May to the fact that tutoring should involve listening to students as well as to her inner voice?
3. Do you think most tutors carry on dialogues with themselves as they tutor? What are the advantages and disadvantages of inner dialogues in tutoring?

Interrupt: Tutoring for the Quiet Tutor
Esther Sam

> Tutoring a talkative, aggressive student poses problems for a quiet tutor. Esther describes how her student dominated the sessions and how, by being more assertive, she might have been a more effective tutor.

I am a quiet person by nature. In most cases, I would rather watch and listen to people than speak. In addition, I have always been taught to be as humble, polite, and obliging as possible. Because of these tendencies, I have difficulty tutoring very aggressive and talkative students, especially my first student this semester. I am writing about this experience so other quiet tutors like me can avoid the kinds of problems I had with this student.

The strongest impression I got from the tutor orientation session at UC Berkeley's Student Learning Center came from watching the videotapes of different sessions. Two episodes stood out in my mind in particular. The first showed a tutor who did most of the talking while her student seemed uncomfortable and hardly spoke at all. The second showed a tutor cutting off his student in mid-sentence, which one of the new tutors immediately pointed out during the discussion that followed. Everyone laughed at how rude this interruption seemed. These videotapes instilled in me a fear of a silent student. They convinced me to let students talk without interrupting their flow of thought.

I was happily surprised when I met my first student, Amy. She seemed incredibly enthusiastic and brought everything she had written last semester to our first meeting. I was thrilled as she talked energetically throughout the entire session. I had been so afraid that my student would not talk at all that I was blind to the fact that she talked too much.

I should have noticed that Amy was not at all open to criticism and almost unwilling to be helped. As she flipped through her papers, she almost shrugged as she read off the grades (mostly C's and at best a B−). In the same breath she told me that she might like to be an English major and read out comments like, "Your writing is at a third-grade level." This seemed strange—not because she couldn't learn how to write well and become an English major but because the teacher's comments did not even make her bat an eye. She seemed not to acknowledge these comments at all but to brush them aside.

Whenever I suggested that she brainstorm for ideas for a paper, she gave me incredibly long plot summaries. When I tried to guide her toward a thesis, she proved too strong for me. Sometimes she even reprimanded me when I asked her a question replying, "I'm trying to tell you . . ." and gave me further plot summary.

Amy went off on every imaginable tangent, and I let her. I didn't want to interrupt her flow of ideas, because I wanted her to feel that they were important, but this made our sessions exhausting and unproductive. I could not help her improve her writing, which was as convoluted as her monologues, because I could barely follow her thinking.

Eventually, Amy started skipping sessions, and to tell the truth, I breathed a sigh of relief when she stopped coming altogether. I knew she needed serious help with her writing, but I was just not ready for her when she came along. Though I now have students who have really improved their writing during the semester, I will always feel a pang for this lost student. Had I known how to be more effective in our sessions together, perhaps this would have turned out differently.

Here are a few things you can do to keep your sessions from getting out of hand when you're tutoring a talkative student:

1. *Establish your presence immediately.* Basically, you can tell from the first or second session what the nature of the relationship between you and the student will be. If you find a student talks a great deal and without focus, you should make an extra effort to keep the discussion focused and in control. Try to establish a more balanced relationship during the first few sessions. The longer it goes on, the harder it is to change.

2. *Tell your student something about yourself in the first session*—what you hope to accomplish in college and why you chose to be a writing tutor. Your ethos is important when you are a reserved person. Don't come across as timid. I don't mean that you should dominate the sessions by any means (collaborating is the goal), but sometimes more active tutoring is called for. For example, you do not always have to defer to your student and hope she can figure out what is wrong with a sentence, paragraph, or paper. You can make direct statements like, "You can't say that," or "That is redundant." Then go on to explain why what she chose does not work or does not work well.

3. *Interrupt.* Be more aggressive than you are naturally. Don't worry about seeming rude; most likely your student wouldn't even notice if you were ten times as rude as you normally are. If your student talks too much, goes off on a tangent, or tries to dodge a subject, remind her that she needs to stick to the topic. And keep reminding her. For example, a simple "Stop" or "Hold on" can do the trick. Or you could say, "That's interesting, and we can discuss it later, but what about the point I was asking you about?" The important thing is that you jump in. Don't wait for the student to pause or finish her idea, because it might not be her own.

4. *Be organized and focused.* If you go into the session organized in your mind, the disorganization of a talkative student might be less confusing to you. Have in mind what you want

your student to get out of each session before you meet, in case the student does not know what she wants to work on. If she brings in a draft of a paper to work on, choose just one particular aspect of it to work on—the thesis, the structure, the grammar, etc. One way to do this is to ask the student to write down a few things she wants to work on and then choose one. Another way is to list a few things the student needs to work on and ask her to pick one of them. But be sure you both stick to the topic.

5. *Keep your journal up to date.* It is really helpful to talk to your supervisor, but sometimes it takes a few days to get around to doing that. By then, you might have forgotten what happened in the session that made it unusual or problematic, so it's a good idea to write down what happens soon after your session.

DISCUSSION QUESTIONS

1. Can you think of ways that Esther might have been helped to understand the differences between working with a quiet versus a talkative student before she started tutoring?
2. Esther blames herself for not being more successful with Amy. Does Esther's attitude seem realistic? Do you think that another tutor could help Amy, or do her problems seem so complex that she should be referred to counseling? Explain.
3. Critically evaluate Esther's four points for avoiding the problems she faced. Do you think they might be useful in your tutoring?
4. Can you think of any other techniques that might help quiet tutors like Esther be more assertive with students?

On Crossing the Tutor-Tutee Line: Toward a New Kind of Relationship
Helen H. Woo

When she tutored a Cambodian refugee student whom she greatly admired, Helen changed her view of the roles of tutors and students.

Going into my second semester of tutoring at the Student Learning Center, I did not expect to have any especially enlightening experiences. I had a rewarding first semester tutoring, but it was not an out-of-the-ordinary experience; our meetings seemed typical in that we discussed purely writing topics such as brainstorming, organization, development, etc. None of my students seemed to be especially different from those described in our training. I therefore assumed that this semester would be more of the same—rewarding but predictable tutoring. However, when I met a student named Sida Booth, I got a fresh outlook on tutoring.

Before meeting Sida, my attitude toward students was limited and, looking back, fairly shallow—shallow in the sense that although I did not see students as mere objects, I think I did tend to objectify them. They were to be the recipients of my carefully balanced role of teacher and peer collaborator. And they in turn fulfilled typical student roles as students struggling with English courses, fellow-collaborators, "good" students making steady progress, or just plain "flakes." I saw them as students with individual problems, but I did not see them as individuals beyond our professional relationship as tutor and student. In fact, I felt no need to know them better because our tutor contracts did not demand anything more.

This was my attitude during the first week of the semester when I met Sida for the first time. Only one word could describe her: bright. Not only was she intellectually bright, but she was literally bright. She seemed to radiate light from her smile to her eyes, even in her walk. However, during our very first warm-up session, we somehow got on the topic of a very dark subject—death. And it was then that I discovered that in her youth she had seen darkness face to face in the form of fellow workers bombed, an uncle killed in battle, and other tragedies. That's when I realized that I had already crossed the boundary of merely being a tutor and was beginning to see her as a whole person.

I gradually learned more about her through our sessions together and by reading an article about her in a university publication. She is the first Cambodian ever to be admitted to Berkeley. She is now one of seven Cambodian refugees at UC Berkeley. To put it mildly, her background was radically different from most Berkeley students. While other children were starting school, she was torn from her family, living in a concentration camp, working on a rice paddy, hearing death cries at night, and, at almost every minute, close to death herself. After fleeing Cambodia, she entered the United States with most of her family. Entering the United States for her was like entering a new war zone, for the West Oakland neighborhood her family settled in was saturated with drugs and crime. And she did not even understand the language here. At the age of eleven, Sida was exposed to formal education for the first time ever. After spending two years in the third grade, she skipped to the seventh grade and eventually graduated from high school. She finally reached Berkeley, where she is now a junior. Partly because I knew so much of her background and partly because we seemed to get along naturally and instantaneously, Sida and I began to build a friendship beyond the bounds of our tutoring contract. She became no longer just the student who needed help organizing her paper or with punctuation. Beyond her role of student, I realized that she was a person with a history, life experience, and feeling, and I developed a deep appreciation for the strength she had shown in surviving the psychological and emotional assaults of her past experiences. In fact, I gained the most from our relationship because she showed me that it is possible to overcome the most difficult circumstances that life inevitably brings. However, we did not only talk about the dark past, we also had lighthearted conversations about personal encounters with people on campus, cooking, midterm anxiety, and other day-to-day things. Moreover, she began to confide in me about her personal relationships and the happiness and heartache they brought.

Although I believe that our relationship went beyond tutoring, our sessions were primarily about tutoring. But I also believe that our tutoring experience benefited from our friendship. I was no longer merely tutoring on development, organization, and grammar. Rather, I began to see writing as being more personally meaningful to the student. Each assignment began to take on new importance because I saw that writing, to her, was a way of expressing herself as well as a measure of her self-worth as a competent student. In other words, I began to care more about each session, not only hers but others as well.

Finally, I believe there are important implications for other tutors in the lessons I learned from Sida. By viewing our students as human beings with their own unique, colorful, and significant histories, we add a dimension to tutoring that otherwise is lacking. However, not everyone is willing to open up, and not everyone is interested in going beyond the tutor-student roles spelled out in our professional contract. Some are just interested in getting help with writing, and that is fine. My point is that underneath the role of student lies a person who not only might turn out to be a friend but also might end up teaching you a thing or two about life itself.

DISCUSSION QUESTIONS

1. It can be very ego enhancing to tutor a brilliant student from an exotic background who has had unusual and exciting experiences. What does Helen's description of Sida tell you about Helen? For example, which of Sida's characteristics seemed to impress Helen the most? How would you expect Helen's experience with Sida to affect her work with other students? Do you think most tutors need a dramatic experience like this to see students as unique individuals?

2. Helen writes, "Before meeting Sida, my attitude toward students was limited and, looking back, fairly shallow—shallow in the sense that . . . I did tend to objectify them." Do you think Helen's self-perception was accurate? Why? What examples can you find to support your opinion?

3. How do you think Sida might have benefited from tutoring? What examples does Helen give of Sida's gains?

4. Describe the advantages and disadvantages of going beyond the tutoring role to that of good friend. What do you think are the greatest dangers of getting into a close relationship with a student?

Ignoring the Voices
Mary O'Connell

Frustrated by many weeks of tutoring a perfectionist who did not improve, Mary realizes that he's very depressed. Here's how she tried to help.

For years I have been plagued by a detestable little man with a very loud voice. He appears unpredictably and in inconvenient places and makes it impossible for me to continue to work. He shows no mercy when I have urgent things to finish. He's an elusive creature—always there when I least expect him and impossible to catch when I finally hunt him down. It took me years to understand his voice clearly, but always the message is the same: "You have boring ideas. Your writing is crap. You're going to fail." Rejecting him is impossible; all I can do is fight his sabotaging voice.

In my tutoring sessions with Ed this semester I've begun to realize that other people also hear negative voices. Some voices are even louder than mine, and some seem more debilitating. Ed's little man has enticed Ed into utter incompetence and has taken over his conversations. I hear statements from Ed like, "This is really a bad paper," "This is a stupid thesis," and "I'm so stupid." Ed's self-analysis results in an almost total paralysis. He cannot seem to put a paragraph down on paper without destroying the idea behind it. After so much frustration with his inability to write anything intelligent, Ed forfeits the game and stops trying.

Ed and I worked for six weeks on an overdue paper. He would bring me a draft of about four pages each week, the product of his free-writing. I felt that he only needed to make the logical connections, reorganize, and polish a few sentences to produce a well-written essay. But Ed rejected the idea of editing these drafts and said he did not like his thesis statement and wanted to start over. I tried to persuade him that starting over might take too long for a paper that was already overdue but to no avail. Ed's little voice was clearly in control. He wanted to make his thesis statement *better* so that he would have a *better* argument. So we started again at ground zero and worked to create the perfect thesis statement. (Ed has never bought the old cliche, "nobody's perfect.")

The next two sessions Ed brought more extensive notes on his readings for the same paper. I asked him what had happened to his thesis, and he replied that he needed a *better* understanding of the characters to write his paper. He then displayed a huge four-page diagrammed map of notes he had taken. Its complexity would put the brilliant heuristic diagrams of *The Practical Tutor* to shame. Trying to estimate the number of hours Ed must have spent compiling his diagram was inconceivable to me, and I began to wonder if he created this monster to prove to me that he was working on his paper. Certainly it was more than enough proof. Unfortunately, he was misdirecting a tremendous amount of energy, because although he seemed to be determined to get his paper done, he was afraid to try to write a finished draft. He feared that his final draft would never live up to what he expected. Nothing would ever be good enough.

Our fifth and sixth tutoring sessions were wasted hours. Not only was I exhausted by the topic, but Ed seemed completely overwhelmed by his many ideas, drafts, and notes. He had by now stopped bringing me tangible proof of his work. In fact, he had stopped writing anything at all, although his overdue paper continued to haunt him. In his eyes, it became another indication of his stupidity. I was at a loss for my next step with him. Offering him large amounts of encouragement was obviously not enough.

Early in the semester, I realized that Ed was not the most happy camper at UC Berkeley, and I suspected this was due to poor study habits. "Ed," I said, "What do you do when you get home from classes?" "I sleep," he answered. "I've been sleeping twelve to fourteen hours a day." I was shocked and asked him why he slept so long and whether he tries to get up on time. His answers convinced me that he was deeply depressed, avoiding problems, and suffering tremendous anxiety. So I suggested that he go and talk to a counselor at the Counseling Center, though he never found one that he felt completely comfortable talking with. I knew that he felt comfortable with me and that we had established a friendly relationship. About 40 percent of our meetings became rap sessions, and we talked about what was going on in his life. Although I felt comfortable in the role of tutor, I did not feel the same way in the role of counselor, so there were certain issues where I deliberately chose not to probe too deeply for several reasons. First, I did not feel qualified to give advice on his emotional problems, and I was afraid that if I did, Ed might have acted on anything I said. (There is something about being a tutor that makes one the great authority, not only about grammar but about life.) Secondly, I was there to help him with his writing, not to advise about personal issues. Thirdly, and to me the most important reason, I did not like the idea of taking on Ed's problems unless I wanted to be involved, and I realized that sometimes I get involved out of a feeling of obligation. Thus, I became more timid as his personal problems became more apparent.

Finally, I decided to let go of my self-created responsibility to fix his life and suggested that he continue confronting his personal problems on his own.

The last time I met with Ed, I read to him the beginning of this story and asked him how I should end the paper. Could I give it a triumphant ending and write that Ed had finally realized the pain he was inflicting on himself and finished and turned in his overdue paper as well as his final exam? Or would the story end in sadness and hopelessness? He told me to write that he turned in his papers and successfully completed English 1B. I hope his prediction will come true. If not, I'm afraid my little man will return once again and scream, "You are a terrible tutor!" in which case I'll have another battle to fight. This time I'll win, I'm sure, for I have now seen worse cases of self-destruction and intend to minimize the damage the little man can do to my own life.

DISCUSSION QUESTIONS

1. Does Mary's argument that a little voice within one's mind that censures and disapproves of what we're trying to create can be powerful and destructive seem feasible to you? Do you think that it's a good explanation of Ed's behavior in trying to write?
2. Are there other ways you might explain Ed's writing paralysis? his putting so much emphasis on the wrong things?
3. What did Mary think Ed's diagrammed map of notes represented? Do you agree?
4. Do you think Mary should have probed more deeply into Ed's life when tutoring reached an impasse? Explain.
5. What do you think was the significance of Ed's suggesting a happy ending for Mary's story about him?

Keeping the Promise
S. Eric Larsen

> What should a tutor do when a student tells him she doesn't need any more tutoring even though she is flunking the course? Eric found that tutors must be assertive and persistent if they are to help those who need the most help.

This semester, my second as a writing tutor, has offered few rewards, particularly in comparison with my first semester. Perhaps this dissatisfaction has resulted because I haven't been taking the long-term perspective, comparing the current work of the students with whom I have been working with the work they were doing at the beginning of the semester. Perhaps the novelty of the first semester has worn off. Perhaps I have forgotten what I was told when I became a tutor: you should not expect overnight success with every one of the students with whom you work and should consider any progress an outstanding achievement.

What I think has happened, however, is that I have lost sight of what I was hoping to accomplish as a tutor, that is, helping students overcome the same problems I have had as a writer and using my experience in overcoming my difficulties to help others. I was particularly eager to help those who, like myself, are using education as an opportunity to give themselves and their children a better life than their parents had.

It was difficult for me to keep these goals in mind when tutoring this semester. I really like all my students, but I have found it hard to rationalize, beyond pure benevolence, why I was giving up my precious time to help them. For instance, Roger, who comes from an aristocratic African family, would have no problem passing Subject A without my help. Quincy, who earned a B in English 1A, is eager to move up to an A in English 1B and then leave writing behind in his studious pursuit of biology or chemistry. Mary, who intends to major in business administration, brings me paper after paper marked with an imperfect A−. I enjoy working with Roger, Quincy, and Mary, but I find it hard to get excited about working with them. I rationalize that, with my help, they will become models in their communities, but deep down, I am dissatisfied.

At the beginning of the semester, I was tutoring a fourth student, Marcy, who was clearly having a very hard time, not only with her writing but also in reading critically and in getting excited about school. After three or four meetings, Marcy, apparently not satisfied with the results, began to stand me up. After her second absence, I called her and she promised to show up for our next appointment. I was eager to avoid alienating her in any way, as I felt that she would not pass her class without outside help. I repeated my request that she call me if she were not able to make it to our next meeting, as I could use the time I spend waiting for her studying in the library. Before our next appointment, she called me and said that she had decided she didn't want to be tutored any more. I was surprised and asked her many times if she were sure of her decision. She insisted she was, and I wished her good luck.

Meeting with Thom, my supervisor, later this semester, I told him about the progress I was making with my students. As an aside, I mentioned that I had dropped one of my students. He asked me if I thought she were in danger of failing. I replied, frankly, "Yes." His eyebrows raised a notch, and he asked if she were a student admitted under Affirmative Action. I replied naively, "Uhh . . . I think so." His eyebrows raised another notch. He suggested that I not only speak with her counselor but also call her back and offer her some last-minute collaboration before the rush of finals. I walked out of his office somewhat sheepishly, feeling I had made a horrible mistake.

I realized later, however, that it was my apathy with the outstanding students with whom I was collaborating that made me forget my goals as a tutor. And when I forgot my goals as a tutor, I also almost forgot Marcy. After two days of busily working on an important paper, I called Marcy and asked her how she was doing, how school was going, and how she was keeping up with her classes. I even lied to her and told her that one of my students had dropped tutoring due to the pressure of upcoming finals. I told her I had some time available and asked if she wanted a little help with her papers before the end of the semester. She was delighted and immediately made an appointment.

There were only a few weeks left in the semester, and she had a good deal of work to do. Marcy had yet to turn in her last paper, had a paper due next week, and had been given the opportunity to rewrite two other papers. I suggested that we concentrate on improving a few of her skills that she could apply broadly to her writing, and she agreed. She was having a tough time coming up with anything to say about any of the books she had been reading, and her assignment was to write about the style used by W. E. B. DuBois in one of the assigned essays. I asked her some questions about DuBois' style and she didn't reply. Trying a different approach, I asked her to compare DuBois' style with that of Mark Twain in *Huckleberry Finn*. This approach was much more successful, and before I was buried in an avalanche of ideas, I asked her to write her thoughts down in a list. Then I asked her to consider what DuBois' purpose was in writing the essay. This produced another list. Then I asked her to keep these purposes in mind and consider why DuBois' style is the way it is. Before the hour was over, not only had she outlined her paper, but she had gained a skill she could apply to the other papers as well. Marcy could now make the nebula of ideas that formed in her head concrete and, when she faced a writing assignment, could consider the relationships between these ideas. Though only two weeks were left in the semester, we made plans to meet twice a week for the rest of the term.

Unfortunately, I don't know whether Marcy will pass her writing class or not. Either way, I think we have both benefited. If she doesn't pass, at least her writing has improved somewhat, and she will be successful if she repeats the course. Furthermore, I hope I left her with the impression that there are people in the university that want her to succeed. I have benefited from working with her in that I no longer feel I have wasted my semester, and she has helped me regain my original goals in tutoring.

DISCUSSION QUESTIONS

1. What does Eric suggest was the reason for his dissatisfaction during his second semester of tutoring?
2. Do you think you would feel the same way about them that Eric did if you were working with Mary, Quincy, and Roger? Why or why not?
3. Why do you think Marcy was willing to make an appointment when Eric called her late in the semester?
4. Do you think that Marcy would continue to see Eric if the semester had not ended? Why or why not?

Violence, Writing, and Control
Frederick Aldama

A tutor gets a frantic call from a student who is facing a personal catastrophe and must talk with him. After tearfully describing her tragedy, Rosa discovers that she has to cope and finish the semester.

December 3, 1991

My body warms as I walk into the Student Learning Center, leaving the cold December morning outside. I sit down in my familiar chair, next to my familiar table, waiting anxiously for Rosa, a student in my writing workshop for English 1A. I think, "Why was her voice so dim, so fragile, when she phoned asking to see me? This didn't sound like the self-assured Rosa in workshop! What was it she couldn't talk about over the phone? Why was she in such a rush to get off the phone?"

As these questions race through my mind, my body becomes restless. I shift around in my chair; my eyes settle on the clock, where I watch the seconds, then the minutes pass. The familiar interplay of sounds, smells, and sights mingle in the expansive tutoring area, inducing a feeling of solace; my body responds by easing comfortably into the chair's shape. I remember . . .

> Karla, patiently standing, chalk in hand, in front of the blank chalk board. Loud thumps at the door, Rosa's flushed face pops around the edge of the door. It's so late I didn't think she'd make it today.
>
> Rosa, out of breath: "Sorry everyone, for being late; they messed me up over at Financial Aid. Money, you know! So what's on the menu?"
>
> I announce, "We're trying to brainstorm on potential themes for analyzing *A Woman Warrior*. Any ideas?"
>
> Rosa: "Yeah, just let me catch my breath."
>
> Mariecela: "We haven't really come up with anything concrete."
>
> Rosa: "What about myth? After class yesterday I started thinking about myths and storytelling in the novel. Don't you remember when your mom told you bedtime stories, like La Llorona?"
>
> Karla: "Yeah, but I don't see how that relates to *A Woman Warrior?*"
>
> Rosa: "This is kind of a shot in the dark, but doesn't Brave Orchid act as a woman warrior by telling myths to the children? You know, pass the stories of her ancestry down to the children?"
>
> Karla writes on the board, "In the novel *A Woman Warrior*,

the character Brave Orchid tells stories to thread the women's history together.''

Rosa: "Yeah, history in *A Woman Warrior* is defined specifically along motherlines, but now we need to find some passages to support our assertion. Any ideas? Don't you think that . . .''

"Good morning, Frederick," Rosa says awkwardly. Sensing a stiffness in her body and tone, I snap into an upright position, prepared to listen and respond attentively. The sights, smells, and sounds suddenly seem discordant. ''What's wrong?''

Sitting now face to face, her sadness, like a strong gravitational force, pulls me toward her. My face changes shape, the skin below my eyes weighs heavily, mirroring her sadness. Tears full of pain burn her flesh, as they trickle slowly down her face, pained, blood-shot eyes too tired to shine, hands shaking with pain. Slowly, calmly, her voice gives shape to her agony, ''My sister was blown away by her husband yesterday.'' More forcefully, ''She's dead. What's going to happen to her children, my family, my studies?'' Her words, her pain hurl themselves into my consciousness and rupture my sense of self, this protective shell so carefully formed in the university. Her words uncover my vulnerability. ''Frederick,'' she cries, ''What shall I do?'' What answer can I give her, what support can I show? Now, swimming in a sea of confusion, where can I find an answer, an anchor within this miasma of thoughts and feelings? I look to past experience, to my workshop . . .

Seven students working together, supporting one another through the writing process. Coming together to find our voice, a sense of identity, within this alienating institution. One African-American man, one Chicano (myself), one Nicaraguan woman, and four Chicanas, building trust in one another, in one another's ideas, in one another's writing. Learning how to effectively and efficiently wield prose, learning about different writing styles, like the passive and active voice, or vernacular and official language. The effect when tense shifts from present into past, or past into future. Using computers to free up our writing voice. Understanding that writing is a process, a process of building, shaping, and refining through many drafts.

(Where is this sense of structure that we brought to the workshop? Tutor, facilitator, advisor, participant in a collective process of learning and changing, I stumble, falling dizzily down into a structureless void . . .)

I hear myself telling the students, "If your writing has a solid structure, fluent and well-controlled, your audience will feel the control."

Where is all of that control? And here before me sits a woman whose tears continue uncontrolled, because of someone else's complete lack of control. Then is the control I discuss in the workshop detached from the world out there? Does the university supply us with tools and structures, only to abstract us from violence, poverty, oppression, reality? Am I, as a tutor, perpetuating this process of abstraction and thus perpetuating the violence? Does Rosa's violent world, her sister "blown away" in East Oakland, really require her words on paper to exist? No! But her words, shaped with pen and paper, can articulate and break the silence of her pain; her words in the shape of letters on a page, give substance to her thoughts and feelings. Now her words can move through the air, from subject to object, explosively impacting the reader's imagination.

Rosa's tears fall, each glistening drop asking for comfort, for answers. "What shall I do, what do I do?" In her silence her eyes reveal a switch in thoughts, feeling. Her eyes, then her voice speak her promise to me, "Frederick, if there's anything I gained from this workshop it's the knowledge that I can use the energy of my emotions to drive the writing of my papers in my own voice. I will give shape to my feelings for my sister, and I will finish this semester."

April 8th, 1992

As I walked into the Student Learning Center to escape the April heat, I bumped into Rosa. She told me that she had finished the fall semester with a high grade in her composition class and was eagerly pursuing her scholarly work. She didn't mention anything about her sister. Perhaps Rosa's grief and anguish over her loss of her sister is fading, but her memory lives on through Rosa's motivation to write, and to continue writing.

DISCUSSION QUESTIONS

1. Do you agree with Frederick and Rosa that writing enables us to gain control over strong emotions? Can strong emotions also interfere with effective writing?
2. If Frederick had presented Rosa with a plan for overcoming her grief and suggested that she do something like joining a support group, do you think the results would have been the same? Discuss.

After Hours
Jennifer Jean Brunson

> Who's to blame a harried tutor, who, after a long, hard semester, indulges in a little fantasy? Jennifer imagines an argument among the silent observers about what is most essential to good tutoring.

The outer door shut with a loud clank that echoed through the silent corridors, its sound bouncing off the wallboards and prancing over the linoleum as it wound its way back into the building. Its ring bounded along merrily, until, suddenly, it tripped on the edge of the carpet before the reception desk of the Student Learning Center and was hushed by the cavernous space and the cathedral quiet of the room.

"'Bout time," grumbled a table near the counter.

"Oh, here we go again," muttered the fluorescents.

"Well, really!" teetered the table. "It's the same thing day in and day out. People come and go, come and go. Do they realize how intrinsic we are to their system? Do they consider our feelings? No!"

"Now, now," soothed a neighboring chair, its voice wrapping a cushy embrace around its subject.

"Don't you start comforting me!" the table swung about and cocked a rim at its squishy mate. "You always take things as they come, letting yourself be dragged about only to have someone turn his back on you. How can you ignore our role in things? Don't you have any self-respect?"

"I always do my best to see that everyone feels relaxed. It can be very fulfilling work," sighed the chair.

"Yes," the table enthused. "But what really is the meaning of it all?"

"Tutoring is, of course," the dictionary rustled with pleasure, "the act or fact of guarding or guiding, i.e., dealing with the guardianship, instruction, or care of others."

The table, ignoring this outburst, tilted back to address the room. "But why are we here in this facility? What is our role in the grand scheme of learning?"

The assembly squeaked and grumbled as it puzzled with this. "Wait," began the chair, its cushions wheezing into new positions. "Doesn't tutoring include comforting a student?" The room froze expectantly. "Both the tutor and his or her student must be relaxed to give and receive ideas critically. Yes," the chair's breathy voice rose in excitement, "being at ease makes one open to trusting those around one."

"Oh, one must, mustn't one," beamed the lighting.

"Feeling that one is in a safe environment," continued the chair, "where one is free to express oneself without fear of being attacked, is very important in a tutoring relationship."

"Why, don't you remember that poor fellow, Jeffrey? He was so shy when he first came here for tutoring in basic writing. So concerned about his grasp of English, only having come to this country a few years ago. And his tutor was just as nervous!" tittered the chair. "She had just started tutoring writing and was unsure of herself. With a little support from us chairs, though, they were able to lean back or sprawl out casually. We helped dissuade their fears."

"And then," it continued, "when they began to discuss their personal experiences, we chairs were there to lean them forward, angling them about the corner of the table so they could work at the same papers while seeing each other clearly. Very nonconfrontational." A roomful of chairs bobbed in agreement.

"You positioned around us?" the table's rim turned a darker hue. "Now see here, the most important work in tutoring takes place on or at the tables; papers are read and critiqued; notes are discussed and written; goals are proposed and met! If it weren't for us tables students might go to a . . . a . . . café," it rasped. The listeners at turns shuddered or blushed. "There was that student, Sue, who had to write five papers for English and hand them in altogether. She and her tutor needed space to lay them out, to read them through, and to discuss their weaknesses."

"They did use me," chirped the dictionary.

"Yes, yes, but reference materials like you are superfluous. It's the bare bones tutoring, that's all that really matters."

"Now, hold on, you elitist. You'd subordinate us as much as you do your clauses if we'd let you!" rumbled the resource files. "You might consider the grammar worksheets, the sample essays, and the training articles from which both your students and your tutors have benefited. Without skills, a tutor cannot function. Without examples, students will often not fully absorb a concept. Pfft," the file cabinet finished with a flourish of a drawer. "All else is ancillary."

"Ahem." A great thrumming filled the room. "I/we think you are all missing the point," spoke the mailboxes.

"Yes, yes!" burst the table.

"Communication is the crux of the system," pronounced the boxes.

The table gasped. "Erp..!" squeaked the flummoxed furnishing.

"Tutoring itself is a manifestation of communication. And tutors are in constant connection with their students, peers, and supervisors. The Center could not meet the demands of one student, not to mention so many, without contact."

"And," the harmonies continued, "you all must remember that tutor the other day who needed to leave her journal for her supervisor, a note for her senior tutor, and copies of a paper for her seminar mates. And she received fliers for her pupils and a cancellation from her student, Steve." The mailboxes smiled smugly. "All thanks to us."

"My foot," grumbled the table.

"For once I agree with the table," thudded a voice. The reception counter took advantage of its full height and peered down at the common furniture. "All of this," it waved a lip at the room, "is because of humans. Humans need organization. I organize."

"I give and receive messages, follow the tutors' schedules, keep the waiting lists orderly, update the center on current announcements, and generally watch over all at the center. I organize your information," said the desk, learning toward the boxes, "and your business." It finished with a glare at the table.

The counter settled back on its walls. "Furthermore, I assist in greeting newcomers to the premises, reassuring them with current news or prompt solutions."

"Oh, but don't you see," drawled the carpet. Normally sedate, it had gone unnoticed as usual by the fervent furniture.

It waved its fibers. "We're all part of a great pattern, filaments of tutoring as a whole."

The lights sniggered behind their baffles. "Silly carpet," it confided to the windows. "Been doing too much grass."

"What?" queried the panes, rattling.

"The carpet does have a point," interceded the chair. The table toyed with this mental image.

The room raised a reluctantly expectant eyebrow.

"All right!" the table finally managed. "We all assist—to various degrees," it muttered, "in the tutoring of many different people on a variety of subjects. But to what end?"

"Job satisfaction?" posed a swivel chair.

"Cheap thrills?" fluttered the lighting.

"Well, maybe if you had the great responsibility that I do," rumbled the reception desk, rippling a counter, "you might achieve such bliss."

"Now, wait a minute," countered the mailboxes in polyphony. "We all contribute to the communication that is instrumental in tutoring."

"Yes, but you must first have something to communicate," the file cabinet clattered. "And obviously the resource files are an irreplaceable part . . ."

The room broke out in a rumble and almost missed a gentle *click* from the hallway.

"Showtime," whispered the flourescents.

The custodian paused for a moment at the door. She shook her graying head to clear it. She had only been hearing things, she assured herself. She knew the room was empty, but it always managed to spook her. She couldn't shake the feeling that she was being watched.

Glossary

Golden Bear Center
Where the Student Learning Center is housed, along with several other student services.

Individual tutoring
Students sign up for tutors whom they meet in regular weekly appointments for the duration of the semester.

Reading and Composition 1A and 1B
A two-semester requirement that can be fulfilled in a variety of departments, including but not limited to English, Comparative Literature, Rhetoric, Asian American Studies, African American Studies, Native American Studies, and Chicano Studies. 1A is meant to be completed in the freshman year, 1B in the sophomore year. Until 1990, both courses were considered freshman courses, and some departments still allow freshmen to take 1B. Students in these courses are tutored either individually or in small groups. Individual tutoring is usually one hour per week, by appointment only, and groups (writing workshops) meet in two one-hour sessions per week.

Senior tutor
An experienced undergraduate tutor who helps train first semester tutors.

Subject A
A composition course required of all entering UC Berkeley students who fail the Statewide University of California Diagnostic Exam given to those who have scored below 600 on the College Entrance Examination Board (CEEB) English Achievement Test. Students must pass Subject A before they can take the required freshman and sophomore Reading and Composition courses. Beginning fall semester 1992, students satisfy the Subject A requirement by taking College Writing 1A, a new course that fulfills both the Subject A and the Reading and Composition 1A requirement. Usually Subject A students are tutored individually, two one-hour sessions per week by appointment, but a few participate in small group tutorials (writing workshops).

Writing workshops
Students sign up for small group tutoring sessions in specific classes

215

and meet weekly for two one-hour sessions. All students, whether in groups or individual tutorials, sign up voluntarily. Some are referred by instructors, but the majority come on their own.

Appendixes

The University of California, Berkeley Student Learning Center's Peer Tutoring Program in Writing: A Brief Historical Description

Thom Hawkins

Whom Do We Serve?

Affirmative Action students on the Berkeley campus are now persisting and graduating at unprecedented high rates. A recent news report (*Berkeleyan,* May 6, 1992) attributes this success to the students themselves, to better preparation for college, and to the efforts of support services such as the Student Learning Center. The center is the university's primary academic support service for Affirmative Action (AA) students. (AA students at Berkeley are Native American, African American, Chicano/Latino, and Pilipino.) AA and EOP (Educational Opportunity Program) students are given priority for services. Other priority groups include disabled students, students on academic probation, Special Action students (qualified students who lack one or more of the requirements for regular admission), reentry students, students repeating a course, and students with an instructor referral. A significant portion of our services go to students who are not in our priority groups. Thus, the Student Learning Center is a diverse, multicultural community both in its users and in those who provide services.

The brochure that appears in appendix B outlines the specific services we provide, and the SLC Mission Statement below describes our goals and philosophy.

> The Student Learning Center offers a variety of free programs that help students expand the knowledge, skills and self-confidence essential to realizing their academic and personal goals. Our programs provide opportunities for students to actively participate as scholars in the academic community and we also strive to function as a resource for instructors and faculty. We serve all students who feel the need for academic support, and we particularly welcome students from historically underrepresented groups and those at critical transition points in their academic experience. Our services are based on a respect for the diversity of students' experiences and a belief in their capabilities to further their own learning while acting as resources for one another. Therefore, we employ principles and methods promoting cooperation, dialogue and inquiry within formats such as individual tutoring, study groups and small classes. Whatever their current level, we hope to help students progress and gain greater independence.

Collaborative learning, students learning from students, is our pervasive approach, taking its form not only in one-to-one and small group peer tutoring but also in courses for credit taught by professional staff. Collaborative learning occurs whenever two or more people learn together as partners on a voyage of discovery rather than in a hierarchical, competitive relationship. A visitor observing students working together in our center cannot, in general, readily distinguish between who is tutoring and who is being tutored. It looks like a giant study hall where silence is not the rule.

In general, the students using our services come voluntarily after hearing about us from fellow students or from announcements in classes or in campus orientations or after seeing our various advertisements. A few, maybe 10 percent, come because the instructor makes a strong recommendation. Four to five thousand students in all subjects use our services each year, and in lower division writing we deliver over 300 hours per week of individual and small group peer tutoring. Most of those hours go to students in the freshman composition sequence who see their tutors by appointment on a weekly basis, although we do offer limited drop-in help in other lower division literature courses. At present, students get no academic units for seeing a writing tutor, but we hope soon to offer credit to students enrolled in our writing workshops (see the description in appendixes N and O). Students also get writing help from separate SLC programs in ESL, the social sciences, and reentry services. (Help with papers is also available from a broad variety of other, smaller, campus tutoring services in some departments and residential living units and from student groups.)

Ever shrinking budgets keep us from providing services for groups that we should be serving. At Berkeley, finite resources force the learning center to focus on lower division, while many of our high priority AA students have a hard time of it when they reach the upper division and fail to graduate at rates comparable to non-AA groups (whites and Asians). Some groups, such as African-American males, are at greater risk than others. Within the lower division population that uses SLC services, the number of males in general is far below the number of females, usually only about a third or less of the total users and tutors. This issue deserves more attention, especially since among African-American, Native-American, Chicano/ Latino, and Pilipino students, the percentage of males that graduates from UC Berkeley is significantly lower than the percentage of females in the same groups, and in recent years the decline is sharpening. Many programs and courses on campus address the problems of equal access. However, not enough is being done to mitigate economic hardship and traditional male restrictions on asking for help. If our diversity is to be truly inclusive, we must find ways to bring more men of color into the learning center and into the intellectual life of the university. How can we continue to allow those very same young men who suffer the highest mortality rates in our society at large to remain the most vulnerable in higher education, where, ironically, they are supposed to be able to increase their chances for survival?

History and Training

Dr. Martha Maxwell started the Student Learning Center in August 1973 by combining her Reading and Study Skills Laboratory with the EOP Academic Support Service. The peer tutoring in writing during that first year was delivered by six volunteer-credit tutors who were supervised by a half-time instructor. Now we have seventy to eighty tutors each semester, supervised by four full-time professional staff, three of whom were undergraduate tutors in this program. Most of the tutors are juniors and seniors, about a third of them hold paid positions, a third are volunteers, and a third tutor for academic credit in English 310, *Field Studies in Tutoring Writing*, sponsored by Professor Donald McQuade of the English Department.

From the beginning we have made tutor training a major emphasis and stressed that training never ends. Each semester every tutor—paid, credit, or volunteer—attends a weekly one-hour training seminar (one-and-a-half hour for first semester), does a video analysis of a tutoring session, reads professional articles, confers with a supervisor, and attends two or three centerwide meetings. (All tutor training in the SLC is discipline specific, but a centerwide orientation and a general meeting to discuss AA and multicultural issues are held early each semester.) First-semester tutors also keep a journal of their tutoring and submit it weekly to the supervisor for comment, and they meet frequently with a senior tutor who is a more experienced peer tutor. Seminars are small (five to eight), so tutors have ample time to discuss their students' writing and draw on each other for solutions, ideas, and support.

We have three basic types of seminars: one for first-semester tutors, one for group leaders (who must have tutored individually for at least two semesters), and one for experienced tutors who are not leading groups. A few first-semester tutors (four to six) also attend weekly one-hour seminars for apprentice tutors, a group of talented freshmen and sophomores whom we start early in hopes they will tutor for us during most of their undergraduate education. The senior tutors (four to seven) have a one-hour weekly meeting, in addition to their weekly training seminar, with the four supervisors to discuss the progress of first-semester tutors.

Recruitment and Selection

We recruit and select tutors with the same awareness of AA that influences the delivery of our services, and we are especially eager to recruit students who have identified themselves as members of an AA group for the apprentice tutor program mentioned above. Usually about half of our writing tutors are students of color, and most of those are AA students. We attribute our success in recruiting tutors of color to the efforts of our experienced tutors of color who visit classes and student organizations to talk about the joys of tutoring. Most of our recruiting emphasizes tutoring for credit, but almost all our AA tutors are paid because they must work to go to college. In general, word of mouth is our best advertising, but we also depend on the usual newspaper ads and saturation of the campus with colorful, catchy flyers written and designed by the tutors. Instructors refer potential tutors to us, and tutors refer their best students. Several current tutors, including senior tutors and even a couple of supervisors, first came to the center to be tutored.

The selection process is as demanding as the training. Prospective tutors submit an application that includes their written response to a case study, two sample academic papers, grade point average, and a faculty recommendation (tutors must be good students and good writers—average GPA is 3.4). If they pass a preliminary screening of their application materials, they are invited to a one-hour group interview: two supervisors interview three candidates. This group interview allows us to observe how candidates interact with peers when asked to collaborate on specific tasks. Once accepted, new tutors receive two hours of general orientation and two hours of an introduction to the basics of tutoring writing. Most are tutoring by the third week of the semester.

Evaluation

Evaluation procedures are standard for all tutors; you will find some of the forms we use in appendixes J–L. In the same sense that training never ends for our tutors, evaluation is built in as a constant part of the learning process. Goal setting and feedback begin and end each tutoring session, individual or group, so that the purpose and results of each session are mutually understood and so that the student knows why he or she needs to come to the next session. Tutors collect written midterm feedback from their students using questions they write themselves or take from a list of those used by previous tutors. They are evaluated by each student at the end of the semester using a standard form. Every tutor receives comments from someone (senior tutor, supervisor, fellow tutors) on a videotape of his or her tutoring session, and the seminars and the open tutoring area provide many other opportunities for supervisors to gain a sense of each tutor's strengths and weaknesses. Many tutors write essays at the end of the semester, some of which you've read in this book, and that process involves bringing drafts to the seminar and getting feedback on both the content and the writing from fellow tutors. Tutors visit their students' instructors and compare notes on their different approaches. (For a full exploration of how tutors and instructors can work together, see the essay, "Teamwork," in chap. 1.) In a final conference with the supervisor, the tutor reviews all the written evaluations, and from a discussion of the tutor's strengths and weaknesses, the supervisor writes notes that go into the tutor's file. We hope that our evaluation procedures help us to be flexible in the way we respond to the fluctuating and changing needs of a diverse student population.

We have refined our selection, training, and evaluation methods over the years and have been rewarded with the marked successes of our tutors and their students. The students, as several studies and reports have shown, have not just persisted, they have excelled. Although it is difficult to know how much of this success is attributable to our tutoring, students keep telling us and their teachers and the administration that the SLC has made an important difference. Many of those tutored have in turn become tutors, and nearly all tutors claim the experience in our program has helped make them even better students and writers.

New Directions in Teaching Composition

We do have to be judicious about how much student success we attribute to the efforts of a tutor, because that tutor provides only one part of a student's educational experience. We also have to acknowledge that the improvements in tutor training over the last twenty years coincided with advances in the study and teaching of composition. A look at our syllabus in appendix F reveals the names of just a few of the many people we rely on, and the pages of our required textbook, *The Practical Tutor,* reveal even more. The very shape and direction of our syllabus and of *The Practical Tutor* reflect the new emphasis on process, revision, peer feedback, and the role culture plays in voice and communication. As instructors have embraced these principles in the classroom by using peer response groups, portfolio grading, and multicultural texts, the job of writing tutors has become more and more part of a joint effort between tutor, teacher, and student.

This larger revolution in the teaching of writing gives a different meaning to the old saw about the goal of tutoring—We want to work ourselves out of a job. When most writing and learning center professionals use this maxim, they mean that they want to teach individual students to grow out of dependence on the tutor, to become *independent* learners. But as long as we supervisors spend less time training tutors so that we can tutor the students our tutors don't have time for, we never will work ourselves out of a job in a larger sense, because for every student we succeed with another takes his or her place. We will never be able to serve all students, and each entering class brings us a new batch of potentially *dependent* learners. Do students in fact ever reach that vaunted state of independence, or is their dependence relative, shifting and changing in intensity according to the relationships they develop with different teachers and other students as they proceed toward a degree? Our job ought to be to help create situations in which students can become *interdependent* learners, fully enfranchised members of the academic community who share in the common processes of making knowledge enjoyed throughout that community. This democratic inclusion can happen only when students find classroom environments that welcome diversity and give every student the opportunity to fully and actively participate.

The Future

We are not working ourselves out of a job but into a new one, because our society is becoming more pluralistic, because a revolution has been taking place in the teaching of writing, and because in many schools around the country the classroom and the writing center are beginning to look more alike than different. Teachers and tutors are consulting more, joining hands of varied hues in mutually supportive activities, and learning from each other just as students are learning from each other. Knowledgeable tutors are making presentations to faculty groups, attending faculty symposia on multicultural and teaching issues, and publishing papers in national forums. Tutors and teachers are coming together to find ways to involve all students in collaborative classroom activities that are as responsive to individual needs and cultural differences as the writing center activities. The only way to work ourselves into this new job is to join with instructors in a lasting partnership that makes the goals of tutoring and teaching synonymous. Our challenge now is to find ways to be more and more effective in each other's environment.

As our college population increasingly reflects our nation's ethnic, cultural, and socioeconomic diversity, such cooperation between tutor and teacher becomes an urgent imperative. New voices are enriching our intellectual life, and nowhere is that more apparent than in academic support services. Many of these new student voices will eventually become teaching voices. For them to be heard, the university has to become a different place, a place where collaborative learning and cross-cultural understanding is the norm rather than the exception. That change is already happening at UC Berkeley and other schools, as students, tutors, and teachers of all colors join together in finding ways to value other voices.

Thom Hawkins

Student Learning Center Brochure

Student Learning Center

University of California at Berkeley
642-7332

Hours of Operation
Monday – Thursday 8am–6pm
Friday 8am–5pm

Special Programs

History 98: Ethnic Perspectives

History 98: Ethnic Perspectives is a course coordinated by students interested in searching for innovative approaches to historical studies. It is designed to provide a wide range of cultural and ethnic experiences that have been overlooked in traditional historical thought. Speakers are chosen who will expose lower division students to alternative and non-traditional approaches to history. The course is offered P/NP.

Each semester positions are available to students who want to become discussion group leaders for the course sections. For more information and an application, please see the receptionist in the Open Tutoring Area of the Golden Bear Center.

Other Voices Mentoring Program in English

This program supports the efforts of students of color who are considering or entering literary studies. We offer individual and small group tutoring and advising, and in the Spring semester coordinate English 97 (*Other Voices: Multicultural Literary Perspectives*). The program is geared towards students of color in sophomore level courses, but all students are welcome to participate.

Each semester positions are available for those students who wish to serve as mentors in the Other Voices program. For more information and an application, please see the receptionist in the Open Tutoring Area of the Golden Bear Center.

The Re-Entry Project

The Re-Entry project provides special services to undergraduates over the age of twenty-five, as well as to graduate students who are twenty-nine and older. Based on a collaborative learning philosophy, the program offers weekly workshops and programs designed to encourage students to work and study together. Other services include peer advising, advocacy, tutorial assistance and information and resource referrals. Work-Study and volunteer internships are available.

Graduate Student Support Service

Academic support assistance is provided to graduate students individually and in groups, as well as for graduate level classes. Graduate students seeking assistance with writing papers, organizing research and writing schedules, preparing for oral exams, preparing a dissertation proposal, or who have other academic concerns are welcome. Assistance is available on a drop-in basis or by appointment.

Tutor for Credit

Students may receive intensive training in collaborative learning and peer tutoring and earn two or more units of credit by tutoring fellow students in languages, mathematical sciences, sciences, social sciences, and writing courses. Applicants for tutorial positions should have strong backgrounds in the subject area(s) in which they wish to tutor.

The Student Learning Center

The Student Learning Center (SLC) is an academic support service of the University of California at Berkeley. The Center is open to all registered students at the University, and services are offered without fees. Over four thousand students utilize the Center each semester. Priority for services is given to:

- Freshmen
- Students who identify themselves as participating in the Educational Opportunity Program (EOP)
- Students who identify themselves as members of an Affirmative Action population (AA)
- Students repeating a course
- Disabled students
- Students with a written referral from an instructor or counselor.
- Students for whom English is a second language
- Re-Entry students

The Student Learning Center offers individual and group tutorial sessions in a number of lower division courses as well as a wide menu of challenging academic workshops and courses for credit. The Center is housed in the Golden Bear Center, located on Lower Sproul Plaza (642-7332).

Tutorial Services

A list of courses for which study groups are offered, as well as the dates and times of group meetings, is available from the receptionist in the Open Tutoring Area.

Languages
Individual assistance is available to students enrolled in lower division French, German and Spanish courses. Study groups are also available in lower division French and Spanish. Demand is high, so an early sign-up is important.

Mathematical Sciences
The SLC offers a wide range of study groups and drop-in assistance in the following areas:
Mathematics: Pre-calculus and first- and second-year calculus.
Statistics: Lower-division courses in the Department of Statistics; introductory quantitative methods courses in other departments.

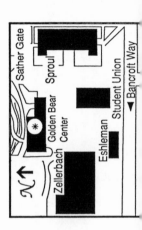

The Student Learning Center is conveniently located on Lower Sproul Plaza next to the ASUC.

Sciences
The SLC offers study groups and drop-in assistance in the following areas:
Chemistry: General chemistry; organic chemistry; introductory biochemistry
Biology: Introductory biology
Physics: Introductory courses

Social Sciences
Individual and small group assistance is available to students enrolled in lower division courses in the following areas: anthropology, business administration, economics, history, political science, psychology and sociology. Demand is high for assistance, so an early sign-up is important. Study groups, open to all students on a drop-in basis, are also available.

Writing
Individual and group assistance in the form of writing workshops is available for students enrolled in Subject A, SANSE (Subject A for Non-Native Speakers of English), and Reading & Composition 1A-1B courses. Demand is high, so an early sign-up is important. Writing Workshops require pre-enrollment prior to the start of the semester.

Courses for Credit

The Student Learning Center offers courses emphasizing strategies critical to academic success at Cal. Topics include: Writing and Public Speaking, Reading and Study Strategies, and Test Taking. Adjunct courses are offered in conjunction with large lower division lecture courses. For most adjunct courses, students must also be enrolled in the large lecture course. The Student Learning Center also offers courses not associated with a specific lecture. Students may earn 1-2 units of academic credit. Sections are taught by Student Learning Center professional staff and UC Berkeley graduate students. A complete schedule of courses is available each semester from the receptionist in the Open Tutoring Area.

APPENDIX C
Introduction to Tutorial Services in Writing

Dear Student,

Welcome to the Golden Bear Center. Like hundreds of other UCB students you've come here to improve your writing. Before you see a tutor, perhaps you'd like to know a little more about us. Writing tutors are students who have gone through a rigorous application and interview process, have been recommended by faculty members, and participate in an extensive training program run by experienced writing instructors. Most tutors are Juniors, Seniors, or Graduates from a wide variety of majors, and they tutor for academic credit, for pay, or as volunteers.

What can you expect from a tutor? Basically, you can expect friendly, competent help in learning skills that will improve your performance in all your writing assignments. A tutor will work with you while you prepare a paper for a course, or in between assignments on areas of writing in which you want to improve. A tutor may go over a returned paper with you, offering constructive suggestions so that you can make your next paper better. A tutor can teach you how to analyze an assignment, develop a strong thesis, organize your ideas, make good use of examples, improve your command of sentence structure, even how to enjoy your writing assignments. A tutor will work with you at your level and at your pace to help you meet the demands of academic writing and the standards of good, clear, concise prose. We'd like to help you write convincingly and in a style you'll be proud of.

What will a tutor expect from you? Conscientious effort is the main ingredient of a successful tutoring session. We've listed your responsibilities on the other side, and your tutor will expect that you've read this handout. Following these guidelines will give you the maximum benefit from our tutoring services. Good luck and have a great semester!

Sincerely,
The Writing Tutors and Staff

How to Get the Most Out of Tutoring

Keep Your Appointments

Your tutor will set up a schedule of weekly appointments with you. Most Subject A students meet twice a week with their tutor; 1A–B students usually meet once a week. Your tutor will do her best to accommodate changes in your schedule and to set up extra appointments when you need them. In turn, if you are going to be more than 5 minutes late or can't make it at all, please let her know as far in advance as possible.

Know Your Rights

1. You have a right to expect your tutor to arrive on time, to keep all scheduled appointments, and to give you his/her full attention for the time scheduled.
2. You have a right to change tutors if you are uncomfortable with the one to whom you have been assigned.
3. You have a right to confidentiality.

Come Prepared

1. Do whatever homework you have been assigned.
2. Bring all relevant assignments, papers, or books to your tutoring sessions.
3. Most important, come to your session with a clear sense of what *you* want to work on during that session.

Actively Participate in Your Tutoring Session

1. Be prepared to write—to take notes, to construct an outline, to revise a paragraph during the session. You will learn more from doing than just listening.
2. Talk! Keep up your end of the dialogue. This is *your* time to talk about *your* work. *Tutors will not do your thinking or your writing for you.*

Remember That Improvement Takes Time

Writing is a skill that improves with time and practice. Each exercise that you do, each conversation with your tutor will carry over into improvement on all your future writing assignments. Be patient with yourself and watch for the unexpected breakthroughs!

Cooperate with Your Tutor

Tutors know about many approaches to writing and many resources on campus that enhance learning. If you are open to their suggestions and are willing to try new techniques, you will be surprised at what you can accomplish. However, the tutor is not a miracle worker. In the final analysis it is your effort and willingness to work that will contribute the most to your success. As one student wrote when evaluating our service: "I expected to have the paper proofread or edited by some English scholar while I sat back; I was glad that I ended up going through the paper with the person who helped me. That way I learned something that I could use in my next writing assignment."

Applications: General, Writing, Information

UNIVERSITY OF CALIFORNIA
STUDENT LEARNING CENTER
198 GOLDEN BEAR CENTER

INSTRUCTIONS FOR GENERAL APPLICATION

Applications for the semester will be accepted until Wednesday of the second week of classes at 5:00 pm. Interviews and selection will be ongoing during the application period. The number of positions available is limited, so please submit your completed application in advance of the due date.

STEP 1: In addition to this general application, you must pick up a color-coded application and information packet:

Writing/NNS	Blue supplement
Ethnic Perspectives	Pink supplement
Other Voices	Purple supplement
Social Sciences	Yellow supplement
Math	Orange supplement
Languages	Brown supplement
Sciences	Goldenrod supplement
Statistics	Cherry supplement
Study Strategies	Green supplement
Bus Ad/Econ	Grey supplement

STEP 2: Before completing any of the application information, read the information packet for the subject area(s) for which you are applying. The information contained in these packets will acquaint you with specific information about our programs and should answer your questions about, among other things, the training you will receive and the commitment we will expect of you.

STEP 3: Once you have read the information packet, complete the general and supplemental applications. General applications, supplemental applications, and any work samples requested must be submitted at the same time to the receptionist in the Atrium. If you are applying to more than one subject area, you must photocopy the general application and return a copy with each supplement. Applications will be accepted until **5:00 pm on Wednesday of the second week of classes.**
A faculty recommendation is required for everyone tutoring at the Student Learning Center; however, you may submit your application and interview for a position before obtaining the necessary faculty signatures.

STEP 4: Once your application has been reviewed, we will contact you by telephone if we wish to schedule an interview. Therefore, your current telephone number and a schedule of times you are available are crucial.

APPLICANTS FOR *PAID* OR *CREDIT-BEARING* POSITIONS: SEE RESTRICTION PAGE 4

UNIVERSITY OF CALIFORNIA
STUDENT LEARNING CENTER
198 GOLDEN BEAR CENTER

GENERAL TUTOR APPLICATION

Name (print)_____Date_____

Local address_____
        address   city   zip

Telephone (   ) _____

Permanent address_____
              address   city   state   zip

Telephone (   ) _____

Subject area(s) in which you wish to tutor_____

Class standing -Fall 1992: ☐Freshman   ☐Sophomore ☐Jr.   ☐Sr.   ☐Grad.
☐ Non-student (Must have obtained bachelor's degree at time of application.)

Major/Department_____GPA in major____Overall GPA_____

Undergraduates: Expected date of graduation (month/year) _____

Ethnicity(for statistical purposes)_____EOP ☐Yes ☐No

Do you want to tutor for ☐academic credit ☐as a volunteer☐for pay? If you are
applying for a paid position, complete the information at the bottom of this page.

Transfer students: Name of previous institution_____
Number of semesters at UCB_____

How did you hear about the Student Learning Center? (Check all that apply.)
☐Daily Cal   ☐Flier   ☐Recruitment table on Sproul   ☐Class
announcement   ☐Previously received tutoring at SLC   ☐Current tutor at
SLC(name)_____☐Other_____

COMPLETE THIS SECTION ONLY IF YOU ARE APPLYING FOR A **PAID** POSITION:

How many semesters will you be available for work?_____

Are you eligible for work-study funds? ☐Yes☐No   If yes, amount_____

How many hours a week, on the average, can you work?_____

If we cannot offer you a paid position at this time, would you be willing to tutor for
☐academic credit or as a ☐volunteer? (If yes, check one.)

THANK YOU FOR YOUR INTEREST. BE SURE TO COMPLETE THE APPROPRIATE
COLOR-CODED SUPPLEMENTAL FORMS AND SUBMIT THEM WITH THIS
APPLICATION. YOU WILL BE CONTACTED BY TELEPHONE IF WE WANT TO
SCHEDULE AN INTERVIEW.   8/92

INTERVIEW SCHEDULE

Name_____ Telephone _____

Best time to call_____

	Monday	Tuesday	Wednesday	Thursday	Friday
8:00					
9:00					
10:00					
11:00					
12:00					
1:00					
2:00					
3:00					
4:00					
5:00					

Please X out times you are __NOT__ available for interviews.

PAID TUTOR POSITIONS:

1. Students may not be employed by the University more than 50% time during the fall spring semester in any combination of titles. Students may work up to 100% time during the summer (from the end of the spring semester to the beginning of the fall semester) and during the winter break.

2. Students employed as Tutors must have received a grade of "B" or higher in the course(s) they will tutor (or an equivalent or more advanced course) and must have a cumulative GPA of at least 3.0.

3. Students employed as Tutors (or any other academic title) can have no more than two incomplete grades.

4. Students on academic probation cannot be employed as Tutors (or in other academic titles)

TUTORING FOR ACADEMIC CREDIT:

Education 197: You must have completed 60 units and be an upper-division undergraduate with a strong academic background in the subjects you wish to tutor. You can enroll for 1-3 units a semester and repeat the course up to a total of 6 units.

Education 97: You must have completed fewer than 60 units and have a strong academic background in the subjects you wish to tutor.

English 310: You must have completed 60 units and be an upper-division undergraduate with strong writing skills. You can enroll for 1-3 units a semester and repeat the course up to a total of 6 units.

Math 301: You must have attained at least sophomore standing and have completed the Math 1A/1B series with a B- average or better.

Chemistry 301: You must have attained at least sophomore standing and have completed the Chemistry 1A/1B series with a B- average or better. You can enroll for 1-3 units a semester and repeat the course up to a total of 6 units.

Students tutoring for 3 units of academic credit in one course may count that 3 unit tutoring course for the Undergraduate Minor In Education 's Fieldwork in Education requirement.

VOLUNTEER POSITIONS

You must agree to tutor for the **entire semester** and attend required tutor training seminars.

UNIVERSITY OF CALIFORNIA
STUDENT LEARNING CENTER
198 GOLDEN BEAR CENTER

TO: ELLEN ROBERT, DIRECTOR

In my professional opinion, _____
name

has the academic background and knowledge necessary to tutor

students in_____.
subject/discipline

Additional comments would be helpful but are not required. *Thank you.*

SIGNED_____DATE_____

NAME (PRINT) _____

POSITION/TITLE_____

DEPARTMENT_____ TELEPHONE_____

8/92

Supplemental Application to Tutor Writing

How to Apply

Step 1   Read our introductory pamphlet attached to this supplement, "General Information for Prospective Writing Tutors," to become familiar with our goals, philosophy, and procedures.

Step 2   Fill out this supplemental application form and attach it to your completed "General Application to Tutor."

Step 3   Attach copies (not to be returned) of two recent samples of your best academic writing. Deliver your completed application to the receptionist in the Golden Bear Center.

Name _____ Date _____

How did you fulfill the writing requirement? (i.e., Sub A, 1A–B) _____

_____

_____

Complete the case study on the following pages.

Case Study

Please read the following case study carefully, and write a detailed response. Rely on common sense and common language. Keep in mind that there are no right answers, only more or less insightful ones.

Elizabeth Rodriguez has received failing grades on the four Subject A essays she has completed during her first month at UC. She has grown discouraged with her writing and begins to wonder whether she can succeed as a Cal student. You have discovered that she is reluctant to meet with a counselor or her instructor and that she finds the instructor's assignments boring and her marginal comments difficult to decipher.

You have met with Elizabeth twice before, and each time you have noticed that her reserve has prompted you to do most of the talking. You hope to encourage her to talk more this time.

When she arrives for her appointment, Elizabeth takes out a copy of the assignment, "What makes for a good essay," and the following response. She asks you to help her make this essay a passing one.

An Essay

The task to complete an understandable, smooth, well-constructed essay is very difficult but, it is an assignment that I hope to accomplish. In order to write an essay, there are three main ingredients needed: Introduction, body, and conclusion. A writer must use descriptive, well-constructed sentences to appeal and interest his reader. In order to write an understandable, informative essay the writer should choose a topic that is interesting to him. Generally, if he has an interest in the topic, he has a certain knowledge pertaining to the subject.

The introduction acquaints the reader with the idea of the essay. An introduction should be the most interesting paragraph. In order to captivate the reader's attention, the first sentence should be descriptive. The use of adjectives enhances the thought of the central idea. It is necessary to include two or three topics which will be explained in detail in the body of the paragraph. At the end of an introductory paragraph, a thesis must be written. A thesis makes a statement or postulate. In order to convince the statement to the reader, a writer must prove his point in the body of the essay.

The body of the paragraph supports the thesis statement. The body may be one to three paragraphs. Each paragraph must contain a topic sentence. A topic sentence states the main thought of each paragraph. In order to prove your theory, the writer will use facts. He will state opinions which will be based upon research and observation. By using examples to express the opinion or thought, the reader will be enabled to relate and understand the essay. Here are some examples: There are many appealing names of lipsticks: Toasted Almond, Cocoa, Cafe, Frosted Melon, etc.

The conclusion of a paragraph is a summary. It restates the topic sentences and thesis. Then the conclusion winds up the statements, theories, facts, and opinions on the previous paragraphs. It states the final outcome or finale of the body paragraphs: Due to these certain factors, the result is the thesis stated earlier.

In order to maintain the reader's interest, the essay should be concise. Although, the main idea should be developed with explicit detail. By using a forceful personal voice, the writer shows an interest. If the writer is fascinated with the topic, the reader will be intrigued. The achievement to write such an essay requires much discipline and practice. However, with much dedication and determination, it is feasible.

Answer questions in sections A and B below:

A. What is your assessment of the essay? Don't confine your response to sentence level problems; feel free to discuss the larger issues of thesis, organization, and development. What does the student need to work on? Is there something in the writer's process or are there any external factors that could be causing her writing problems?

_____

_____

_____

_____

_____

_____

_____

_____

_____

_____

_____

_____

_____

_____

_____

_____

_____

_____

(continue on next page)

B. Explain how you would structure an hour with Elizabeth. What activities would you engage this student in, and why?

_____

_____

_____

_____

_____

_____

_____

_____

_____

_____

_____

_____

_____

_____

_____

_____

_____

_____

_____

_____

_____

_____

_____

Student Learning Center
Golden Bear Center

General Information for Prospective Writing Tutors

Tutoring for English 310 Credit or as a Volunteer

In this course you will receive training and experience in tutoring college students in writing and/or literature courses. You will learn how to respond constructively to student writing, and you will develop and polish tutoring skills. By guiding others towards clarity and precision in prose, you will sharpen your own writing abilities. You will tutor in the Golden Bear Center under the supervision of an experienced writing instructor. In order to enroll, you should be a junior or senior who has a strong academic background and demonstrated writing competence. To earn three units (the course may be repeated for a total of six units) you are required to:

1. Spend four hours per week in individual tutoring.
2. Attend a weekly seminar and occasional training workshops.
3. Keep a journal of your tutoring experiences and write a final paper.
4. Read assigned articles, videotape your tutoring, and familiarize yourself with the resources available in the Golden Bear Center.

Note: This course is offered only on a Pass/Not Pass basis.

To the Volunteer

The exact nature of your contribution will depend on your experience, the amount of time you have available, and the needs of students. However, you will be asked to make a full commitment to at least 3 students for a minimum of 4 hours per week. You are also required to attend a weekly seminar, to keep a journal, and to meet other program requirements. Your work will be evaluated at the end of the semester. In return for satisfactory service, we will provide you with a suitable letter of recommendation.

Tutoring for Pay

Each semester there are a limited number of paid positions available. Preference is given to registered UCB juniors and seniors, to students with work/study eligibility, to those with successful records in English 310, and to previously employed tutors. *Students of color are encouraged to apply.* We also prefer hiring tutors who can commit themselves to tutoring for a minimum of one full academic year and who can work at least eight to fifteen hours per week. Paid staff are expected to fully involve themselves in the activities of the Student Learning Center, for they are the core of the tutorial program.

Qualifications

You must be proficient in your knowledge of writing and language to tutor students in Subject A and the Reading and Composition (1A–B) sequence.

Personal qualifications are as important as academic ones. Patience, ingenuity and the ability to get along with many different kinds of people are qualities that most of our tutors possess.

To All Prospective Writing Tutors

Welcome to the Student Learning Center in the Golden Bear Center! We're glad you're interested in becoming a writing tutor, and we appreciate the time and effort you put into the application process. To make this process quicker, we have compiled answers to questions frequently asked by prospective tutors. We recommend that you *read this packet* thoroughly before filling out the application.

Writing Program Staff: Anya Booker
Yvette Gullat
Melanie Hahn (ESL)
Thom Hawkins
Liz Keithley

Q: *Who will my students be?*

A: We enjoy a large ethnic and socio-economic diversity. Most students come to the Golden Bear Center voluntarily, although many students are referred by their instructors. Well over 50% of our tutees are enrolled in Subject A and most of the others are in the Reading and Composition 1A, 1B courses (English, Rhetoric, Comp. Lit., Ethnic Studies, etc.). Every tutor, therefore, tutors students in Subject A, but you will most likely have at least one student in 1A or 1B. Typically, by mid-semester most tutors have two to five regular tutees.

Q: *How will I be assigned students?*

A: You will be fully responsible for keeping an up-to-date appointment schedule at the reception counter in the Tutoring Area, and you will note on your schedule which courses you prefer to tutor. When a student comes in for the first time, a receptionist will look through the book of schedules for an available tutor in the appropriate course. Should you find that you can't help a particular student, you can talk with your supervisor about referring the student to another tutor or writing specialist.

Q: *Will I have to recruit students?*

A: There is generally no need to recruit, but you may be asked to call students or instructors.

Q: *How often will I see each student?*

A: Regularly scheduled one-hour sessions help tutees the most, and you will discover more about teaching and learning if you can follow the progress of individual students over a span of many weeks. Most students will benefit from one regular weekly appointment with you, but you should plan to see Subject A students two times a week. You are responsible for arranging regular weekly meeting times and making certain your student understands what "regular" means.

Q: *How long are tutoring sessions?*

A: The tutors' schedules are set up for hour-long appointments, and most tutors find that an hour is sufficient for the average student. Beyond that you will find your efficiency drops rapidly; one-to-one instruction can be a very demanding way to teach.

Q: *What can I do to prepare myself for my first student?*

A: To help put you on firm ground, your supervisor will give you essential reading material and may make recommendations for further reading. Our library and file cabinets contain many additional resources. Browse and be flexible in your reading. You might also get a lot out of spending some time hanging around the Golden Bear Center and casually listening to other tutors at work. Remember that you're not alone with your jitters, and make the effort to introduce yourself to the other tutors, both new and experienced. Before you see any student, you will have gone through a 2 hour training session where you'll be introduced to many of the techniques and principles that will enable you to tutor effectively. Also keep in mind that we admit students into the course only after we satisfy ourselves that the potential tutor has the necessary writing skills, personal qualities, and analytical abilities to competently help fellow students improve as writers. You have just passed a careful examination of your qualifications; feel confident that you can successfully meet the challenge of working with your first tutee.

Q: *What kind of training will I receive?*

A: Much of your training is "on-the-job"; in other words, you will be learning as much, if not more, from doing the actual tutoring as from our seminars and resource materials. However, we are concerned that you grow through your tutoring experience in the Student Learning Center, stretching your learning and writing skills and developing your knowledge, just as you in turn will expect your tutees to grow and learn. A great percentage of our time and energy in building this program is spent in providing tutors with outstanding resources and in offering each of you encouragement and support.

We will do our best in the interview to answer any question that this pamphlet has not dealt with, but there are certain questions which you will learn the answers to only through participating in our training program and making full use of the resources we offer you. Such questions as "What does a tutor do?" "Can I correct my student's paper?" "What shall I write in my journal?" "How can I be an effective tutor?" can be answered tentatively when you read the handouts in our resource file, peruse the essays of previous tutors, and talk with our professional staff, but will only be fully answered once you have tutored many hours, attended seminars, and received feedback on your videotapes and your journal.

In the seminars you will read and respond to student writing, study interpersonal skills that contribute to effective tutoring, and learn how to apply theories from the latest research on composing. You will be expected to do some outside reading and to write brief papers and reports.

Q: *What will my record-keeping responsibilities be?*

A: The Student Learning Center is a free service to registered Cal students, and it is supported in part by their money (education fees). Like any other campus agency, we must report exactly how our money is spent in order to receive continued funding. Thus, each tutor must report the number of hours he/she spends tutoring in the form of weekly time sheets. Tutors are also responsible for keeping personal records of instructors' office hours, students' phone numbers and of each student's academic progress.

Q: *How will I be evaluated?*

A: We will look chiefly at your work in the tutoring sessions, but we will also consider how well you utilized the support and resources made available to you and met the other program requirements. At the end of the semester you and your supervisor will fill out an evaluation form together.

Interview Format

I. Introductions and general information (five minutes)

Interviewers introduce themselves; speak about why we hold a group interview (found it creates a more relaxed atmosphere, brings forth more ideas, gives us a chance to see them interact with other people); and emphasize that they are not competing with one another.

II. Body of interview (forty to fifty minutes)

A. Experience and Philosophy (ten minutes)

We ask applicants to introduce themselves to the group and tell whatever they'd like about their major, interests, goals, etc. We ask why they want to tutor. We ask them to each talk about their experience teaching, if any, and their experience working on their own writing: what have they found to be the most important factor in someone improving his or her writing?

B. Case Study Discussion (twenty minutes)

For this part of the interview, we return the applications so that they can review the case study and their responses. We ask the applicants to discuss among themselves how they assess the essay (part A of the case study); we instruct them to try to pretend that the interviewers are not in the room and stress that they do not have to come to a consensus about the case study. After they discuss their assessment, we ask them to discuss how they would handle their next session with the student (part B of the case study).

C. Educational Opportunity Program and Affirmative Action (ten minutes)

We explain SLC's commitment to EOP and AA students; clarify if necessary the definitions and the nature of EOP and AA at UC Berkeley; and ask each applicant to share their experiences, observations, and thoughts regarding EOP and AA.

III. Wrap-up (five minutes)

We answer any questions about the particulars of the program: hours, procedures, training, etc. We emphasize the intense nature of commitment to this program. We check to see that they can, if accepted, make the initial training meeting. We let them know when they'll be notified (check phone numbers) and thank them for their interest in the program.

English 310 Syllabus and Reading List

English 310 Course Syllabus

English Department sponsor: Professor Donald McQuade
Student Learning Center tutor supervisors and course instructors: Thom Hawkins, Liz Keithley, Yvette Gullatt, and Anya Booker

Texts: Emily Meyer and Louise Smith, *The Practical Tutor;* English 310 reader (available from tutor supervisors); Phyllis Brooks, *Working in Subject A Courses* (available from tutor supervisors); Grammar handouts (distributed during seminars); Jackie Goldsby, *Peer Tutoring in Basic Writing: A Tutor's Journal*

Journals: Your supervisor will tell you the weekly due date for your journal.

Final paper: If you are taking this course for credit, you are required to write a four-page term paper. In the fifth week of the course, your supervisor will provide you with suggestions for topics you might consider exploring in your paper. A rough draft is due in seminar the thirteenth or fourteenth week. The final draft is due the last day of class or as indicated by your supervisor. If you plan to submit your 310 paper to our newsletter, *The Bear Facts,* an early draft will be due in the seventh week.

Week 1 and 2

Interviews: Ongoing

Writing assignment: Write a 500-word essay (about two pages, typed, double spaced) that analyzes your process of learning to write in the context of your introductory readings. Bring a rough draft of your essay when you meet with your senior tutor during the third week of classes. *Be sure your draft is rough, not finished.* In this meeting your senior tutor will model a tutorial by tutoring you using your draft as a paper in progress.

Reading assignments: *PT,* Chapters 1 and 2; Goldsby, "Teamwork"; Brooks, *Working in Subject A Courses;* "Keeping Your Journal"
These readings contain important concepts chosen to prepare you for your first tutoring session.

Half-hour orientation: Sign up for an orientation with a senior tutor. You will learn how to arrange your tutoring schedule and how to locate many useful resources in the Golden Bear Center as well as other information on the operation of the Student Learning Center and our tutoring program.

Two-hour training session: During this initial training session, you will examine the tutor's role, watch videotapes and live tutoring demonstrations, and analyze student writing. You will learn who your supervisor and senior tutor will be and to which seminar you have been assigned. This training seminar is mandatory for anyone who plans to tutor in the program.

Week 3

Tutoring begins: Schedule a tutorial with your senior tutor. Bring your rough draft of the writing assignment from Week 1.

Seminars begin

Seminar Overview: Attendance is mandatory. Each ninety-minute seminar allows time for discussion on a prearranged topic or topics. Tutors are expected to come to seminars having finished all reading assigned and to come prepared with questions about tutoring and samples of their students' writing. In these weekly seminars, you will have ample opportunity to talk with other tutors about what is going on in your tutoring sessions and about your students' writing.

Seminar topic: Overview of Subject A and Reading and Composition 1A/1B (also includes goal setting, dialogue, relations with instructors)

Reading assignment: Halpern, "Goal Setting for Writing Tutors," SLC tutor paper. Be sure you've read Goldsby and *PT.*

Initial conferences: Schedule a conference with your supervisor.

Week 4

Seminar topic: Composing process: prewriting strategies and writing block

Reading assignment: *PT,* Chapters 3 and 4; Karliner, "Collaborator or Evaluator?"; Rose, "Rigid Rules"

Week 5

Seminar topic: Composing process: drafting and reader response

Reading assignment: *PT,* Chapters 5 and 6; "Reader Response Sheet"; Student Paper; Rose, "Reclaiming the Classroom," from *Lives on the Boundary*

Week 6

Seminar topic: Composing process: revision

Reading assignment: Berry, "Fear of Failure"; Fiore, Chapters 1 and

2; Hawkins, "Intimacy and Audience"; Jordan, "Nobody Mean More to Me Than You and the Future Life of Willie Jordan"

Week 7

Seminar topic: Subject A instructor's visit; grammar self-test; Subject A marking system

Reading assignment: Subject A Department, "The Subject A Diagnostic Essay Exam"; Brooks, *Instructors' Guide to Marking Symbols and Grammatical Terms*

Videotaping: Make a videotape of a tutorial and watch it with your senior tutor. Complete this assignment no later than the ninth week. Keep your tape for viewing in seminar during the ninth week.

Midterm feedback: Have your students provide you with written comments on how the tutoring is going. Prepare your own forms and questions using handouts provided.

Midterm conferences: Schedule a conference with your supervisor. Be prepared to discuss your videotape and the videotape write-up by your senior tutor.

Week 8

Seminar topic: Grammar

Reading assignment: *PT,* Chapter 8; grammar self-test; Additional reading: *PT,* Chapters 9 and 10 and Clark, 55–77

Week 9–11

Videotaping: Watch videotapes of your tutorial sessions in seminar.

Seminar topic: Multicultural education: Myths and realities

Reading assignment: Pollitt, "Delusions of a Meritocracy"; Dean, "Multicultural Classrooms, Monocultural Teachers"; Mura, "Strangers in the Village"; Shen, "The Classroom and the Wider Culture: Identity as a Key to Learning English Composition"; Bernstein, "Academe and Orthodoxy"

Week 12

Seminar topic: Visit by a reading specialist

Reading assignment: *PT,* Chapters 11–12

Week 13

Seminar topic: Response to 310 papers, responding to advanced writing

Assignment: Drafts of 310 papers. Bring your rough draft with copies for each of the seminar members.

Week 14

Seminar topic: Response to 310 papers

Final evaluations: Distribute to your students the final evaluation forms, which they will use to assess your effectiveness.

Assignment: 310 papers; final evaluation instructions.

Week 15

Seminar topic: Summary of your tutoring experience

Reading assignment: Conroy, "Think About It"; Brown, "Teaching: Whatever Works"

Final conference: Both your supervisor and your senior tutor will want to schedule 30 to 60 minutes to spend wrapping up the semester.

Reading List

Required texts:

Goldsby, Jackie. *Peer Tutoring in Basic Writing: A Tutor's Journal.* Berkeley: University of California, Bay Area Writing Project, 1981.

Meyer, Emily, and Louise Z. Smith. *The Practical Tutor.* New York: Oxford University Press, 1987.

Other readings:

Beery, Richard G. "Fear of Failure in the Student Experience." *The Personnel and Guidance Journal,* December 1975, 191–203.

Brooks, Phyllis. *Working in Subject A Courses.* Berkeley: University of California, Subject A Department, 1990.

——. *Instructors' Guide to Marking Symbols and Grammatical Terms.* Berkeley: University of California, Subject A Department, 1977.

Clark, Beverly Lyon. *Talking About Writing: A Guide for Tutor and Teacher Conferences.* Ann Arbor: The University of Michigan Press, 1988.

Conroy, Frank. "Think About It: Ways We Know, and Don't." *Harper's Magazine,* November 1988, 68–71.

Dean, Terry. "Multicultural Classrooms, Monocultural Teachers." *College Composition and Communication* 40 (1989): 23–27.

Goldsby, Jackie. "Teamwork." Paper presented to Conference on College Composition and Communication, Annual Convention, San Francisco, 1982.

Hawkins, Thom. "Intimacy and Audience: The Relationship Between Revision and the Social Dimension of Peer Tutoring." *College English* 42 (1980): 64–69.

Jordan, June. "Nobody Mean More to Me Than You and the Future Life of Willie Jordan." *On Call*, 1985, 123–39.

Karliner, Adella. "Collaborator or Evaulator? The Role of the Instructor in the Individualized Writing Conference." University of California, San Diego, Muir Writing Program, 1979. Unpublished.

Mura, David. "Strangers in the Village." In *The Graywolf Annual Five: Multicultural Literacy,* edited by Rick Simonson and Scott Walker, 135–53. St. Paul, MN: Graywolf Press 1988.

Rose, Mike. "Rigid Rules, Inflexible Plans, and the Stifling of Language: A Cognitivist Analysis of Writer's Block." *College Composition and Communication* 31 (1980): 389–400.

Shen, Fan. "The Classroom and the Wider Culture: Identity as a Key to Learning English Composition." *College Composition and Communication* 40 (1989): 459–66.

Introducing Your Senior Tutor

First semester tutors like yourself are assigned a Senior Tutor who will be an important resource to you during the term. Supervisors try to be everywhere at once, but no one really expects them to and Senior Tutors provide a valuable additional source of wisdom and knowledge about tutoring. Get to know your Senior Tutor. A Senior Tutor is someone who has years of tutoring experience in both individual and small group tutorials, and who has been selected from among his/her peers for his/her outstanding tutoring skills and leadership qualities.

The primary role of your Senior Tutor is to be there for you whenever you want to sit down and talk about your tutoring or your students or your writing. It is important that you know each other's phone numbers and schedules so that you can keep in touch.

You will probably be bumping into your Senior Tutor around the Student Learning Center, and he/she can help you get acquainted with the tutors and staff. There are a lot of materials and activities to support you in your tutoring, but the people in the Student Learning Center—tutors, receptionists, supervisors—represent your most valuable resource for ideas and suggestions that will help you realize your full potential as a tutor.

Most of your contact will be pretty informal, but there are some structured meetings that everyone is required to make.

Videotape

In the fourth week of your tutoring you will record one of your tutoring sessions and watch the tape with your Senior Tutor. He/she will talk with you about the tape, discuss tutoring strategies, and write a summary of the tape and your discussion. The written summary provides you and your supervisor with a record of the taping experience.

Opening and Closing Conferences

1st Week—Meet for one hour to get acquainted and be tutored.
Mid-semester—Half hour to check in on your students' progress.
Last Week—Sum up the semester.

Journals

Once, during the semester, you will turn your journal in to your Senior Tutor instead of your supervisor. He/she will read it and make written comments.

We encourage you to take an active role in establishing a productive relationship with your Senior Tutor.

Keeping Your Journal

1. Your weekly entries should be at least one full page in length. Your journal should be of a size that will fit into your mailbox; a spiral standard size notebook is best. All entries should be turned in each week.
2. Each entry should include your student's name, course, instructor, and date of session.
3. Your entries should consist of the following: an overview of each session, details of the session, and reflection on the session or on tutoring. These elements do not have to be in any particular order, but should be present in each entry. You are free to use any writing style you like.
4. Avoid using vague phrases such as *we worked on . . . we came up with . . . we discussed . . .* etc. Be very specific when writing about your sessions.
5. At least one entry must be about your visit to a student's instructor.

Your journal is due weekly on _____ by

_____ .

Your journal will be returned to you each week on _____

_____ .

Happy tutoring!

Videotaping

1. Plan to videotape as early in the semester as possible; you *must* video-tape before the 9th week of classes. Taping is intended to help you in your work with your student and your skills as a tutor; the sooner you make the tape the sooner you can apply what you learn from it.
2. Schedule yourself on the "Taping" schedule in Room 173 for the hour you plan to videotape. The schedule fills up fast, so do this as soon as you think you know which session you want to videotape.
3. Check out a tape from the front desk, and follow the instructions posted in the videotaping area. You may want to arrive a few minutes early so that you can get everything set up before your student arrives. Ask your supervisor or a Sr. Tutor to check to see that the equipment is set up correctly. (Sitting down later to watch a blank or soundless tape is not much fun!)
4. After you've finished your masterpiece, schedule a time on the "Play-back" schedule to watch it with your Sr. Tutor. *Do not* turn the tape in. Keep it to watch by yourself and with your Sr. Tutor, and possibly to show cuts of in seminar.

Possible Questions for Midterm Feedback

Tutors: Please consider these questions when formulating your midterm feedback questions for your students. You are free to select questions from these possibilities or to write your own. Be sure to obtain written midterm feedback from each of your students. Hang on to the responses; you will turn them in at the end of the semester.

Please describe what we have done to establish long- and short-term goals (i.e., discussing things to work on during the whole semester as well as things to work on at the next meeting).

How have we met the goals we set?

In what ways do we work on what you need to work on?

Describe your role in organizing our meeting time.

How would you like to change our sessions?

What do you feel has been most helpful about tutoring?

What has been least helpful about tutoring?

Why did you come to today's tutorial session?

Which has been your favorite tutorial session or part of a session so far and why?

Which has been your least favorite? Why?

Please describe things that you do differently as a writer that you have learned in our tutorials.

How directive am I with my questions and comments?

Do you have plenty of time to think about and then answer the questions that come up?

What would you like to concentrate on in the tutorials for the remainder of the semester?

How would you describe the communication between us?

If you were explaining tutoring to someone who hadn't been tutored, how would you characterize the tutor's role? How would you characterize your role?

How do you feel before the tutoring sessions?

How do you feel about your writing at this point?

What have you learned about writing so far?

How have your writing goals changed since the beginning of the semester?

Do you have any problems getting along with me? Do you feel you could talk with me if you do/did have problems relating to tutoring or complaints about our sessions?

Do you have any additional comments or thoughts about tutoring?

Evaluation of Individual Tutoring: Writing

Please do not sign this form. Be as specific as possible. When you have completed this form, fold it and put it in the envelope labelled "Writing Tutor Evaluations" at the reception desk.

I was tutored in _____ by _____
                           (course)   (tutor's name)

_____ .

I met with my tutor _____ times during the semester.

Semester/Year _____ .

Please list the two or three most important things you learned from your tutor:

1.

2.

3.

What did you like most about your tutor and your tutoring sessions?

What would you recommend that your tutor do to improve?

My tutor:

Knew what I needed to work on	1 2 3 4 5 (always)
Asked questions that stimulated my thinking	1 2 3 4 5 (always)
Listened carefully	1 2 3 4 5 (always)
Explained things clearly	1 2 3 4 5 (always)

Explained things clearly   1   2   3   4   5 (always)

Cared about me and my progress   1   2   3   4   5 (always)

How would you rate the overall effectiveness of your tutor? (Circle one)

Excellent   Good   Average   Fair   Poor

Thank you for helping us improve the quality of our services!

Evaluation of Writing Workshops

Workshop Leader: _____ Course: _____

Date:_____

PART I

How often did you attend workshop meetings? (circle one)
Most of the time (80–100%)   Sometimes (40–80%)   Rarely (less than 40%)
In your writing workshops do you . . . (Place an "X" at the appropriate place on the line.)

Find other workshop members
  helpful . . . .

	1	2	3	4	5
	never		sometimes		always

Intitiate topics for discussion 1   2   3   4   5

	never		sometimes		always

Respond to other students 1   2   3   4   5

	never		sometimes		always

Come prepared 1   2   3   4   5

	never		sometimes		always

What did you like best about the workshop?

Could you have improved your participation in the workshop? How?

PART II

Please list two or three ways you think the workshop could be improved:

1.

2.

3.

Please list the two or three most important things you learned in workshop this semester:

1.

2.

3.

Please rate the workshop by circling one of the following:

1	2	3	4	5
Poor	Fair	Good	Superior	Outstanding

PART III
Does your workshop leader . . . (Place an "X" at the appropriate place on the line.)

Care about the people in the work-shop and their writing difficulties

1	2	3	4	5
not at all		somewhat		very much

Explain things clearly . . . .

1	2	3	4	5
never		somewhat		always

Organize workshop time effectively

1	2	3	4	5
never		somewhat		always

Listen carefully . . . .

1	2	3	4	5
never		somewhat		always

Allow time for you to think . . . .

1	2	3	4	5
never		somewhat		always

Ask questions that stimulate your thinking . . . .

1	2	3	4	5
never		somewhat		always

Please list two or three ways you think your workshop leader could improve:

1.

2.

3.

Please list two or three things you liked best about your workshop leader:

1.

2.

3.

Please rate your workshop leader by circling one of the following:

1	2	3	4	5
Poor	Fair	Good	Superior	Outstanding

Anything else we should know?

Personal Checklist of Tutoring Skills

Listening

	Infrequently	Sometimes	Most of the time

I try to be an *attentive listener* by practicing the following techniques:

1. I show that I am interested in what the student is saying by:

	Infrequently	Sometimes	Most of the time
a. Making regular eye contact.	1	2	3
b. Smiling, nodding, and making other gestures that signal my concentration and receptiveness.	1	2	3
c. Leaning forward in interest, undistracted by anything else.	1	2	3
d. Sitting beside the student, not hiding behind a desk or table.	1	2	3
2. I avoid interrupting, even for the purposes of clarification, until a student has completed her message.	1	2	3
3. In order to indicate trust in the tutee's abilities to make thoughtful judgments, I allow a period of calm silence (wait time) after a student has apparently finished talking. In this way I can avoid cutting off a tutee's statements, and provide enough time for reflection and self-criticism.	1	2	3

4. I give my full attention to what the student is saying by:

	Infrequently	Sometimes	Most of the time
a. Taking notice of how he is delivering his message, including noverbal cues.	1	2	3
b. Thinking chiefly about what he is saying, not reveling in my own thoughts on the topic or planning my next brilliant statement.	1	2	3
c. Framing my response in the context of the student's experience, whenever possible.	1	2	3

	Infre-quently	Some-times	Most of the time
d. Yet sharing my own experiences with writing, to show the student that he is not alone.	1	2	3
5. I encourage a student to answer her own questions, or at least to try to answer them.	1	2	3
6. To check my understanding of what the student has said, I briefly paraphrase the tutee's idea(s) in my own words.	1	2	3
7. Using the following techniques, I ask questions in a manner that stimulates thinking and reveals a student's strengths and weaknesses:			
a. I avoid verbosity and make my questions brief but specific.	1	2	3
b. I don't overwhelm my student with too many questions.	1	2	3
c. On the average, I wait more than five seconds between asking a question and saying something myself.	1	2	3
d. I avoid answering my own questions.	1	2	3
e. I try to ask open-ended questions, sometimes directive (Socratic) and sometimes nondirective (discovery)—not questions that require simple "yes" or "no" answers.	1	2	3
f. The intention of my questions is to enlighten, not to intimidate.	1	2	3

	Infre-quently	Some-times	Most of the time
Explaining			

I try to give *clear explanations* by practicing the following techniques:

	Infre-quently	Some-times	Most of the time
1. Since I don't want to do all the talking (or the work!), I give short explanations with appropriate examples or demonstrations.	1	2	3
2. I ask the student to perform a task that will help me measure his grasp of the concept or skill.	1	2	3
3. In addition to giving my own examples, I also ask students to provide examples after they have understood my explanation.	1	2	3
4. Although I sometimes share my experiences with the student, I am cautious about insisting on approaches based on my own experience because I am aware that the student's background may be different from mine.	1	2	3
5. I observe the student's learning habits and structure my teaching approach to her needs.	1	2	3
6. Whenever possible I model a useful behavior rather than give a long explanation.	1	2	3
7. When it comes to learning/ teaching, I am suspicious of all panaceas and flat "yes" or "no" answers.	1	2	3

	Infre-quently	Some-times	Most of the time
8. Once I identify a tutee's typical learning style, I point out his strengths and weaknesses in the hope that the student will become more aware of how he learns best.	1	2	3
9. I delay my correction of a "wrong answer" so that I can first question my own preconceptions. (There may be another way that I've never considered to look at the issue, and it may be more important for me to understand *why* a student answered the way she did. Sometimes, with enough wait time, a student may self-correct.)	1	2	3

Summary

	Infre-quently	Some-times	Most of the time
1. I try to make each tutoring session a joint effort with at least 50 percent of the work coming from the student.	1	2	3
2. I try to make sure the student has as much or even more access to the paper we are discussing and the pen or pencil.	1	2	3
3. I find out what the student already knows, I discover what she needs to know, and then I show her how to learn what she needs to know in a way that best suits her individual learning style.	1	2	3
4. I try to concentrate on real learning and self-improvement, not just on earning better grades. (I am aware that certain types of growth are not measured by grades.)	1	2	3

Thom Hawkins, University of California, Berkeley, © 1978.

ENROLL NOW!
SPACE IS LIMITED!

HOW TO ENROLL

Deadlines for enrolling are concurrent with class registration deadlines.

1) Pick up a workshop enrollment form at the reception desk in the main tutoring area of the Student Learning Center. This form will list both class and workshop times and will let you know how to use Tele-BEARS to enroll in workshop sections.

2) Read and complete the form. It contains valuable information about the workshops and your responsibility as a student participant.

3) See the Administrative Assistant in the Student Learning Center to schedule an appointment for your enrollment in a workshop. Bring your registration forms and your workshop enrollment form to this appointment. When you are admitted to a workshop section, you will receive a Course Entry Code (CEC) that will allow you to enroll through Tele-BEARS.

ENROLL IN A WRITING WORKSHOP!

*I know the workshop was the reason I got such a good grade in my 1A class.
(Daphne O. sophomore)*

*African American Studies 1A and 1B
Chicano Studies 1A and 1B
College Writing 1A (satisfies both Subject A and 1A)
English 1A and 1B
Native American Studies 1A and 1B*

**UNIVERSITY OF CALIFORNIA AT BERKELEY
STUDENT LEARNING CENTER
642-7332**

ABOUT WRITING WORKSHOPS

The writing workshop provides the resources that you can use to strengthen and improve your writing skills. In the workshop you will collaborate with other students and learn techniques for mastering college-level work. Workshops offer a cooperative, supportive environment in which you can experiment with new approaches to your writing. Your participation will help deepen your understanding of all that goes into good writing.

THE ADVANTAGES

✐ participate in small groups (no more than 8 students per workshop)

✐ learn together with other students

✐ work with trained group leaders

✐ decide how and what you learn

✐ explore topics of your choice in depth

✐ develop your leadership skills in a supportive environment

✐ improve your course grade

My best students are in writing workshops.
(Kim D., instructor, English 1A-1B)

WORKSHOP STRUCTURE

Each 1A and 1B writing workshop consists of up to 8 students from the same class. Each College Writing 1A workshop will be composed of 6 students from different sections. Priority for workshop enrollment is given to EOP and AA students but all students are encouraged to apply. Each workshop is led by a trained group leader and meets for two one-hour sessions on a weekly basis.

The workshop focuses on writing as a process that involves

✐ reading and comprehension skills

✐ pre-writing techniques

✐ organization of material

✐ revision

✐ constructive peer response to your writing

✐ developing your self-confidence

You will learn techniques to strengthen

✐ essay structure and style

✐ grammar

✐ time management

✐ critical thinking skills

My writing workshop discussions help me to think more analytically and that makes me a better writer.
(Eliza P., sophomore)

YOUR COMMITMENT

Because the workshops are collaborative, student participants set the pace and control the agenda. Workshops sessions are frequently dedicated to looking at papers written by student workshop members. At other times, workshops spend time discussing paper topics in order to help students develop their ideas. Workshops are effective only when students commit to

✐ regular attendance at two one-hour sessions each week

✐ active participation in the workshop

✐ development of cooperative learning skills

My workshop was small enough that by the end of the semester we were all good friends.
(Angel V., freshman)

The Student Learning Center offers workshops for a variety of departments. The departments currently represented are: African American Studies, Chicano Studies, English, Native American Studies, and the College Writing Program (satisfies both Subject A and 1A).

I wish my entire class could be in a writing workshop.
(Myrtha C., Instructor, Chicano Studies 1A-1B)

Introduction to Writing Workshops

Dear Student,

You will probably find that a Writing Workshop is unlike any class you've ever participated in. The Workshop allows you and the other members to learn from each other rather than from a professor; the Workshop leader will guide rather than teach. The emphasis will be on cooperation, not competition, as you work together to develop your skills as writers and critical thinkers. You can expect to do a lot of talking and to get to know your fellow Workshop members well. These fellow Workshop members will become valuable resources to you as you learn to work together as a group.

The Workshop is also likely to differ in some ways from other Student Learning Center workshops in subjects such as math and chemistry. You will discuss your readings and paper topics in an atmosphere that encourages you to experiment with your ideas before you start writing. Once you start writing, you will learn how to revise early drafts by trying them out on your Workshop group. You will read your draft aloud and receive helpful suggestions and support from your peers and the Workshop Leader. In turn, you will listen while other members of the group read drafts of their papers, and you will offer constructive verbal comments using a method of response introduced by the Workshop leader. This is a new process for most students, and it takes some practice to learn how to benefit from it. The rewards are great, but you must attend regularly, come prepared, and participate fully in group discussions and decisions.

No Workshop will succeed without this full commitment from all its members. This is your Workshop, not the leader's. It is your energy and enthusiasm that will create the opportunity to learn. Therefore, we ask you to carefully read and follow the instructions on the following page and to be fully aware of the commitment you are making before you sign and submit the pre-enrollment application. Signing the application is your contract with us and your agreement to forfeit individual writing tutoring during the semester if you stop attending Workshops regularly without consulting with your Workshop leader. This penalty will be stringently enforced because many more students sign up for Workshops than we can accommodate. We don't want to turn people away who really want to participate, only to find that some of those who did sign up had no intention of doing the work.

Hundreds of students have participated in these workshops since they began in 1980. They have learned that by helping others with their writing they are helping themselves to become better writers. It makes sense to talk with each other about your writing, because communication is what writing is all about—getting your message across to an audience. We look forward to seeing you.

Sincerely,
The Workshop Leaders

Writing Workshop: Authors' Guidelines, Readers' Guidelines, Reader Response Model

1. You will benefit the most from the workshop if you come prepared with a *complete* first draft (intro, thesis, body, conclusion).
2. Your readers' comments will be more specific and precise if you provide them with Xerox copies of your complete draft.
3. Briefly introduce your essay by noting the improvements you wish to make over your previous papers (you're working on paragraph structure, you want to vary your sentence patterns, etc.), but refrain from making apologies or self-criticisms.
4. Read your paper aloud, *slowly*, without interruption.
5. Ask readers open-ended questions (see below).
6. Take notes based on your readers' comments.
7. In general, remain silent and listen to your readers. Don't defend your paper.

Some Questions for Writers to Ask

Questions like these help focus the discussion so that you can learn what effect your writing has had on readers. Don't subvert your readers' opinions by loading the questions: "I know my thesis doesn't make sense, but what do you think?" Avoid making any statement that will prejudice your reader either for or against your paper.

1. What does my writing say to you? How do you react to it? Why does it affect you the way that it does?
2. Do you see a form to my essay? Can you describe it? Can you see parts, divisions? What does each part do? Do the parts create a movement?
3. Were you surprised by anything you read?
4. What is the strongest feature of my writing? What is the weakest feature?
5. Is this a subject or issue that you find interesting? Are you entertained, irritated, or bored? Do you agree or disagree with my point of view? Do you think I have done justice to my subject?
6. Did any parts of my writing jump out at you as you read? What do you think made them jump out at you?
7. Did you notice any distracting mechanical errors?
8. Would you like to tell me anything else about your experience of reading my writing?
9. Do you want to ask me about anything?

Some of the above questions were adapted from the article, "Peer Response: Feedback Script," by Wendy Lapidus-Saltz (*The Writing Instructor*, Fall 1981, 19–25).
Copyright, 1982—Thom Hawkins

Readers' Guidelines for Writing Workshops

1. Hold your comments until the author has finished reading the paper aloud.
2. Take notes and mark your copy while the author is reading so that later you will be able to refer to specific parts of the essay when you talk to the author. A simple check in the margin or a circle around a passage will be enough to bring your attention back to something you wanted to comment on.
3. Address your comments directly to the author and take responsibility for your opinions. Look at the author and say, "*I* don't understand what *you* are trying to do in the second paragraph." Don't look at someone else and say, "He doesn't seem to have a point to his second paragraph."
4. Work at giving tactful, sympathetic criticism, both positive and negative, but be demanding enough to help the author improve. Be honest, thorough, and respectful. Your group should be cooperative, not competitive. Remember that you hope other critics will put just as much effort and concern into responding to your work, so try to be as helpful and useful as possible.
5. The order of your response should move from large issues, such as content (subject or idea), thesis, organization, unity, coherence, and logic, to smaller issues, such as paragraph structure, sentence structure, grammar, and spelling. In other words, first ask yourself these questions: "Is this an essay?" "Does it hold together?" Then move on to questions like: "Do the paragraphs and sentences work?" "Are there mechanical errors?" If you reverse the order of these questions, you may find yourself suggesting corrections to paragraphs and sentences that will have to be deleted in the second draft.
6. The content of your responses should move from supportive, positive comments about the strengths of the essay to constructive criticisms of weaknesses and to suggestions for improvement. Make sure the author knows what you think she is doing well before you tell her what should be changed.
7. The way to make your comments supportive and constructive is to be as specific as possible. *Point* to the exact *place* in the essay that you like or dislike, and try to say exactly *why* it works or doesn't work.
8. Ask the author for her comments on your responses to her essay. Find out which responses were the most helpful, which the least helpful.

READER RESPONSE MODEL

I.

WHAT IS BEING SAID? *CONTENT & IDEAS* YOUR REACTION,
FEELINGS, OPINIONS,
ASSOCIATIONS. DO YOU AGREE OR DISAGREE? FURTHER THOUGHTS
ON THE SUBJECT. ARE YOU INTERESTED, EXCITED,
OR BORED WITH THE SUBJECT?

II.

ESSAY STRUCTURE *THESIS* ORGANIZATION *LOGIC*
DEVELOPMENT PARAGRAPH STRUCTURE

Strengths → Improvement

III.

SENTENCE STRUCTURE GRAMMAR, STYLE,
PUNCTUATION, VOCABULARY

Strengths → Improvement

"No Sweat Writing"

No Sweat Writing

It's four o'clock in the morning and you're on your fourth pizza, your fourteenth cup of coffee, and your fortieth No Doz, and the page in front of you is still blank. You're beginning to hate yourself for not starting the paper four weeks ago when it was first announced. But that doesn't help: the page in front of you is still blank, and the paper is still due tomorrow morning.

Does this sound familiar? If it does, it's not surprising because most of us find that one of the most difficult things about composing an essay is *beginning.* Our fears of writing seem to prevent us from being able to put pen to paper. However, these fears can be resolved through the use of simple techniques which represent a more relaxed and productive way of thinking about the writing process.

There are many types of fear which confront the writer. Probably one of the most basic is the simple fear of blankness, the fear that you will never have anything to say about the subject. Assigned to write a paper about your favorite subject, for example, music, you go home and sit at your desk only to find that you can't even think of the name of your favorite song. (Nor does it occur to you that your own background in music, your own tastes and interests, could be relevant.) Thus, you continue to stare at a blank page. Equally paralyzing is having an overabundance of ideas. You may have so many things to say about your subject that all your ideas seem to be a jumble. You don't know where to begin; or you become convinced that you have so much to talk about that you can't possibly fit it all into one essay. In a case like this, you may be inclined to give up before you begin.

Although these two fears may sound like opposites, they are actually caused by the same thing. Most of us are afraid to put down words on paper. We think that once we write something down, we are committed to it, and there is no opportunity for future change or improvement. It seems permanent in a way that an oral statement does not. Once we write something down, moreover, we feel that it is exposed to public view and therefore to criticism from outsiders. We feel vulnerable because our thoughts are nakedly exposed to the world, instead of protected within our minds. Perhaps it is because we regard writing as simultaneously permanent and public that we all need to take the written word more seriously than the oral statement. Because it is in print, it is there to be looked at again and again, and we expect that people are going to evaluate it and reevaluate it. It's no wonder, then, that we find it hard to write.

However, while our fears may seem insurmountable, there are ways of

---

Handout from the Writing Center, Assumption College, Worchester, Mass.

resolving them. We must get rid of our old idea of writing as something which necessarily involves sitting at a desk and seating uncomfortably, and develop a new idea of writing as something which is the outgrowth of relaxed, creative moments. But considering these fears, how do we allow such moments to happen? We can do this by understanding writing as a process, as something which can and should be done as a series of manageable steps rather than all at once.

The first step may involve simply mulling over your ideas. It's important to recognize that there is a necessary period which comes *before* writing, when you develop your thoughts on your subject. This isn't procrastination, because you are actually thinking about what you may write rather than trying to escape from your work. You may find it difficult, of course, to feel relaxed enough to let your mind work efficiently. If this is the case, try taking a walk while you think about what you want to write, or talking to your friends about your subject. If it makes you more comfortable, you can jot down the ideas that come to you. However, don't try to explain them or put them in order, just make a list.

The next thing you can try is drafting your ideas on paper. Don't worry about matters such as technique or organization at this point. Try writing anything that comes to your mind, just discussing each idea as if you were talking to a friend. You may even want to try setting a time limit: tell yourself that you're just going to write down anything that comes to your mind during a given time period. Keep writing and don't stop until your time is up. The important thing during the drafting phase is to realize that you're actually making progress even though your material is not in its final form—you're getting your thoughts down on paper.

Now that your ideas have been put down in a rough draft form, the next thing you will probably want to do is to focus. In other words, you have probably collected a real assortment of points on your subject and you will need to decide how to narrow your analysis. One way to do this is to look at the draft you have produced during the "free-writing" period and underline each point you have raised. By reviewing this sequence of ideas, you may be able to notice a pattern: Do several of the issues seem to have some connection to one another? By putting them together into an essay, could you arrive at a meaningful conclusion? If so, you have found a basic outline for your paper. Alternatively, you could go over your array of ideas and choose the one that seems most significant, or the one you feel you have the most to say about. Then you can write a paragraph in which you state and fully explain this idea, going as much as possible into what it means or why it is important. Use examples or other evidence to support your point if you have them available. Once you have completed this point, you can go back to your free-writing to see what other ideas emerged there which might be connected to your point. In this way, you could use the point you are most comfortable with to find a general direction for your essay.

Of course, you don't need to follow these steps when writing; you can and should feel free to invent your own approach to the writing process. If you find that taking long walks doesn't allow you to relax and generate ideas but that doing the backstroke in a vat of warm Crisco does, then it's your duty to go out and buy the Crisco. The main thing is to find an alternative to the old idea of writing as sweating. In general, a constructive (rather than destructive) approach involves several requirements. It's necessary that you refrain from criticizing yourself each step of the way. It is especially important to give yourself time off from criticism during the early phases of writing because the most crucial thing is to get your ideas to flow. Once you have something down on paper you will have plenty of time to select, revise, develop, arrange, and rearrange. Nothing has to be permanent just because it's down on paper. (It's just a word; it can't hurt you.) Remember, too, that in writing you only need to do one step at a time—and some steps may involve just sitting in a comfortable place and thinking.

So why not invent a writing process that works for you? Invent one that is relaxing, non-critical, and takes things one step at a time, and instead of wasting your money on coffee, pizza, No Doz, and Pepto Bismol, you could be enjoying yourself and getting more done.

break the silence

TUTOR WRITING

*opportunities to meet and work with instructors
and make departmental contacts
*improve your writing
*improve your ability to construct arguments, think
critically, and explain your ideas to peers
*participate in a diverse community of writers and
educators

volunteer or earn English 310 credit

1-3 UNITS

FOR MORE INFORMATION
STUDENT LEARNING CENTER
OPEN TUTORING AREA
THE GOLDEN BEAR CENTER
642-7332

Works Cited

Beery, Richard G. "Fear of Failure in the Student Experience." *The Personnel and Guidance Journal*, December 1975, 191–203.

Brooks, Phyllis. *Instructors' Guide to Marking Symbols and Grammatical Terms*. Berkeley: University of California, Subject A Department, 1977.

———. *Working in Subject A Courses*. Berkeley: University of California, Subject A Department, 1990.

Clark, Beverly Lyon. *Talking about Writing: A Guide for Tutor and Teacher Conferences*. Ann Arbor: University of Michigan Press, 1988.

Flower, Linda. "Writer-Based Prose: A Cognitive Basis for Problems in Writing." *College English* 41 (1979): 19–37.

Flower, Linda, and John R. Hayes. "A Cognitive Process Theory of Writing." *College Composition and Communication* 32 (1981): 365–87.

Goldsby, Jackie. *Peer Tutoring in Basic Writing: A Tutor's Journal*. Berkeley: University of California, Bay Area Writing Project, 1981.

———. "Teamwork." Paper presented to Conference on College Composition and Communication, Annual Convention, San Francisco, 1982.

Hawkins, Thomas. "Intimacy and Audience: The Relationship Between Revision and the Social Dimension of Peer Tutoring." *College English* 42 (1980): 64–69.

Karliner, Adella. "Collaborator or Evaluator? The Role of the Instructor in the Individualized Writing Conference." Unpublished paper, Muir Writing Program, University of California, San Diego, 1979.

McKeachie, Wilbert J. "Research on College Teaching: The Historical Background." *Journal of Educational Psychology* 82, no. 2 (1990): 189–200.

Meyer, Emily, and Louise Z. Smith. *The Practical Tutor*. New York: Oxford University Press, 1987.

Murray, Donald M. *The Craft of Revision*. Fort Worth: Holt, Rinehart, and Winston, Inc., 1991.

North, Stephen M. "The Idea of a Writing Center." *College English* 46 (1984): 433–46.

Rodriguez, Richard. *Hunger of Memory: The Autobiography of Richard Rodriguez*. South Holland, IL: Bantam Book, 1983.

Sommers, Nancy. "Revision Strategies of Student Writers and Experienced Adult Writers." *College Composition and Communication* 31 (1980): 378–88.

Further Reading

Brooks, Phyllis, and Thom Hawkins, eds. *Improving Writing Skills.* New Directions for College Learning Assistance, no. 3. San Francisco: Jossey-Bass, 1981.

Bruffee, Kenneth. "Collaborative Learning and the 'Conversation of Mankind.'" *College English* 46 (1984): 635–52.

Clark, Irene Lurkis. "Collaboration and Ethics in Writing Center Pedagogy." *The Writing Center Journal* 9, no. 1 (1988): 3–13.

———. *Writing in the Center.* Dubuque, IA: Kendall Hunt, 1985.

Ede, Lisa. "Writing as a Social Process." *The Writing Center Journal* 9, no. 2 (1990): 3–15.

Harris, Muriel, ed. *Tutoring Writing: A Sourcebook for Writing Labs.* Glenview, IL: Scott, Foresman, 1982.

Hawkins, Thom. "Training Peer Tutors in the Art of Teaching." *College English* 40 (1978): 440–49.

Lichtenstein, Gary. "Ethics of Peer Tutoring in Writing." *Writing Center Journal* 4, no. 1 (1983): 29–34.

Maxwell, Martha. *Improving Student Learning Skills: A Comprehensive Guide to Successful Practices and Programs for Increasing the Performance of Underprepared Students.* San Francisco: Jossey Bass, 1979.

McKeachie, Wilbert J. "Research on College Teaching: The Historical Background." *Journal of Educational Psychology* 82, no. 2 (1990): 189–200.

Murray, Donald M. "The Listening Eye: Reflections on the Writing Conference." *College English* 41 (1979): 13–18.

Okawa, G. Y., T. Fox, L. J. Y. Chang, S. R. Windsor, F. B. Chavez, Jr., and L. Hayes. "Multi-Cultural Voices: Peer Tutoring and Critical Reflection in the Writing Center." *The Writing Center Journal* 12, no. 1 (1991): 11–33.

Rose, Mike. *Lives on the Boundary: The Struggles and Achievements of America's Underprepared.* New York: Penguin Books, 1989.

Sommers, Nancy, and Donald McQuade, eds. *Student Writers at Work.* New York: St. Martin's Press, 1984 and 1986.

Winnard, Karin E. "Codependency: Teaching Tutors Not to Rescue." *Journal of College Reading and Learning* 24, no. 1 (1991): 32–39.

Writing Lab Newsletter. Muriel Harris, ed., English Department, Purdue University, West Lafayette, IN 47907.

Editor's note: For an extensive annotated list of relevant readings, see Beverly Clark, "Selected Bibliography," in *Talking About Writing* (Ann Arbor: University of Michigan Press, 1985), 211–25.